Gender, Sexuality and Global Politics

Series Editors: **Ali Bilgic**, Loughborough University, UK, **Synne L. Dyvik**, University of Sussex, UK, **Gunhild Hoogensen Gjørv**, UiT The Arctic University of Norway, Norway, **Thomas Gregory**, The University of Auckland, New Zealand and **Swati Parashar**, University of Gothenburg, Sweden

Expanding the boundaries of International Relations, this series reflects on politics globally with innovative and transdisciplinary perspectives.

With a focus on feminist, lesbian, gay, bisexual, trans and queer activism, the series critically examines existing hierarchies, practices and power relations, investigating the often violent effects of these on different peoples, geographies and histories.

Also available

Bodily Fluids, Fluid Bodies and International Politics
Feminist Technoscience, Biopolitics and Security
By **Jenn Hobbs**

Queering Conflict Research
New Approaches to the Study of Political Violence
Edited by **Jamie J. Hagen**, **Samuel Ritholtz** and **Andrew Delatolla**

Forthcoming

Gender, Identity and Conflict
Theorising Gender, Peace and Security in the Eastern Himalayan Borderland
By **Dipti Tamang**

Black Masculinities and Colonial Legacies
The Global Politics of Jamaican and Diasporic Constructions of Gender
By **Shardia Briscoe-Palmer**

For more information about the series and to find out how to submit a proposal visit
**bristoluniversitypress.co.uk/
gender-sexuality-and-global-politics**

International Editorial Board

Linda Åhäll, University of Gothenburg, Sweden
Terrell Carver, University of Bristol, UK
Shine Choi, Massey University, New Zealand
Bina D'Costa, Australian National University, Australia
Paula Drumond, O Instituto de Relações Internacionais PUC-Rio, Brazil
Cynthia Enloe, Clark University, US
Des Gasper, Erasmus University, Netherlands
Inanna Hamati-Ataya, University of Cambridge, UK
Catarina Kinnvall, Lund University, Sweden
Rauna Kuokkanen, University of Lapland, Finland
Peace Medie, University of Ghana, Ghana
Annie Paul, University of the West Indies, Jamaica
Manuela Picq, Amherst College, US
Vicki Squire, University of Warwick, UK
Cemal Burak Tansel, University of Sheffield, UK
Maria Tanyag, Australian National University, Australia
Cai Wilkinson, Deakin University, Australia

For more information about the series and to
find out how to submit a proposal visit
**bristoluniversitypress.co.uk/
gender-sexuality-and-global-politics**

BOUNDARIES OF QUEERNESS

Homonationalism and Racial Politics in Sweden

Katharina Kehl

First published in Great Britain in 2024 by

Bristol University Press
University of Bristol
1–9 Old Park Hill
Bristol
BS2 8BB
UK
t: +44 (0)117 374 6645
e: bup-info@bristol.ac.uk

Details of international sales and distribution partners are available at bristoluniversitypress.co.uk

© Bristol University Press 2024

British Library Cataloguing in Publication Data
A catalogue record for this book is available from the British Library

ISBN 978-1-5292-2352-1 hardcover
ISBN 978-1-5292-2353-8 ePub
ISBN 978-1-5292-2354-5 ePdf

The right of Katharina Kehl to be identified as author of this work has been asserted by her in accordance with the Copyright, Designs and Patents Act 1988.

All rights reserved: no part of this publication may be reproduced, stored in a retrieval system, or transmitted in any form or by any means, electronic, mechanical, photocopying, recording, or otherwise without the prior permission of Bristol University Press.

Every reasonable effort has been made to obtain permission to reproduce copyrighted material. If, however, anyone knows of an oversight, please contact the publisher.

The statements and opinions contained within this publication are solely those of the author and not of the University of Bristol or Bristol University Press. The University of Bristol and Bristol University Press disclaim responsibility for any injury to persons or property resulting from any material published in this publication.

Bristol University Press works to counter discrimination on grounds of gender, race, disability, age and sexuality.

Cover design: Blu Inc
Front cover image: Unsplash/sharonmccutcheon
Bristol University Press uses environmentally responsible print partners.
Printed and bound in Great Britain by CPI Group (UK) Ltd, Croydon, CR0 4YY

För Ylva, Even, och Tove

Contents

About the Author		viii
Acknowledgements		ix
1	Introduction	1
2	Homonationalism Revisited: Gay Rights and Queer Complexities	11
3	Theoretical Explorations I: Boundary Making and Intelligibility	30
4	Theoretical Explorations II: Racialization	46
5	The How To: Queer and Feminist Methodology	60
6	Pride Järva: LGBTQ People in Right-Wing Nationalist Discourses	76
7	A Flag Worth Defending? Rainbows, Pride and the Swedish Armed Forces	92
8	Racialized Grids of Intelligibility in Swedish LGBTQ Contexts	107
9	Conclusions and Ways Ahead	125
References		138
Index		163

About the Author

Katharina Kehl holds a PhD in peace and development studies and is affiliated to the Department of Gender Studies at Lund University, Sweden. Her research focuses on questions of gender, sexuality and race in relation to migration, nationalism and politics of belonging. Her work has previously appeared in peer-reviewed outlets including *International Feminist Journal of Politics*, *Sexualities* and *Social Identities*.

Acknowledgements

Many people have read and commented on this manuscript, and listing them all would by far exceed any acceptable page count. Thank you to my colleagues at the School of Global Studies at Gothenburg University, particularly Swati Parashar, who encouraged me to submit the initial book proposal. At Lund University, I would like to thank all my colleagues at the Department of Gender Studies, who never ceased to encourage me to actually *finish* the book even during times with heavy teaching loads and little research. A special thank you goes to Andrés Brink Pinto for introducing me to the world of writing stipends, thus making it possible for me to see this project through. The completion of this book was generously supported by stipends from the foundation Åke Wibergs Stiftelse as well as the Stiftelsen Torsten Amundsons fond at the Royal Swedish Academy of Science.

At Bristol University Press, I thank Stephen Wenham, Zoë Forbes and the series editors of the Gender, Sexuality and Global Politics series for their patience, support and insight. I would also like to extend thanks to the anonymous reviewers for their incredibly detailed and engaged commentary on earlier versions of the manuscript. Their kind encouragement, critical eye and extensive knowledge of the literature and context has made this a much better book.

Finally, my family, particularly my partner Ylva, has suffered through me having to go back to the manuscript "just this one more time" very many times and has been incredibly supportive and encouraging throughout.

Attentive readers will notice that some sections in this book have appeared elsewhere: parts of Chapters 2 and 4 have previously been published as Kehl, K. (2020) 'Homonationalism revisited: race, rights, and queer complexities', *Lambda Nordica*, 25(2): 17–38, while parts of each of the empirical chapters have been published in the following three articles:

- Kehl, K. (2018) ' "In Sweden, girls are allowed to kiss girls, and boys are allowed to kiss boys": Pride Järva and the inclusion of the "LGBT other" in Swedish nationalist discourses', *Sexualities*, 21(4): 674–91.

- Kehl, K. (2020) '"Did queer Muslims even exist?" Racialised grids of intelligibility in Swedish LGBTQ contexts', *Social Identities*, 26(2): 150–65.
- Kehl, K. (2023) 'A rainbow flag worth defending? Swedish Armed Forces' pride campaigns 2017–2022', *Tidskrift för genusvetenskap*, 43(2–3): 61–81.

1

Introduction

It is July 2016 in Rinkeby, one of Stockholm's northern suburbs, the week of Stockholm Pride. Jan Sjunnesson, right-wing publicist and member of the populist party the Sweden Democrats (SD), is standing on a makeshift stage, speaking to a small audience of people who are waving both rainbow and Swedish flags. He talks about tolerance towards lesbian, gay, bisexual and transexual people as a compulsory part of what it means to be Swedish; about how people coming from other countries, particularly Muslims, are inherently homophobic and intolerant; and about how 'the left' has abandoned White Swedish LGBTQ people in favour of political correctness towards immigrants, thus leaving it up to forces on the right to protect them. This speech is the climax of his very own 'Pride Järva', organized, as he puts it, to teach the many migrants and racialized Swedes living in this area a lesson on "what it means to be Swedish" (Avpixlat, 2016).

Later that same year, the Swedish Armed Forces (SAF) launch their marketing campaign 'Thou New, Thou Free' (*Du Nya, Du Fria*), in which they explicitly use LGBTQ rights and the rainbow flag as markers of liberal Swedish values. According to the campaign, these values are increasingly under threat from 'the outside', thus requiring protection from the military and, in turn, rearmament. Similar campaigns appear in the following years, drawing repeatedly on LGBTQ rights in order to define Swedishness and stressing the need for the SAF to protect these rights.

A third observation from the same period puts these nationalist mobilizations of LGBTQ rights into perspective: across social media platforms, racialized Swedish LGBTQ activists start to organize, building community spaces both online and offline and claiming and creating more visibility for their experiences. They are a vocal part in the counterdemonstrations against Sjunnesson's Pride Järva – they organize separatist blocs in pride parades across the country and share their experiences in panel events and conversations with other parts of the LGBTQ community. Their testimonies make it more than clear that notions of Swedishness, including different ways of defining it through LGBTQ rights, are far from readily available to everybody.

What happens when actors and institutions best known for their affinity to national flag waving suddenly start to raise the rainbow flag? How do people who continue to endure stigma and discrimination end up being mobilized as poster children for the values of the very societies, politics and institutions that have excluded and oppressed them? And what does this inclusion in nationalist narratives mean for LGBTQ people and movements? Since the 1990s, lesbian, gay, bisexual and (usually with a pronounced delay) transgender people have successfully fought for civil and reproductive rights across many Western states. They have gained access to rights that normalize their sexual orientations, gender identities and family relationships within the confines of existing social institutions, awarding them the protection of the state in return. This inclusion of LGBTQ people into the nation has been conceptualized as homonormativity (Duggan, 2002) and homonationalism (Puar, 2007), and it is usually considered to be conditional. It depends on one's LGBTQ-ness not fundamentally challenging or disturbing social norms and conventions regarding binary gender, monogamous relationships and parenting. Or, to put it differently, on not being 'too queer'.

In the wake of fights for LGBTQ rights, these rights have also assumed new meanings beyond their immediate relevance for LGBTQ communities. Internationally, states have started to use their stance on LGBTQ rights to position themselves as either 'good' states that support these rights (Rao, 2020) or as defenders of 'traditional family values', challenging LGBTQ rights (Edenborg, 2023). The question of how LGBTQ people are and should be treated as well as which rights and protections they should enjoy has therefore become a boundary marker, both on an international stage and domestically.

In Western European contexts, LGBTQ rights have frequently been used in debates on immigration and domestic minorities in order to delimit who belongs and who does not (El-Tayeb, 2011; Haritaworn, 2015; DasGupta and Dasgupta, 2018; Altay, 2023). Anti-LGBTQ attitudes are projected on to communities and people who are already externalized because of the ways in which they are also ascribed racialized 'Otherness'. Notable here are the intricate ways in which these processes of racialization also seem to include religion – particularly Islam – as an ethno-cultural signifier of (non-)belonging. People racialized as non-White and/or Muslim are assigned the position of the 'constitutive outsides' to a newly LGBTQ-friendly West, with their communities embodying the homo-, bi- and transphobia that Western societies claim to have left behind. The inclusion of some LGBTQ people into national communities of belonging therefore not only depends on them not being 'too queer'; it is also used to further the exclusion of other minorities. The explicit *exclusion* of LGBTQ people from national communities of belonging in the name of the protection of 'traditional family values', on the other hand, is equally employed to delimit belonging and to justify the persecution of all kinds of queerness. Most recently, this rhetoric plays a prominent role in ongoing Russian attempts at expanding its sphere of influence, including the invasion and occupation of Ukraine (Brock, 2023; Kratochvíl and O'Sullivan, 2023).

Along with existing and emerging research across a number of fields and disciplines, this book argues that boundary-making processes around sexuality and gender in relation to race are important at different levels of society. They have (geo)political implications, when LGBTQ rights are used to frame certain actors (or whole countries) as morally superior and more advanced than others; they play an important role for individuals and groups in their processes of identity formation; and they materialize in institutional frameworks and decision-making processes such as reproductive health, transgender health or asylum-seeking processes. Since these aspects are interrelated and mutually reinforcing, the stakes involved are high – critically engaging with these constructions not only enables us to question dominant national narratives upheld through processes of boundary making but also to highlight the violent effects they have on individuals and groups through the construction of 'right' and 'wrong' kinds of queers. In this book, I therefore investigate attempts at national boundary making through queer notions of subjectivity and identity, crucially advancing our understanding of the intricate and complex relationship between the two.

Aims and questions

By studying contemporary constructions of Swedishness in relation to LGBTQ rights, this book aims to explore the relationship between acts of boundary making around national communities of belonging and the various grids of intelligibility they draw upon and enable. While national communities of belonging are always contested, they do have an impact on how we identify and understand ourselves as well as each other. The question of who is recognizable as the 'right kind of queer' within the context of a contemporary politics of belonging might be particularly explicit for some, but it is in various ways present in the lives of all of those challenging norms regarding Whiteness, heteronormativity and binary gender. I therefore draw on Judith Butler's conceptualization of the term 'grids of intelligibility' in order to account for the ways in which social norms and expectations enable, but also circumscribe, our ways of being recognizably human within a given social context (Butler, 1990).

By introducing this aspect of normative intelligibility to literature on borders, boundary making and the politics of belonging, the book looks to expand and destabilize binary notions of (non-)belonging. It stresses the importance of analysing geopolitical aspects of sexual politics in studies of gender and sexuality, paying particular attention to questions of how the inside/outside are constructed in current narratives on belonging. It also aims to (re-)focus our attention on the importance of analysing processes of racialization whenever we engage analytically with sexuality and gender as markers of belonging.

In order to untangle this theoretical puzzle, the empirical section of the book relies on Sweden as a political arena where boundary making around LGBTQ rights is both common and contested. Attitudes towards gender identity and sexuality are drawn upon by a number of actors in order to create and reinforce powerful narratives of Sweden as particularly progressive. This 'Swedish gender exceptionalism' (Habel, 2012; Martinsson et al, 2016; Alm et al, 2021) is central to defining (non-)belonging and crucially relies on notions of intolerance, sexism and LGBTQ-phobia being located in far-away places and racialized communities (Molina, 2005; Mulinari and Neergaard, 2017; Cuesta and Mulinari, 2018). While there has been criticism of normative ideas of gender exceptionalism and accompanying notions of Sweden as an anti-racist, colour-blind country from both academics and activists, the political right has in turn employed a rhetoric of gender equality having gone 'too far' (Martinsson, 2020). The tensions between these different positions provide potential for analytical insights that go far beyond the specific empirical context, as they engage overarching issues concerning the discursive mobilization of sexuality, gender and race in contestations around (non-)belonging and (un)intelligibility.

Three main questions guide this analysis of the complex relations between belonging and intelligibility: How are LGBTQ rights mobilized in contemporary constructions of Swedishness? What role does racialization play in these constructions? Which subject positions are made available in these constructions, and how are they negotiated by LGBTQ people racialized as non-White and/or Muslim?

These questions are investigated across three research sites, introduced briefly in the opening vignette of this introduction and reflected in the book's empirical chapters. They consist of a 'pride parade' organized by the Swedish populist right, SAF marketing material published in relation to Stockholm Pride, and a Swedish Instagram account for racialized LGBTQ people. Inspired by queer and feminist methodologies, the book analyses data from the three sites using a discursive approach that accounts for the performative nature of both textual and visual material. All three research sites constitute discursive events in which the intersection of race–sexuality–gender manifests particularly clearly in the context of boundary making around notions of Swedish gender exceptionalism and homonationalism. By investigating them, we gain an understanding of how certain subjectivities and positionalities become more easily available through normative grids of intelligibility enabled by processes of boundary making and how people manoeuvre and navigate these grids in different ways. The coexistence of these sites in both time and space enables us to approach constructions of Swedishness qua LGBTQ-friendliness from what appears to be widely diverging political standpoints. It also serves as an indicator of the ways in which many of the narratives are in fact long-lasting and built on well-established notions of Otherness.

Even though it might be confusing to see populist right wingers like Sjunnesson or traditionally hetero-masculine institutions like the SAF pick up the rainbow flag, defining 'the body of the nation' in relation to normative notions of sexuality and gender is a long-lasting European tradition. Not least because it was through reproductive heterosexuality that citizens (and nations) were said to be, quite literally, reproduced. Likewise, the ascription of race to some bodies and not others, as experienced by racialized Swedish LGBTQ activists, has a history as a well-established method for the production of respectable genders and sexualities considered worthy of recognition and protection. In European literary and medical discourses from the 19th and early 20th centuries, the Black colonial Other (Laskar, 2007), as well as Roma and Sinti (Laskar, 2015b), features prominently as a racial and sexual 'threat', producing 'counter-images and deterrents to the majority society's ideals of gender, sexuality, class and race' (Laskar, 2015b, p 138). As part of early 20th-century social engineering, these discourses also legitimized practices like forced sterilization and the removal of children from families (Mottier and Gerodetti, 2007; Laskar, 2015a). While transgender people in Sweden have only been freed from the spectre of sterilization since 2013, when it was finally removed as a legal requirement for undergoing gender reassignment, the era of eugenics is generally considered to be over in Western Europe. The use of sexuality, gender identity and race to mark the boundaries of national communities of belonging, however, seems to only have gained momentum again in recent years. Since the empirical data I discuss cover a period from 2015 to 2023, the shifting nature of the ways in which sexuality, gender identity and race are used in projects of national boundary making becomes particularly clear. During this period, Sweden went from having a social-democratic government which introduced the much-discussed doctrine of a feminist foreign policy to the international stage in 2014 (Aggestam et al, 2019) to being a country led by a conservative government coalition backed up by the SD. A party on the far populist right, SD are well known for xenophobia and virulent anti-LGBTQ sentiments among their supporters as well as for consistent anti-LGBTQ law making. Their rise to actual political power in 2022 has in many ways changed the public debate on sexual and reproductive rights even in the mainstream Swedish media and exposed LGTBQ activists and organizations to threats and violence (RFSU, 2020; Lagerman, 2023b). In comparison to the early and mid-2010s, right-wing actors have backed away from making homonationalist statements, instead refocusing on a public rejection of many more kinds of queerness. Pride Järva seems far away in the Sweden of 2024.

Russia's full-scale invasion of Ukraine in 2022 and the escalation of the war, on the other hand, has profoundly changed the security landscape in Europe. This has seriously accelerated what was a slow re-armament and reterritorialization of the Swedish defence in the late 2010s. The government's decision to give up any notions of 'neutrality' (Agius, 2013) and join NATO has been accompanied by a normalization of militarized imagery and discourse, visible not least in the SAF's pride-related campaigns. In the summer of 2023, they presented a metal pride flag that was forged out of tank armour, which was supposed to symbolize that the flag is 'as undestroyable as our defence of human rights, everybody's equal value, and our right to live as we ourselves chose' (Voss, 2023). At the same time, Eastern European feminist and queer perspectives on the war in Ukraine have pointed to the complex relationship between the defence of LGBTQ and women's rights against Russian aggression under the label of 'traditional values' and the pressing need for a military organization capable of such a defence in a situation of occupation (Kratochvíl and O'Sullivan, 2023). Their calls for military action from the West have been phrased both through emancipatory notions of sexuality and gender and via decolonial analyses of the Ukrainian relationship to both the EU and a renewed Russian imperialism (Graff, 2022; Hendl, 2022; Tsymbalyuk, 2022).

Contributions

In a shifting political landscape, this book hopes to speak to a number of different issues and audiences by making empirical contributions as well as theoretical interventions. First, it expands existing research on 'Swedish gender exceptionalism' at a time when the Swedish claim to gender exceptionality is under renegotiation both within and outside the country. The notion that Sweden is particularly progressive with regard to gender equality, sexual and reproductive health and LGBTQ rights, and the way in which this progressiveness is performed in opposition to various Others, has so far been overwhelmingly investigated with regard to gender equality (Martinsson et al, 2016; Bergman Rosamond, 2020; Alm et al, 2021). This book opens up notions of 'Swedish exceptionalism' to include both gender and sexuality.

Secondly, the book's explicit concern with questions of racialization in relation to the mobilization of LGBTQ rights also contributes to the literature that discusses constructions of Swedishness as Whiteness (Mulinari and Neergaard, 2017; Alinia, 2020; Keskinen et al, 2021; Hübinette et al, 2023) by analysing how acts of boundary making around race–sex–gender make people variously intelligible. It thus adds new insights to studies of queer migration in the Nordic countries more generally. While engaging critically with questions of sexuality and gender identity in relation to migration in the Nordic countries (Akin, 2019; Hedlund and Wimark, 2019; Lunau, 2019; Wimark, 2020; Sólveigar- og Guðmundsdóttir, 2023), this field has lacked more systematic interrogations of race and racialization (see Ahlstedt [2016] for one of the exceptions). This might potentially be because of an institutionalized doctrine of 'colour-blindness' that can make it hard to access data on racialization and ethnicity (Hübinette et al, 2023).

While the Swedish case is no doubt intriguing, the book's core contribution, and what I hope to be its wider appeal beyond specific academic circles, lies in its theoretical exploration of how attempts at national(ist) boundary making draw upon and enable normative grids of intelligibility, as well as how both of these are to be understood as inherently unstable. The book provides insights not only into how various boundary-making processes around sexuality, gender and race work; it also expands our knowledge with regard to the role these processes play in the constructions of collective identities and individual subject positions.

Since the introduction of homonormativity and homonationalism, the literature has quite extensively conceptualized the inclusion of some parts of the LGBTQ community into nationalist narratives through normative understandings of sexuality and gender in relation to race. However, there is a pressing need to also understand how these exclusive inclusions affect people by circumscribing what subject positions are made available as (non-)intelligible. This book, therefore, builds on existing research on what homonationalism *is* (that is, the development of the concept as such) and expands it towards what homonationalism *does* (that is, the ways in which it positions people differently with regard to how they can negotiate and manoeuvre their 'being-intelligible' within a given context).

To explore what homonationalism does, I put three main bodies of literature in conversation with each other: literature on political boundary-making processes (Hall, 1997a; Yuval-Davis, 2011; Basham and Vaughan-Williams, 2013; Edenborg, 2020c) with conceptualizations of the constitution of intelligible subjectivity (Butler, 1990, 2015; Stern, 2006), read through theories on social processes of racialization and the ascription of race and religion as ethno-cultural signifiers, of 'Otherness' (Ahmed, 2007a; Collins, 2009; El-Tayeb, 2011; Weheliye, 2014). Their combination deepens our understanding of how boundary-making processes that aim for the construction of collective identities draw upon and enable certain grids of intelligibility for (non-)belonging, which in turn privilege certain ways in which individuals 'make sense' of themselves and others. It becomes apparent that the ways in which narratives of 'Selves' and 'Others' underlie the construction of communities of belonging through boundary-making processes have an affinity with constitutions of the Self at an individual level, not least because it is through the encounter of the social that we become recognizable to ourselves and those around us. Looking at boundary making through literature on the performative nature of grids of intelligibility also points towards the instabilities inherent in attempts at boundary making, as this performative aspect, crucially, includes the constant potential for contestation and re-signification. Finally, reading boundary making and grids of intelligibility through literature on racialization is crucial. It draws our attention to the fact that intelligibility historically has been and still is more readily available for some, radically conditional for others and remains out of reach altogether for yet others, based on the hierarchized ascription of racialized Otherness which in itself remains a precondition for the construction of the intelligible Self.

The way in which the book puts these concepts in conversation with each other therefore expands our theoretical understanding of how attempts at boundary making around sexuality, gender and race never completely manage to distinguish inside from outside, Self from Other, despite their normative potential. Approaching homonationalist boundary making through queer understandings of the Self (as enabled by grids of intelligibility) stresses the inevitable instability in these boundary-making moves. It directs our analytical attention to the ways in which queer people challenge the normative grids of intelligibility enabled by these attempts at boundary making by carving out liveable lives for themselves. By doing so, it contributes to ongoing academic debates dealing with current political developments across the globe on gender rights and sexuality. More importantly, however, I hope it provides insights as well as methodological and analytical tools to activists fighting for liveable queer lives around the world.

Situating the book

This research project rests on post-structuralist epistemological and ontological assumptions about the nature of language, the way it shapes social realities and our 'making-sense' of these realities. In line with much of queer and feminist research, I take language to be the means by which we access social reality, as well as the way in which we speak ourselves (and others) into being. Discourse, in its wider meaning, is thus something through which meaning is constructed and can be studied (see Jørgensen and Phillips, 2002). This understanding makes the study of language and the various (normative) discursive formations into which it is organized particularly suited to approach the kinds of questions this book investigates.

Inspired by postcolonial scholars' critical engagement with history, I do not consider the discursive processes I analyse to be a recent phenomenon. Instead, I read them in the context of existing genealogies of Otherness in relation to gender, sexuality and race in Sweden, Europe and beyond.

These include narratives of linear progress, openness and tolerance as well as ways in which certain sexualities and gender identities are constructed as respectable, innocent and deserving of protection through processes of racialization. Continuities in the construction of difference feed into more contemporary concepts such as homonormativity and homonationalism. Being aware of continuities and creating a genealogical understanding of certain terms and concepts enables us to see how contemporary discussions and debates are made meaningful or obscured by references to past events, narratives or tropes which are in turn related to practices and ideologies of colonialism and imperialism (Said, 1978, pp 41–2; Hall, 1992). While the Nordic countries have often been conceptualized as existing 'outside colonialism' (Keskinen et al, 2009), they were and are by no means mere bystanders when it comes to these (re)constructions of racialized differences. A central part of this project is to make clear the deep historical connections and continuities of racialization, colonialism and sexuality in the European, and more specifically the Swedish, context. These are directly connected to the way in which 'the right kind of queer' can go from being an Other to becoming part of a normalizing discourse which continues to exotify, other, even punish 'wrong kinds of queers' and other minorities.

Finally, sexuality and gender identity are here treated as socially constructed phenomena which are historically and geographically specific, expressed in the context of this book through the acronym LGBTQ. This understanding also applies to the social processes called 'racialization' through which people are constructed as different and categorized hierarchically based on various conceptualizations of 'race'. An understanding of the ways in which these categories and the discriminations and inequalities connected to them intersect is central to my analysis.

Some crucial delimitations have to be made with regard to the ground covered by this project. First, the book uses the notion of the 'right kind of queer' predominantly to refer to normative grids of intelligibility in relation to racialization. There are of course other social norms making people intelligible as the 'right kind of queers'. These include normative understandings of parenthood and family relations (Dahl, 2017, 2018; Dahl and Gabb, 2019), (dis)ability as discussed within the field of crip theory (McRuer, 2006; Rydström, 2012; Long, 2018; Mery Karlsson, 2020) and norms around romantic and sexual relationships (most frequently in relation to same-sex marriage [Warner, 1999; Spade, 2013; Conrad, 2014; Wilkinson, 2017]). None of these are explicitly addressed here beyond cursory references. Secondly, while this book's theoretical approach speaks to racialization processes at large, the empirical material mostly covers experiences of racialization connected to migration (experienced or ascribed) into Sweden, very much in line with the 'externalization' of the racialized Other from both Sweden and notions of Swedishness. Swedish (post)coloniality as lived and experienced by the indigenous Sámi population, one of the main internal racialized Others throughout Swedish history, is not explicitly addressed. For those interested, there is a growing feminist, queer and decolonial literature on Sámi experiences of sexuality, gender and racialization (Dankertsen, 2019; Knobblock, 2021; Kokkola and Siltanen, 2021; Kyrölä and Huuki, 2021; Bjerknes, 2023; Brovold, 2023; Huuki and Kyrölä, 2023).

I therefore do not claim to provide a 'complete' overview of the different ways in which boundary-making processes around various notions of Swedishness happen or the implications they have for normative grids of intelligibility around sexuality, race and gender. Since these constructions are constantly (re-)shaped, this would be an endeavour destined to failure – there is no conclusive discursive formation, no consistent 'whole' to be approached here. Not least the changing political landscape in Sweden and beyond proves how volatile discursive constructions of (national) belonging and intelligibility around sexuality, gender and race are. Instead, this project is driven by existing research, my theoretical approach and my experience of having lived as a queer activist and researcher within the Swedish context for over ten years.

Outline of the book

This introductory chapter is followed by a review of literature that discusses homonationalism and homonormativity as well as Swedish gender exceptionalism. Chapters 3 and 4 introduce the theoretical-analytical framework by discussing the three main concepts: boundary-making processes and the politics of belonging, the construction of subjectivity through grids of intelligibility, and racialization as a process for social differentiation and the ascription of (in)humanity. In Chapter 5, on queer and feminist methodology, I discuss research design and methods as well as ethical considerations and challenges stemming from my own positionality as a queer 'researcher-activist'. This chapter also offers insights into what the empirical analytical work looked like, including a section on writing as part of the analysis. Chapters 6 to 8 each engage with a specific empirical case: Pride Järva, the SAF's pride campaigns, and the activist Instagram channel. The final chapter provides concluding thoughts on the contributions of this book, as well as some pointers with regard to future research avenues. While ideally read as a whole, I have done my best to make each of the book's chapters accessible individually for any reader who is pressed for time or who only wants to focus on particular aspects of the book's broader analysis.

2

Homonationalism Revisited: Gay Rights and Queer Complexities

Beginning in the early 2000s, queerness and the social movements associated with it have experienced an unprecedented move into the societal mainstream of particularly North American and Western European democracies, with LGBTQ people gaining the legal right to marry, raise children and serve in the armed forces. As certain right kinds of queers are integrated into various heteronormative social institutions, heteronormativity increasingly seemed to have run its course as queer theory's main adversary. But what in many ways looked like 'the best of times' (Dhawan, 2013, p 191) for queer politics has been critiqued by those who question the exclusive inclusions upon which these moves into the mainstream are predicated and the contradictory ways in which queerness is celebrated, instrumentalized and fiercely policed.

Analyses of how notions of normative and deviant sexualities and gender identities play into practices of (national) boundary making have extended queer theory's reach into various academic fields, such as migration studies, human rights studies and, most recently, international relations. However, as critiques of homonormative and homonationalist narratives have become more established within (and outside) academic discourses, they have also been subjected to scholarly scrutiny and criticized for a tendency towards simplifications and generalizations that obscure the contingencies, ambiguities and complexities of particular formations of knowledge/power/pleasure (Weber, 2016b; Rao, 2020).

This chapter asks how we can develop these concepts in order to maintain their relevance for much-needed analyses of the role that different versions of L–G–B–T–Q play in projects of boundary making as well as the ways in which LGBTQ people are variously positioned to deal with these projects. I argue that we need to take into account the ways in which homonationalism and adjacent concepts have developed as they have entered new academic disciplines. By connecting new perspectives to core aspects of the original critique, we will be able to better account for the complexities and messiness of contemporary queer positionalities as they relate to various exclusive inclusions, as well as for the question of which queer bodies can and cannot afford to 'not want rights'.

The following section provides an introductory summary of the concepts of homonormativity and homonationalism as well as discourses on gay-rights-as-human-rights and their global implications. The chapter will then nuance and develop these critiques, focusing on two main aspects. First, I discuss the potential of gay-rights-as-human-rights discourses as more than just expressions of (neo)colonialism and (neo)imperialism, as well as queer communities' inability to not want rights. Secondly, I employ writings by Cynthia Weber, Rahul Rao and Nikita Dhawan in an attempt to challenge seemingly straightforward narratives on homonationalist and homonormative processes of boundary making and to expand our view beyond issues of legal recognition.

Homonationalism and homonormativity

This book's investigation of current inclusions of the right kind of LGBTQ people into projects of (nationalist) boundary making relies on a body of literature building on two concepts that have their roots in the United States: homonormativity and homonationalism. Introduced by Lisa Duggan and Jasbir Puar respectively, they initially dealt with the specific ways in which certain LGBTQ people became integrated into nationalist narratives about the United States. They have since been applied across a number of fields by researchers interested in how normative notions of race, sexuality and gender play into the formation of (non-)belonging.

Duggan conceptualized the incorporation of the right kind of queer into the national fold through the notion of homonormativity (Duggan, 2002). The homonormative gay mainstream, she argues, does not contest heteronormative assumptions and institutions but upholds and sustains them by aiming for inclusion within them (Duggan, 2002). In embracing what Rao calls a 'non-redistributive recognition politics' (Rao, 2020, p 153), they therefore promise conservative politicians the possibility of a demobilized, depoliticized and privatized gay constituency (Duggan, 2002, p 180) that is more interested in living an undisturbed private life as part of the majoritarian (heterosexual) nation and its institutions than in furthering progressive politics or opposing state-sanctioned violence against or expulsion of other minorities. Building on Duggan's conceptualization, Puar goes on to argue that those domesticated queers not only have been included into the nation at the expense of racial and sexual Others but that they are indeed part of a 'collusion between homosexuality and American nationalism, generated both by national rhetoric of patriotic inclusion and by gay, lesbian, and queer subjects themselves: homo-nationalism' (Puar, 2006, p 67). The folding of homosexuality into the 'us' in the 'us–them' rhetoric (Puar, 2006, p 70) enables Western countries such as the United States to project themselves as gay-safe in comparison to the Middle East. These patterns of inclusion and exclusion, however, are not only implemented by state actors. Puar shows in her analysis of the post-9/11 public discourse in the United States (2006, pp 71ff) how LGBTQ activists and organizations are actually a part of homonationalist discourses. These discourses turn certain LGBTQ people into markers of a civilized, tolerant, liberal West vis-à-vis a barbaric, anti-modern and anti-liberal East (Butler, 2008). As Puar argues, homonationalism, therefore, creates certain national homosexual subjects or positionalities which in turn can police or sanction non-nationalist, non-normative sexualities (Puar, 2006). Or, as Sabsay puts it, rather than queer activists managing to challenge the nation, nationalism has 're-inscribe[d] the queer into its own narrative' (2012, p 607) by way of various exclusive inclusions, something which holds true for both Anglo-American and Western European contexts.

Inspired by Duggan's and Puar's analyses, a growing number of scholars interested in issues such as migration, human rights, development aid and geopolitics have engaged with what Rahul Rao calls the rise of 'the queer question' on to the international arena (Rao, 2014a) and the various ways in which LGBTQ issues have become part of boundary making on a domestic level as well as international geopolitical powerplay. This includes research on the conditionality and direction of development aid (Laskar, 2014), critiques of the normative power of 'gay-rights-as-human-rights' discourses (Bosia, 2020a; Rahman, 2020; Langlois, 2022) and analyses of how homophobia is located in specific countries and bodies (Rao, 2014b, 2020). Haritaworn, Kuntsman and Posocco direct their gaze to 'those lives and deaths (queer or otherwise) that fall outside of inclusive citizenships and into erasure, violence and abandonment' (Haritaworn et al, 2013, p 446; see also Lunau, 2019). Their question 'inclusion into what?' – and, I would add, at what cost? – guides many academic enquiries into how LGBTQ rights have become mobilized in processes of boundary making, including this book.

Homonationalism(s) in European contexts

The concept of homonationalism has been used to analyse various debates on 'European values' and the construction of overarching European as well as specific national identities. Initially, the focus of these debates was on the so-called cultural conflicts regarding LGBTQ rights that were said to appear between racialized and/or Muslim immigrants and 'native' Western European populations (frequently characterized as White and secular) (El-Tayeb, 2012; Haritaworn, 2012; Jungar and Peltonen, 2015; Kosnick, 2015). Increasingly, however, LGBTQ rights have also been at the centre of debates over how actors engage in boundary drawing between notions of Western and Eastern Europe and the geopolitics associated with these. While countries such as Poland, Hungary and Russia are constructed as backwards in relation to countries such as the Netherlands, Germany or Sweden, they are at the same time seen to be actively positioning themselves as defenders of traditional values against what they perceive as a promotion of what is considered to be unhealthy family constellations and an attack on natural gender roles on the part of 'liberal Western elites' (Rexhepi, 2016; Edenborg, 2023; Plakhotnik and Mayerchyk, 2023; Shevtsova, 2023). As this book's empirical chapters show, contemporary constructions of LGBTQ-friendly Swedishness rely both on the construction of cultural conflicts and the geopolitical boundary drawing between Western and Eastern Europe.

Similar to the North American context, certain members of LGBTQ communities are understood to achieve symbolic entry into citizenship by providing living examples of the self-definition of Western European countries as sexually progressive and morally superior (Edenborg, 2023), as their sexual liberation is being used to create a temporal segregation between European modernity and supposedly more traditional (that is, conservative) societies. Crucially, in this narrative, the 'West' exists in the present, with everyone else living in the past (Butler, 2008, p 2). This teleological narrative is familiar to, among others, critical development studies scholars: the notion of a linear and universal path to progress, based on an Enlightenment logic according to which the 'West' have come further towards 'civilization' than the 'rest' of the world, which is forever lagging behind (Fabian, 1983, quoted in Hall, 1992; Rao, 2020).

Not only do these Others live in the past – they live in a specific, Western past (El-Tayeb, 2011, p 90). This story, Dhawan reminds us, neglects to account for the immense costs at which the construction of the West as a normative power has come for those non-Western Others, including the establishment of violent and exploitative systems of government and extraction across the world (see Dhawan, 2013, pp 201–2). Communities and individuals racialized as non-White and/or Muslim are connected to this narrative – they are 'positioned within a spatial and temporal paradox – ... permanently frozen in the moment of arrival, as eternal migrants' (El-Tayeb et al, 2015, p 771). Within the context of this book, the externalized positionality of the 'eternal migrant' (also in its specific temporality) becomes particularly clear in Chapters 6 and 8. Sjunnesson's rhetoric at Pride Järva relies on it as a mechanism of Othering, while the experiences shared by racialized LGBTQ people on the Instagram account capture this in their use of the term *blatte*. In Sweden, the term *blatte* has been claimed as a self-identifier by those who constantly experience being assigned this position as an 'eternal migrant' (El-Tayeb, 2011, p xxv), even if they are Swedish citizens, born and raised in Sweden.

Butler describes 'a certain paradox ... in which the coerced adoption of certain cultural norms becomes a requisite for entry into a polity that defines itself as the avatar of freedom' (Butler, 2008, p 4). This paradox is particularly acutely present in the fate of LGBTQ asylum seekers who fail to perform the right kind of queer in the face of migration authorities and asylum boards, thus being refused access to Europe's alleged havens of LGBTQ rights and freedoms. Research has shown how access to asylum is connected to the asylum seeker being able to present a coherent story about their sexual orientation or gender identity, frequently framed in terms that make sense first and foremost in a Western European context. The expectation to deliver a convincing story about one's coming-out, but also expectations regarding stable relationships and sexual intercourse, features prominently in many asylum seekers' stories about their experiences of being interviewed by migration authorities (Akin, 2019; Lunau, 2019; Tschalaer, 2021; Wimark, 2021).

LGBTQ rights and subjectivities have also become 'entangled with New Cold War sentiments' (Rivkin-Fish and Hartblay, 2014), as parts of Eastern Europe are constructed as backward and not civilized enough (Kulpa, 2014; Kahlina, 2015). Baker's analysis of the Eurovision Song Contest shows how a 'progressive Western' Europe is distinguished from a 'traditional Eastern' Europe, with the bearded drag queen Conchita Wurst providing the watershed benchmark of European modernity (Baker, 2017, see also 2019). At the same time, various Eastern European countries have proclaimed themselves to be defenders of the very same 'traditional values' that are problematized as being anti-LGBTQ (and thus anti-European). Wilkinson and Edenborg have identified such a project of 'traditional values' undertaken by Russia through legislation such as the 'anti-homopropaganda law' (Wilkinson, 2014; Edenborg, 2020a). Poland and Hungary have employed similar discourses, promoting state homophobia and transphobia in the name of protecting children, the traditional nuclear family and the continuity of the nation state (Petö and Kováts, 2017; Żuk and Żuk, 2019; Korolczuk, 2020b; Graff and Korolczuk, 2021). Even though these narratives are profoundly anti-LGBTQ, they do simultaneously (through their resistance to it) reproduce discourses about Western European countries as particularly LGBTQ-friendly, thus adding to notions of 'the West and the rest' with regard to LGBTQ rights.

Rescue narratives, hate crimes and hateful Others

As homonationalist and homonormative boundary making in European contexts frequently has been focused on questions of so-called cultural difference, a number of narratives around communities racialized as non-White and/or Muslim and their attitudes towards sexual rights have recurred across national contexts. These include the rescue narrative (Bracke, 2012) and the homophobic hate crime with racialized/Muslim youth as perpetrators (Klatran, 2021), both of them enabled by the more generalized notion of the hateful racialized Other (Haritaworn, 2015). The rescue narrative also ties in closely with the previously discussed temporal segregation of civilization, modernity and development from barbaric and backward societies. According to this narrative, LGBTQ people racialized as non-White and/or Muslim have to be liberated and saved from the patriarchal, static and oppressive societal structures which are said to also exist in migrant 'ghettos' in Europe's larger cities (El-Tayeb, 2012, p 80). One example of this narrative is the way in which separate accommodations for LGBTQ refugees have been discussed and partially implemented in a number of European countries (for example, Sweden and Germany) in the wake of the so-called refugee crisis in 2015/16. LGBTQ refugees were to be separated from the majority of refugees (the Other) for their own safety, after a number of violent attacks and incidents of sexual harassment occurred in refugee accommodation. Initially a measure requested by LGBTQ activists and LGBTQ refugees, this was frequently framed in a way that yet again located the threat and the violence exclusively within racialized minority communities (Wimark, 2020; Hiller, 2022). Even though homophobic, transphobic and racist violence has a long history and a lively presence in European societies, and while one of the main threats to LGBTQ asylum seekers is deportation from said societies, Western Europe was thus once more constructed as safe.

The rescue narrative is a well-established and longstanding practice of Othering (see for example Spivak, 1988, p 297). In public debates on migrants and sexual rights in Europe, Muslim women in particular have been framed as 'faceless victims' or 'notable exceptions', the latter being someone who has emancipated themselves from their oppressive patriarchal background, thus becoming 'a brown woman saving brown women' (Bracke, 2012, p 242). As research from various European contexts shows, similar narratives have also been employed by White gay rights activists. Paraphrasing Spivak, these are 'white homosexuals saving brown homosexuals from brown homophobes' (Rao, 2010, p 145).

The narrative of the homophobic racialized and/or Muslim migrant perpetrating violence against White LGBTQ people plays a central role when it comes to debates on hate crimes and anti-discrimination legislation (Haritaworn, 2015; Klatran, 2021). Queer-of-colour collectives have called out not only right-wing actors and mainstream LGBTQ organizations but also left-wing organizers for focusing too much on homophobia in communities racialized as non-White and/or Muslim instead of dealing with homo- and transphobia among White majority populations (see for example Girma and Atto, 2017).

The figure of the 'hateful Other' is closely connected to and to some extent essential for the emergence and new acceptability of the respectable, the right kind of queer, who is 'visibilised and valorised as injured' (Haritaworn, 2015, p 85), who appears as 'victim subject' (Kapur, 2005) and who is 'innocent and [thus] worthy of inclusion and recognition' (Haritaworn, 2015, p 130). Queer intimacy, symbolized for example by the romantic, innocent (and always monogamous) kiss, is said to deserve protection 'precisely because it is under attack from hateful Others who form the constitutive outside of the newly gay-friendly community' (Haritaworn, 2015, p 85). The right kind of queer thus once more becomes a boundary marker in a multitude of discourses revolving around essentialized notions of 'Western' and 'other' cultures and their views on sexuality and gender identity.

Within these narratives of threat and protection/oppression and liberation, the process of coming-out has been identified as playing a decisive role (Horton, 2018; Edenborg, 2020b). In order to be electable for inclusion into the safety of gay-friendly liberal-secular Western communities, one has to break with the oppressive traditions ascribed to racialized and/or Muslim communities. But while some bodies might be able to access that transition, others remain unrecognizable, ambiguous, out of place. The coming-outs that are possible are therefore 'neither universal nor incidental' (Haritaworn, 2015, p 84). Muslim and gay, for example, become mutually exclusive subjectivities to the extent that there appear to be 'no points of cultural contact between sexual progressives and religious minorities that are not encounters of violence and exclusion' (Butler, 2008, p 6; see also Puar, 2013).

While those racialized as Muslims first and foremost serve as a 'constitutive outside – as a location of backwardness and deficiency that needs to be educated, assimilated or quarantined' (Haritaworn, 2015, p 103), those who are seen as both Muslim and queer become a case of exceptions to the rule (Peltonen and Jungar, 2018; Rahman, 2020). As El-Tayeb argues, this not only essentializes Islam as a cultural phenomenon, thereby extinguishing all variations in the way in which this religion is interpreted and practised; it also makes it extremely difficult for queers racialized as non-White and/or Muslim to be recognized and to participate in the political debate. They are constantly asked to take sides in this imaginary clash of cultures (El-Tayeb, 2012, p 85), with the expectation to either denounce their Muslim/racialized identities or not be taken seriously in their LGBTQ identities.

Finally, as Puar points out, when bodies racialized as non-White and/or Muslim are described as inherently straight, and LGBTQ people as always White, difference becomes carefully separated and managed (Puar, 2013, p 32). The relegation of racialized/Muslim and queer to mutually exclusive realms via acts of discursive boundary making also forecloses the potential political solidarity and alliance building between disenfranchised minorities.

Rather, it might incite alignment with axes of privilege, leaving those behind who cannot (or are unwilling to) align with any of these axes. As this book's empirical sections will show, the rescue narrative, the notion of the hateful Other and the right to/need for coming-out all play a central role in the boundary-making processes analysed here and in the ways in which these processes enable specific grids of intelligibility, particularly for LGBTQ people racialized as Muslim and/or non-White.

Swedish gender exceptionalism, cultural racism and hegemonic Whiteness

As we have seen, homonationalist and homonormative boundary making has (re-)appeared across Western European societies, including France, the Netherlands, the UK and Germany. When turning to the Scandinavian countries and, in particular, Sweden, this picture becomes if anything even more pronounced. Attitudes towards gender identity and sexuality are drawn upon by a number of different actors in order to create and reinforce more overarching Scandinavian identities but also specific national identities that come with their very own inclusions and exclusions (Loftsdóttir and Jensen, 2012; Alm et al, 2021; Keskinen et al, 2021).

Notwithstanding the rise of a conservative government, propped up by support from the populist right-wing Sweden Democrats (SD) in 2022, there still exist powerful narratives of Sweden as particularly progressive with regard to gender equality and LGBTQ rights. These narratives are partly based on Sweden being an early adaptor of legislation protecting same-sex partnerships and reproductive rights, as well as having a well-established and vocal (if predominantly White) LGBTQ and sexual rights movement. There is also a history of 'state feminism' (Dahl, 2011, p 144), expressed, for example, by the Swedish government publicly adopting what they labelled 'a feminist foreign policy' (Nylund et al, 2022; Rosamond and Hedling, 2022). This policy was promptly discontinued by the conservative government in 2022, but its narrative legacy lives on. Additionally, Sweden has long enjoyed an image of being something of a good agent in international relations, represented, among other things, through development aid and peacebuilding initiatives. This might change with its recent turn towards NATO and away from historical notions of neutrality in the wake of Russia's full-scale invasion of Ukraine in 2022 (Eduards and Jansson, 2023). Despite its past as a colonizer of its Scandinavian neighbours, its indigenous population and foreign territories abroad, Sweden is also frequently considered to be somewhat of an outsider to global (post)colonial power relations – an image fiercely criticized by Scandinavian scholars (Loftsdóttir and Jensen, 2012; Andersen et al, 2015; Dankertsen, 2021; Knobblock, 2021).

While gender equality and LGBTQ rights are important parts of discourses on Swedish nationhood, central to defining who belongs and who does not, they seem to be inevitably accompanied by notions of 'bad patriarchies' located in distant places and racialized bodies (Mulinari et al, 2009, p 24). This points to one of the central building blocks of these narratives of Swedish gender exceptionalism (Habel, 2012; Alm et al, 2021): the homo-/transphobic and gender-unequal Others that constitute the outside and thus mark the borders of this particular notion of Swedishness. Thus, notions of Swedish gender exceptionalism (like homonationalism) are shown to effectively define, regulate and exclude (or externalize) bad, dangerous or hateful Others, while Sweden itself is 'envisioned as a country saving … queer subjects, instead of a country deporting … queer subjects' (Jungar and Peltonen, 2016, p 729).

Martinsson et al (2016) show how gender equality is called upon as a national trait in a wide range of Swedish policy discourses, thus constructing a homogenous gender-conscious identity which risks making invisible and depoliticizing gender-based discrimination in Swedish society. In line with the (colonialist) developmental temporalities discussed earlier, promises are made about continued evolution and progress ahead for women and LGBTQ people (Alm et al, 2021). This well-maintained myth of the gender-exceptional country not only has the potential to conceal discrimination and harassment based on sexuality and gender within Sweden. Martinsson et al (2016) suggest that Swedish gender exceptionalism is also easily appropriated by a form of cultural racism that once more makes possible a by-now-familiar hierarchical ordering of nation states and cultures according to Western definitions of progress and modernity. Certain people and communities are portrayed as being in need of help, education and guidance from a modern, highly developed and White Swedish 'we' (Habel, 2012; Andreassen and Vitus, 2015).

In their seminal work on 'the different (dis)guises of power' (de los Reyes et al, 2002), de los Reyes, Molina, and Mulinari introduced a postcolonial critique of the ongoing production of Swedish nationality and an imagined Swedish exceptionalism through normalized gender-equality discourses. They show how an imagined 'Swedish White We' is reproduced through ongoing processes of Othering in various spheres of social life (de los Reyes et al, 2002, p 189). To maintain this notion of Swedish gender equality, which is produced as unique and exceptional, somebody else has to be marked as non-Swedish and non-gender equal. Playing on well-established racist and Islamophobic stereotypes, that role as a constitutive outside is even here frequently attributed to those racialized as non-White, and particularly people considered to be Muslims, who are also represented as being homophobic and/or particularly oppressed. Gender equality and LGBTQ-inclusiveness as a Swedish national trait can thus be understood as intrinsically linked to processes of racialization and hegemonic Whiteness.

Hübinette and Lundström argue that hegemonic Whiteness and associated processes of racialization have a 'double-binding power' over large parts of Swedish society, based on the two images of the 'old Sweden' (built around the notion of the *folkhemmet*, the social democratic ideal of the equal, safe and harmonious home of the people) and the 'good Sweden' as being both anti-racist and (exceptionally) feminist (Hübinette and Lundström, 2011, p 43). By identifying three major phases of Swedish nation building, they illustrate how Whiteness became the 'master signifier of Swedishness' – meaning that 'a Swede is a white person, and a non-white person is therefore not … a full Swede' (Hübinette and Lundström, 2023, p 15). After a phase of White purity (1905–68) came a period of White solidarity (1968–2001). During that time, the Swedish state occupied a position as White supporter of decolonization and anti-apartheid, as well as driving social justice and gender-equality policies. This post-racial Swedish society was also portrayed as free from any colonial past (and guilt). Claiming the international position of anti-racist Sweden thus also meant proclaiming a 'good whiteness' (Hübinette and Lundström, 2023).

White anti-racism, Ahmed argues, is in fact central to regenerating and upholding White hegemony in a time marked by increasing diversity (Ahmed, 2006, p 121), and research shows that feminist movements in Sweden have been and remain spaces of Whiteness, where bodies racialized as non-White might be made invisible or become hyper-visible through their role as providers of diversity despite these movements proclaiming themselves to be anti-racist (see also Ahmed, 2009; Knobblock and Kuokkanen, 2015; Cuesta and Mulinari, 2018; Liinason, 2018; Liinason and Alm, 2018; Brovold, 2023). The final phase according to Hübinette and Lundström is one of White melancholy or mourning, which is characterized by the dismantling of the welfare state, colonial nostalgia, Islamophobia and feelings of fear and anxiety concerning everything that is regarded as foreign (Hübinette and Lundström, 2023, pp 22ff). Mourning the 'old White Sweden' and fearing for the 'good feminist Sweden', both the political left and right construct a (White) homogeneous past when the threatening racialized, non-gender equal and homophobic Other was kept at a safe distance (Hübinette and Lundström, 2023).

How closely hegemonic Whiteness and notions of gender equality are intertwined in the Swedish national narrative becomes clear for example when SD, time and again, have attempted to portray themselves as the protectors of Swedish women (and LGBTQ people) against supposedly violent, patriarchal and homophobic Muslim migrants (Mulinari and Neergaard, 2013; Sager and Mulinari, 2018). At the same time, there is also an increasing tendency to refer to gender and sexuality issues as a threat to a traditional Swedish identity, in line with anti-gender movements on the political right across Europe (Martinsson, 2020).

The historical perspective of different periods of Swedish race relations reveals how Whiteness has worked as a continuous structuring principle of Swedishness over the past century and how closely connected it is to ideas of Swedish exceptionalism, particularly with regard to gender and sexuality. The underlying historical continuities of different paradigm shifts, from scientific racism and race biology to anti-racist colour-blindness and cultural racism, will be discussed in more detail in Chapter 4 on racialization. However, this section has already shown that processes of racialization continue to inscribe certain people as White, good, Swedish, feminist and LGBT-friendly anti-racists, whereas others are marked as non-White, defined according to characteristics such as traditional, patriarchal, homophobic, criminal and violent. Studies show racialization processes to be just as present in Swedish society as in other Western countries, including the use of colonialist-racist imagery and vocabulary (Alinia, 2020; Mulinari and Neergaard, 2022; Hagerlid, 2023). While the notion of a colour-blind and anti-racist Sweden forecloses and silences everyday experiences of racism/being racialized as non-White (Osanami Törngren, 2022; Hübinette et al, 2023), the twin narrative of gender exceptionalism simultaneously projects gendered and sexual oppression on to racialized communities. This seems to continuously put feminists and queers racialized as non-White and/or Muslims into a position where their experiences are not accounted for in hegemonic narratives of belonging in Sweden.

However, despite Hübinette and Lundström's description of the current period as White melancholy, the 2010s and 2020s have also been shaped by the increased visibility of racialized positionalities and experiences and by challenges to and critiques of hegemonic gender-equality discourses related to Whiteness and racial hierarchies. Relying on critical race theory and intersectionality, researchers have scrutinized the Swedish welfare state's gender-equality policies, the exclusionary nationalist implications of exceptionalism narratives, hegemonic Whiteness in all spheres of society and the ways in which Sweden's anti-racist, feminist and queer movements are implicated in these exclusions (Jungar and Peltonen, 2016; Tlostanova et al, 2019; de los Reyes and Mulinari, 2020; Dahl, 2021; Dankertsen, 2021). At the same time, a diverse mix of activist groups has sprung up, challenging and disrupting hetero-, cis-normative and White gender-equality norms as well as the Swedish self-image as anti-racist and LGBTQ-friendly.

LGBTQ activists racialized as non-White and/or Muslims have started to vocalize their concerns in the form of groups outside of the major Swedish LGBTQ organizations. These include local and regional initiatives such as Gays in Angered or Swedish Queer Initiative Syd, as well as groups with a more dispersed reach, such as Black Queers Sweden and Rainbow Refugees Sweden. Their focus is on creating community and representation for racialized queers but also on contesting racism and exotification, fetishization and victimization of racialized queers within White LGBTQ spaces (Girma and Atto, 2017). While building on existing critiques of homonormativity and homonationalism, they frequently describe hegemonic Whiteness as the main problem rather than a binary political distinction between assimilated (right-wing) gays and transgressive (left-wing) queers. This is only a small selection of the groups and organizations that currently exist, but all reject and challenge the positions assigned to them within the narrative of a gender-exceptional Sweden: as victim icons and markers of Western freedom and modernity. These narratives, they argue, justify exclusionary, penalizing, violent and potentially deadly measures against dangerous Others, and their projection externalizes and thus hides the continued existence of racism, islamophobia, sexism, trans-, homo- and biphobia within all spheres of Swedish society.

Questioning gay-rights-as-human-rights narratives

Narratives of a progressive West versus an oppressive East can also be identified at an international level, as part of geopolitical hierarchies and power struggles in connection to an understanding of sexual and gender rights as part of the global human rights discourse (Janoff, 2022). A growing body of literature deals with the ways in which struggles for LGBTQ rights have come to act as performative of nation states and as a symbolic marker of countries' in/tolerance and constructions of modernity and/or backwardness (Weber, 2016b; Bosia, 2020b; Edenborg, 2023). Sexual minority rights are also part of international conditionality, highlighting how, for example, the Middle East, certain African countries and parts of Eastern Europe are constructed as backward and not civilized enough in relation to both Western Europe and North America (Haritaworn, 2015; Agius and Edenborg, 2019; Rao, 2020; Boulila and Browne, 2023).

One frequently cited instance is then-US Secretary of State Hillary Clinton's declaration in 2011 that "gay rights are human rights", and how this became a leverage point in the Obama administration's foreign policy (Rao, 2014a; Weber, 2016b). Since then, the rights of sexual and gender minorities have been formalized internationally through mechanisms such as the 2016 establishment by the UN Human Rights Council of an Independent Expert on Sexual Orientation and Gender Identity, a role that was renewed in 2019 (Langlois, 2022). Against the background of this values-based international rights structure, Rao draws our attention to how LGBTQ rights have been harnessed in support of hegemonic projects not only by Western powers but also by elites in the Global South. He shows how through transnational practices of locating homophobia certain countries in the Global South became places of hope (India, South Africa, Brazil), while others are places of phobia (Iran, Uganda, Jamaica), and how these classifications are intimately connected to flows of economic and political power, both internationally and domestically (Rao, 2020). In the face of new conservative nationalisms waxing and waning across the globe, any country-specific assessments might need to be reconsidered. The overall mechanisms analysed by Rao, however, remain acutely relevant.

Beyond analysing how demands for LGBTQ rights by state and non-state actors can be anchored in homonormative and homonationalist narratives, many approaches express a general critique of the notion of sexual citizenship underlying 'gay-rights-as-human-rights' discourses. Based on Euro-American understandings of a universal liberal subject as claimant of human rights, it is considered to be a concept steeped in Western colonial and orientalist history, disregarding the sociocultural specificity of notions of sexuality and gender identity. Instead, it produces a universalist epistemology through which certain ways of being and certain ways of making claims are normalized, while others are erased and excluded. The global spread of specific definitions and forms of LGBTQ activism is therefore sometimes said to result in a Westernization of LGBTQ identities and politics in non-Western contexts at the risk of ignoring local understandings and cultural meanings about sexualities as well as obscuring local political activism (Richardson, 2017).

While Puar's and Duggan's early analyses of homonationalism and homonormativity were essential to a critical engagement with LGBTQ politics' seemingly triumphant entry into the realm of the accepted and the respectable, and thus to a broadening of queer theory beyond an earlier focus on heteronormativity (see for example Cohen, 1997 for an early critique of this), they have themselves not gone unchallenged. Aiming for further development and refinement of the analysis, I will now critically engage with Puar's conceptualization of homonationalism in particular, as well as some of the works that employ her concept directly to specific local contexts.

Queer critiques and the potential of cautiously deploying universalism

While many of the original critiques of homonormative and homonationalist tendencies discussed earlier seem to see the inclusion of normative (White) queerness through, among others, 'gay-rights-as-human-rights' discourses as unambiguously detrimental, they have themselves been called out for risking dangerous simplifications in their analyses. Nikita Dhawan takes Puar to task for her anti-statist view on queer politics and LGBTQ rights, which she sees as coming from positions of comparable transnational privilege that enable her to 'reject "pragmatic" politics in favour of more "radical" interventions in the face of queer imperialism' (Dhawan, 2013, p 215). Seeing the state – and, I would argue, state-adjacent civil society actors – mostly as a malevolent monolithic power means not acknowledging the importance of the state 'for those citizens who do not have access to transnational counterpublic spheres to address their grievances' (Dhawan, 2013, p 217) and who thus might be dependent on social recognition and legal protection by its institution. This risks disregarding the state and its rights-granting powers as a potentially important arena of political activism in favour of a sole focus on the damage done by the selective granting of these rights (Dhawan, 2016). In the context of the Russian full-scale invasion of Ukraine, this question of state-related power and protection has reached a new urgency, as queer and feminist researchers and activists from Eastern Europe call on Western states to arm Ukraine (Graff, 2022; Hendl, 2022; Tsymbalyuk, 2022; Kratochvíl and O'Sullivan, 2023). Their assertion of the crucial role played by the military in the protection of LGBTQ people against an aggressor waging war in the name of 'traditional family values' (Brock, 2023; Shevtsova, 2023) complicates straightforward claims about the dangers of homonationalist boundary making.

Other authors have taken up the question of whether it is at all possible to 'not want rights' (Langlois, 2015; Weber, 2016b). They reflect less categorically on the paradoxical way in which the extension of human rights to LGBTQ people grants certain entitlements and protections while simultaneously creating exclusionary normative standards, thus further entrenching 'existing institutions ... which even purporting to be emancipatory, often constrain freedoms, generate inequality and entrench injustice' (Langlois, 2015, p 27). Human rights, Langlois argues, 'are about establishing particular normative boundaries', which seems at first sight to create a theoretical paradox in relation to queer theory – 'queer, if it is anything, is anti-normative. Establishing and policing boundaries is not supposed to be its brief' (Langlois, 2015, p 28). However, Rao has challenged this understanding of queer theory and human rights as mutually exclusive, despite being himself a fierce critic of universalizing gay-rights-as-human-rights discourses (Rao, 2020). He acknowledges that in some cases, 'cautious deployment of universalism' can have its place, in order to fulfil states' requirements for identifiable subjects, thus enabling the legal protection of at least some LGBTQ people (Rao, 2018, p 146). He points out that this does not, as frequently assumed among human rights scholars, exist in total opposition to queer theory by going back to what he calls 'the most influential work in queer post-structuralism' (Rao 2018, p 146) – Butler's *Gender Trouble*.

In the preface to the second edition, Butler acknowledges how their practical work on the International Gay and Lesbian Human Rights Commission had made them appreciate 'the strategic utility of universalist categories so long as they were understood in nonsubstantial and open-ended ways, leaving them amenable to expansion through the claims of those who were not yet included within them' (Butler, 1990, quoted in Rao, 2018, p 146). This means that as long as we remain aware of the risks of 'seizing the tools of empowerment and emancipation available to us' (Rao, 2018, p 146), we should not be afraid of doing so based on an overly simplified understanding of queer approaches as inherently disinterested in political recognition. As Wilkinson reminds us, even the most accepted queer is still a queer, conditionally included, and thus remains in danger of being stripped of their rights (Wilkinson, 2017). This puts the ability to not want rights in favour of more radical solutions into perspective, and it is a poignant reminder particularly at a time when political powers on the right are pushing to roll back LGBTQ rights. Falling back on Puar's own initial analysis, we also know that those queers who are additionally subject(ed) to processes of racialization are most acutely affected by this conditionality, an aspect I discuss in more detail in Chapter 4. Langlois sees an active awareness of this queer vulnerability, of feeling backwards to past (and present) injuries suffered, as one way of combining a queer critical reflexivity about gay-rights-as-human-rights discourses with 'the compromised but real opportunities' that are afforded to LGBTQ people by international human rights regimes (Langlois, 2022, p 177).

Rao encourages those engaged in critical analyses of both the role of the state and queer theory and politics to 'conspire to use queer thought to introduce irresolvable tensions' (Rao, 2018, p 147), such as the ambiguity that is involved in not being able to not want rights, while also being aware of the normative, exclusionary and constraining aspects of these rights. As Langlois puts it:

> Queering our politics, then ... is to refuse the seduction and embrace of the state at that point when the state seems to come on side; it is to recognize the *queerness of that point*: a moment of deep danger as well as one of liberation; a moment destabilizing in its possibilities for *both* emancipation and requisition. (Langlois, 2012, p 35, my emphasis)

Being aware of the complexity of this duality and making this complexity a part of our analyses, I argue, is necessary to ensure the continued relevance of concepts like homonationalism for critiques of how LGBTQ positionalities are used in processes of (national) boundary making. We need to be able to maintain an awareness of the dangerous seduction of conditional inclusion but also the politics involved in inhabiting a position of not being able to not want rights, rather than just focusing on the dangers of seduction and condemning the seduced.

Maintaining complexity through queer logics of analysis

If we want to attend more rigorously to the particular queerness of that point, that is, the ambiguity and complexity of gay-rights-as-human-rights discourses and their practical implications on the ground, the works of Weber and Rao provide useful starting points. In her book *Queer International Relations*, Weber critiques claims about the human rights industrial complex. Drawing on Langlois, Brown and Zivi, among others, she cautions us to acknowledge the 'extent to which our [rights] claims both reference and reiterate social conventions and norms, and yet have forces and effects that exceed them' (Zivi, 2011, p 19, quoted in Weber, 2016b). Not only can we not *not* want rights, by focusing exclusively on the homonormative and homonationalist aspects of claiming LGBTQ rights as human rights, we also risk missing the numerous ways in which these claims might 'practically and performatively exceed homonormativity, homonationalism, and (neo)imperialism' (Weber, 2016b, p 120). By not paying attention to this excessive potential, we run the risk of making these concepts more monolithic and universal than they are, thus endangering their critical analytical potential.

This appeal for more complexity also appears in Dhawan's work, which points to the dangers of focusing solely on homonationalism in the Global North when it leads scholars to neglect homophobia in diasporic and postcolonial contexts, 'which are explained away as having been caused by, and as a reaction to, Western racism' (Dhawan, 2013, p 192; see also Rao, 2020). This, she says, is particularly dangerous not only because it exposes those who are 'vulnerable to "normative violence" … from both queer racism as well as postcolonial homophobia' (Dhawan, 2013, p 192) but also because it means we might miss occasions where actors, both colonial and postcolonial, as well as across the religious–secular spectrum, collaborate with each other when it comes to furthering heteronormative agendas. The brief re-criminalization of homosexuality in India between 2013 and 2018 (Tonini, 2016) or the political process leading up to the Ugandan Anti Homosexuality Act (Rao, 2020) are examples of this.

Dhawan asks for a more multidimensional critique that allows us to see the (neo)imperialist, (neo)colonialist and racist aspects of homonationalism and homonormativity, while keeping track of the fact that historically speaking, 'both the empire and its antagonist, the anticolonial nation, are profoundly heteronormative projects' (Dhawan, 2013, p 205). Instead, we need to be able to critically engage with more than one power structure at a time, neither neglecting the homonormative violence perpetrated by Western states, the persecution of non-normative sexualities and gender identities within postcolonial societies nor the ways in which these interact. Rao makes a powerful case for looking at the postcolonial present of queer lives (especially those outside of Western contexts) by acknowledging the influence of a colonial past as much as the promise of a prosperous future, both of which are equal parts resource and terrains for struggles over nation, sexuality and gender (Rao, 2020, pp 10–11). By doing so, he argues, responsibility for ongoing oppressions can be more correctly apportioned between colonial and postcolonial actors, accounting for the mutual constitution of core and periphery (Rao, 2020, p 9). He also points to the importance of understanding the specific grammar of a given context when trying to make sense of how the institutions of (postcolonial) states encounter queerness (Rao, 2020, pp 216–17).

Both Rao's and Dhawan's calls for complexity can be connected to Weber, who also points out that homonormativity and homonationalism are specific both in their geopolitical and historical location. This is something which Duggan took up when first coining the term homonormativity (Duggan, 2002; Weber, 2016b, p 116) and which Puar has stressed when talking about how homonationalism as a concept has travelled (Puar, 2022). However, since their increased popularity within and outside of academia, these concepts have sometimes been applied by scholars and activists in ways that have neglected geographical and historical specificity, leading to 'universalized, reified understandings … that seemingly apply in the same ways across time and space' (Weber, 2016b, p 116). By treating homonormativity and homonationalism as if they were global phenomena, these analyses 'flatten the subjectivities they investigate' (Weber, 2016b, p 116). Figurations like 'the gay rights holder', the 'gay patriot' as well as 'the unwanted im/migrant' or 'the terrorist' become equally reified and monolithic in both their formations and resistances.

Weber illustrates how these figurations are never stable, 'for every performance of a figuration depends upon innumerable particularities' (Weber, 2016a, p 16). These particularities include historical and sociocultural context, geographical location, but also how individuals perform certain figurations as well as how these perfomativities are read by others. Universal figures are therefore 'never as universal as they may at first appear to be' (Weber, 2016b, p 137), and 'institutional arrangements of power/knowledge/pleasure – be they heteronormativities and/or homonormativities – are likewise less stable than they appear to be' (Weber, 2016a, p 17). Weber suggests that if we want to account for these instabilities, we need to move from binary either/or logics of power to and/or logics. Many existing analyses of homonationalism and homonormativity, she argues, are built on either/or logics, which portray the normal and the perverse as being mutually exclusive while also being constitutive of each other.

By applying this logic, we miss that someone (or something) might not be understandable through one single fixed meaning but might require an understanding of how 'a person or a thing is constituted by and simultaneously embodies multiple, seemingly contradictory meanings' (Weber, 2016b, p 9). Her main example is that of the bearded drag queen Conchita Wurst/Tom Neuwirth, the winner of the 2014 Eurovision Song Contest, whom she sees as 'a performative embodiment of a plural logoi' and who has been read through 'vast matrices of sexes, genders, and sexualities' (Weber, 2016a, p 20).

Rao's rich analysis of contestations around queerness in different postcolonial contexts crucially adds to this argument by exploring how queerness 'mutates' in different configurations. His work shows how queerness becomes a signifier for 'anti-imperialism and imperialism, paganism and Christianity, whiteness, embourgeoisement and subordinate caste status' respectively, as a result of collaboration and transaction across the North–South divide (Rao, 2020, p 12). He adds an aspect of temporality to plural logics of either/or by destabilizing and disorienting also the now/then trajectory that underlies many narratives about gay-rights-as-human-rights, pointing instead to the 'heterotemporality of the global queer political present' (Rao, 2020, p 81).

I argue that these approaches can together be read as queer logics of analysis, since they are not limited to describing the ways in which the performatively perverse creates the appearance of the performatively normal or vice versa. Nor do they follow a linear temporal trajectory or a clear binary notion of colonial domination and postcolonial resistance. Relating this back to gay-rights-as-human-rights discourses, and their homonormative, homonationalist, homocapitalist, homocolonialist implications, it is the application of this kind of queer logic that allows for an adequate exploration of the excessive political potential of these discourses, as well as seeing specificities, ambiguities and contingencies of the figurations and subjectivities it is performed through, mobilizes and produces.

Acknowledging appeals for queer theory to account more rigorously for ambiguities and complexities in our analyses of homonormative and homonationalist formations, how do we continue to move forward in ongoing attempts to analyse and critically engage with the various ways in which LGBTQ issues have become entangled in projects of boundary making? While the contributions discussed in this chapter add crucial complexity, it seems that one central aspect of Puar's initial conceptualization slips in and out of focus: the various ways in which sexualized/gendered difference is *always* also racialized, and how this matters for the messiness of contemporary inclusions/exclusions as well as for the question of which queer bodies can and cannot afford to not want rights. This is particularly crucial in contexts where the law might be seen as something neutral, extra-racial, rather than being a big part of 'assemblages of racialisation' (Weheliye, 2014). There is therefore a continued need for queer theory to (re-)engage more deeply with questions of racialization, precisely in order to account for the ambiguities and complexities writers like Weber, Rao and Dhawan remind us of.

Conclusions

The literature on homonormativity and homonationalism, and the ways in which it has developed since the early 2000s, has managed to question and open up what has often been a single-issue focus on heterosexuality and its binary gender norms, increasing our ability to see beyond heteronormativity and to more fully account for the intersectional complexity of queer positionalities. In this chapter, I have both introduced and developed these analyses, arguing that if we want to understand the role figurations of L–G–B–T–Q play in projects of national and international boundary making as well as the ways in which LGBTQ people across the globe are variously positioned to deal with these mobilizations, we need to both expand our theoretical conceptualization of homonationalism and re-focus on some central aspects of the original concept. In the following chapters, I do so by engaging with theoretical explorations of boundary making and (queer) intelligibility while specifically connecting these concepts to social processes of racialization.

3

Theoretical Explorations I: Boundary Making and Intelligibility

This chapter and Chapter 4 engage with the main theoretical concepts that guide the analysis in this book: boundary making, grids of intelligibility and racialization. *Boundary making* enables a theoretical engagement with the discursive-performative creation of communities of (non-)belonging that characterizes the ways in which LGBTQ rights are mobilized in constructions of Swedishness. The concept *grids of intelligibility* attends to notions of identity and subjectivity created by boundary-making processes, and the need to appear or present oneself in certain ways in order to be eligible for belonging to a certain community. It enables a critical discussion of the necessity of becoming intelligible – and the limitations this imposes – and explores how intelligibilities are multiple and fluid, providing opportunities for contestation and re-signification. Finally, as the literature discussed in Chapter 2 shows, many Self/Other distinctions on which boundary making relies are highly dependent on the ascription of Otherness through race, requiring a theoretical engagement with *racialization* as a social process. Racialization will be discussed in Chapter 4.

The main theoretical concepts are first discussed separately. Each discussion includes a final section that collects the most important insights with regard to the particular concept and how it helps our theoretical understanding of the issues at hand. In the final part of Chapter 4, I tie the concepts together and clarify how the combination of and conversation between the theoretical approaches guides and enables analysis of the empirical material.

Boundaries, borders and (non-)belonging

Social scientists have concerned themselves with the dynamics of boundary-making processes from the starting point of nationalism and nationalist imaginaries (Anderson, 1991), the politics of belonging that accompany and enable these imaginaries (Yuval-Davis, 2011), as well as the b/ordering practices that attempt to contain them in relation to certain spatial-historical locations and geographies (van Houtum, 2005). Feminist, postcolonial and queer studies scholars have nuanced these discussions by pointing out crucial ways in which processes of bordering, boundary making and belonging draw upon gender, sexuality and race (Agius and Edenborg, 2019) by looking at their inherent instability (Weber, 2016b) as well as how these processes mobilize emotions (Ahmed, 2014).

While all of these fields of research are concerned with the socially constructed differentiation of 'Self' from 'Other' by way of various characteristics in order to achieve (the appearance of) social coherence, they contribute from different angles to this book. Feminist theories on the politics of belonging help us to understand not only the ways in which projects of belonging are socially constructed but also the power dynamics inherent in these constructions. Those parts of critical border studies that are concerned with symbolic bordering functions and symbolic borderwork (Edenborg, 2020c) enable us to account for the work that racialized, sexualized and gendered imaginaries do with regard to constructing the meaning and boundaries of Sweden/Swedishness, as well as how these are connected to material-territorial aspects. Finally, as touched upon in Chapter 2, recent contributions from the field of queer international relations continuously trouble the binary approach inherent in concepts like boundaries/borders and look beyond those binaries.

The politics of belonging

Yuval-Davis's concept of the politics of belonging defines belonging as something that 'tends to be naturalized, and becomes articulated and politicized only when it is threatened' (Yuval-Davis, 2006, p 197). *Politics of belonging*, on the other hand, are concerned with the specific political projects that aim to construct belonging (to particular collectives) in specific ways while, crucially, simultaneously constructing these collectives. This analytical differentiation between belonging and the politics of belonging is central to our ability to critically engage in analyses of nationalism, racism or other politics of belonging. The term politics of belonging emphasizes that boundary making is by definition a politically contested process, which shows the construction of communities through boundary making to be inherently related to power struggles, patterns of domination and unequal social positionalities. This means that rather than simply looking at constructions of belonging, we can also critically engage with how people are variously positioned to participate in these discourses and to contest them. Yuval-Davis repeatedly points to the importance of applying an intersectional lens to our analysis of these different social locations, for example when she questions

Anderson's influential notion of nations as 'imagined communities' (Anderson, 1991). She points out that imagination should also be acknowledged as situated, an active practice which differs in its effects depending on social location, experiences and resources. We do not all imagine communities in the same way, we are not all affected by imaginations in the same way and not all of us are given the authority to decide on which side of the imagined boundary we will be placed (Yuval-Davis and Stoetzler, 2002).

The question of what is involved in one's placement on either side of imaginary boundaries, what is required from a person in order for them to be considered part of a collective, points us to another strength of the concept 'politics of belonging', and it fits well with the way in which contemporary mobilizations of LGBTQ rights construct 'right' and 'wrong' kinds of queers. In comparison to other approaches which take specific categories such as citizenship, race or nationhood as their points of departure, it remains analytically open as to which categories of belonging are most relevant to the object of study at hand in any given context. Yuval-Davis identifies three analytical levels on which to study belonging: social locations (among them race, ethnicity, class, religion, gender, sexuality, all of which should be understood intersectionally); identifications and emotional attachments; and ethical and political values (Yuval-Davis, 2006). She sees the boundaries constructed by these to be more or less permeable, with boundary making based on social locations being the least permeable, and ethical and political values (such as 'democracy' or 'human rights') being the most permeable (Yuval-Davis, 2006).

However, others have argued that political projects of belonging which emphasize shared ethical and political values, that is, normative ideas regarding the organization of social life, usually reflect ethnocentric norms which in turn rely upon implicit or explicit devaluations of Others (Bhaba, 1994). I would add that seemingly more permeable notions of ethical and political values are deeply intertwined with (less permeable) ethnic, racial and religious signifiers of belonging. The latter ones often define whose adherence to common values is taken for granted and who is (implicitly or explicitly) being asked to demonstrate their loyalties to shared ethics (Haritaworn, 2015). Additionally, allegedly emancipatory values such as women's and LGBTQ people's equality and rights can be transformed into naturalized personal attributes assigned to particular national or regional communities (Sweden, Scandinavia, the 'West'), thus becoming acutely exclusionary signifiers of these communities' boundaries (Edenborg, 2023; Liinason, 2023; Shevtsova, 2023).

Boundary making through the spectacle of the Other

If we consider political projects of belonging to be a form of boundary making, a continuous and dynamic (re-)constitution of the boundaries of a given collective, and thereby of the collective itself, the next step is to engage with what has been conceptualized as the constitutive outside, the strange Other which is essential to defining belonging by demarcating its opposite (Hall and Gieben, 1992). Since processes of boundary making and the constitutive maintenance of Andersonian 'imagined communities' rely on the continuous differentiation between 'us' and 'them', discourses about strangers are central to discourses about belonging. These Others frequently become a 'spectacle' by way of stereotyping – they are ascribed a limited number of naturalized, essentialized and thus fixed characteristics which can be easily differentiated from the community in question (Hall, 1997b, pp 257ff). They can create fear but also more ambivalent feelings like desire and fetishization (Laskar, 2015a). One example of this is the sexualized exotification of the colonized Other discussed by postcolonial scholars as the 'colonial gaze', which purifies the gazer in their *not*-being the colonized Other (McClintock, 1995). This attempt at symbolic purification through the projection of difference and disorder within on to the outside (Butler and Spivak, 2010) reproduces not only the boundaries between inside and outside; it also reinforces the idea of a Self, stabilized through various notions of alterity.

Importantly, as the boundaries of political projects of belonging shift, so might the people, values, bodies, objects embodying the constitutive outside of these boundaries. When boundaries of belonging become contested, it is often those who dwell on the margins of communities of belonging who become the central points of contestation (Yuval-Davis et al, 2018). This development is well demonstrated by the ways in which LGBTQ people have become boundary markers for communities of belonging constructed around widely diverse notions such as Europeanness (El-Tayeb, 2012), progress (Rahman, 2014), Swedishness (Polkov, 2023) or traditional values (Edenborg, 2023). And even when these boundaries are successfully re-drawn, re-enforcing the alterity of the Other, this Other can still be found 'haunting' notions of sameness (Laclau and Mouffe, 1985), threatening the alleged coherence of the community. This idea of 'haunting' will re-appear later when I discuss the formation of subjectivity through normative grids of intelligibility. The more vigorously projects of belonging try to maintain a picture of homogeneity through boundary making vis-à-vis an externalized Other, the more obvious the futility of these projects can eventually become. One contemporary example of this can be seen in the attempts by the conservative-nationalist government in Poland to exclude LGBTQ people from notions of 'traditional Polishness' (for example, by local authorities declaring parts of the country to be 'LGBTQ-free zones'), which in turn has led to an increased international awareness of the precarious situation of LGBTQ people in the country, as well as support for LGBTQ organizations and activists (Korolczuk, 2020b).

Despite agreeing in principle with Yuval-Davis and Anthias's (Anthias and Yuval-Davis, 1992) assessment that there is no *inherent* difference between ethnic, national or racial collectives if we consider all of them to be constructed around boundaries that divide the world into 'us' and 'them', there are additional analytical insights to be gained by moving into the territory of bordering. This literature adds to the specific nationalist aspect of studying constructions of Swedishness, as well as the material-territorial aspect connected to them. These are particularly relevant in relation to the Swedish Armed Forces' (SAF) recent campaigns and their renewed focus on territorial defence, even more so at a time when European geopolitics are conducted under the impression of Russia's territorial war against Ukraine.

Boundary making as/through bordering

Critical border studies understands bordering as a practice rather than theorizing borders as static dividing lines (Parker and Vaughan-Williams, 2012). This procedural understanding of borders sees the border not primarily as a 'thing' but rather as 'continually performed' and 'bound up with the identity-making activities of the nation-state and other forms of political community' (Parker and Vaughan-Williams, 2012, pp 729–30). Crucially, therefore, bordering practices are made logical by the discourses that underpin and rationalize them, but these discourses in themselves are also part of the act of bordering; they make the border, mediating and negotiating subjectivities and spaces.

While their focus on the procedural, performative, discursive and imaginary aspects of bordering works well with understandings of boundary making as related to politics of belonging, critical border studies remain more aware of the physical-material aspect of bordering that are supported and enabled by these sets of practices, and by the territoriality that connects borders, nation states and (nationalist) politics of belonging. This is crucial for understanding processes of boundary making that relate to notions of belonging built around a *national* identity, which is located not only within an imaginary community but is also connected to a specific space or territory. This connection is present throughout the empirical material discussed in this book, especially with regard to Pride Järva and the SAF campaigns. Understanding this is crucial in two ways. First, boundary making around notions of Swedishness in relation to LGBTQ rights among other things informs and enables grids of intelligibility with regard to who becomes 'recognizably LGBTQ' in a certain context. As discussed previously, one of these contexts is the asylum-seeking process, where decisions about the right to cross the actual physical border into Sweden are made based partially on asylum seekers being able to perform their queerness in ways that place them 'on the inside' of discursively produced boundaries around notions of Swedishness. Any theoretical understanding of boundary making therefore needs to be able to account for this territorial materiality.

Secondly, nationalist boundary making based on shared spatiality connects notions of 'us–them' to another binary – 'here–there' – thus situating the political contestations of belonging more or less firmly within a 'homeland'. This connection, in turn, opens for narratives based on temporality, which (discursively and emotionally) connect the members of a specific collective with others that 'came before' and those who will 'come after', reinforcing the need for these communities to be, in fact, 'imagined', but also increasing the potential for 'naturalization' of their boundaries. Edenborg argues that we can see this as a form of 'myth' as Barthes defines it: a narrative that depoliticizes and naturalizes historical contingencies, excludes complexity and contradictions and thus, when successful, 'transforms history into nature' (Barthes, 1973, p 129, cited in Edenborg, 2016, p 38; see also Martinsson et al, 2016). Again, it is important to remain analytically aware that these 'myths' and the absolute binaries on which their boundaries rely remain unstable no matter the degree of naturalization of a certain origin story or a particular threat to a community. Weber's engagement with Barthes' plural logics of the and/or shows how particularly those figures existing on the borders of communities of belonging might be read in multiple, complex ways that defy binary notions of either/or (either us or them, either in or out), thus complicating any attempted act of boundary making (Barthes, 1974; Weber, 2016b; see also my discussion in Chapter 2).

Making sense of: boundary making

Boundary making is performative – it creates the communities whose boundaries it claims to describe: understanding boundary making as a performative dividing practice helps us avoid any kind of essentialized understanding of notions of belonging. While boundary-making processes are located in specific contexts of political negotiation over belonging which (re)produce specific understandings of identities (individual and/or collective), space and time, there is no ontological 'truth' to the question of being 'inside' or 'outside', 'Self' or 'Other'. Stressing the *making* in boundary making, while maintaining an awareness of how it relates to material aspects – such as the actual borders of national territories – points us towards analyses of how belonging is continually produced and performed but also challenged and contested.

Boundary making needs to be looked at intersectionally: the construction of Otherness that underlies practices of boundary making and the notions of belonging that are created through these practices are produced intersectionally, deploying categories of racial, gendered and/or sexual difference. In our analysis of them, we therefore need to look at how different power structures and various forms of positioning and social categorization interact with each other, co-constructing specific social locations.

Boundary making is forever unstable: while attempts at boundary making are characterized by a desire for closure and coherence, the separation of inside/outside never works as seamlessly as the discourses underlying it might suggest. The continued haunting presence of externalized others, but also various cases of and/or as well as conditioned inclusions, shows that boundary making and belonging are frequently more complex, ambivalent and contested than the obvious either-or binaries it promotes. Additionally, we need to remain aware that social coherence and homogeneity crucially rely on erasure and exclusions (and therefore ultimately violence).

Subjectivity, grids of intelligibility and normative violence

As discussed, I understand boundary making as creating – and being created through – the construction of Self–Other distinctions that demarcate the boundaries of communities of belonging, which rely (simply put) on defining some people as being 'inside'/included and others as being 'outside'/excluded. This is relevant to analyses of how LGBTQ rights are employed in nationalist projects of boundary making in two ways: first, it provides a tool to analyse how contemporary constructions of Swedishness employ LGBTQ rights in order to mark boundaries in particular ways, relying on particular notions of what defines 'inside' and 'outside' with regard to these issues. Secondly, and potentially more importantly, it enables us to look at how the making of these boundaries enables specific grids of intelligibility (Butler, 1990), particularly for LGBTQ people racialized as non-White and/or Muslim. These grids make people more or less recognizable as members of a community of belonging, but they also position people differently with regard to how they manoeuvre issues of intelligibility/recognition.

They are relevant with regard to the construction of individual subjectivities and identities because of the ways in which we, through them, become recognizable as the inside, the outside, neither of these or both, to both ourselves and to others. Existing research on the Swedish context shows that being non-intelligible has (material) implications far beyond questions of identity, when asylum statuses are denied, relationships remain legally unrecognized (and thus unprotected) and access to healthcare is made difficult (Linander et al, 2019; Dahl and Andreassen, 2021; Wimark, 2021). This is a field that has been extensively conceptualized by researchers within queer theory, particularly in engagement with Butler's work. I draw on an eclectic selection of works from various other fields – including post/decolonial studies, feminist security studies and queer international relations – to complement and nuance Butler's conceptualization of grids of intelligibility.

While literature on belonging, boundary making and bordering largely focuses on making sense of the constitutive power of binary Self/Other distinctions, queer theorists have explicitly turned their attention to questions of fluidity and the instabilities involved in such distinctions. Combining these approaches might at first sight seem counterintuitive. However, I argue that it allows for a more nuanced understanding of boundary-making processes and the grids of intelligibility they enable.

Belonging and performativity

While processes of boundary making in the way I have discussed so far seem to have their most direct bearing on the construction of *collective* political communities of belonging, they also play an important role with regard to how all of us construct our *individual* sense of self, by making certain identities, subjectivities and positionalities more or less feasible, recognizable, visible, *intelligible* within the context of a certain collective. Yuval-Davis points out that 'constructions of belonging have a performative' dimension, which means that there exist 'specific repetitive practices' which 'link individual and collective behaviour' and which are 'crucial for the construction and reproduction of identity narratives' (Yuval-Davis, 2006, p 203). Identity narratives (for example, regarding a shared homeland, history or a common future destiny) are important to notions of belonging and to related processes of boundary making because they are the 'stories people tell themselves and others about who they are (and who they are not)' (Yuval-Davis, 2006, p 202).

Identity narratives often relate, directly or indirectly, to our own and/or others' perceptions of what being a member of a certain community might entail, connecting individual life stories to overarching and more collective narratives. While collective narratives, in particular, are constantly challenged and renegotiated, the way in which they make up a continuous part of people's everyday lives means they have an important meaning-giving function, ordering experiences and events in patterns that 'seem to make sense' (Edenborg, 2016, p 42). They can, therefore, be considered constitutive of the world as it appears to the people who tell these stories to and about themselves and others. Importantly, the striving for linearity, continuity and coherence that characterizes many of these narratives is not only troubled by omissions and silences; it also glosses over the various ways in which they are performative, politically contingent and continually contested (Bhaba, 1994; Brown, 2006). Instead, people's emotional investment in narratives of belonging (that is, in constructions of themselves and their identities) means that the more threatened and less secure the community and the individuals it is composed of perceive themselves to be, the more they become willing to sacrifice in order for the narratives of their identities to continue to exist

(Ahmed, 2004a; Stern, 2006). Notably, the constructions of Otherness along lines of sexuality, gender and race that we encounter in this book almost all employ notions of threat and protection.

Queer studies scholars, post/decolonial scholars and Black studies scholars have long studied the manifold everyday ways in which grids of intelligibility have determined which populations have qualified as subjects with 'liveable lives' and which have not (Haritaworn et al, 2014; Weheliye, 2014; Butler, 2015). They have also pointed out the violence that is continually (and sometimes very acutely) present in these processes. In the next section, I therefore engage more closely with the concepts grids of intelligibility and mis/recognition to help make sense of the ways in which the boundary making involved in political projects of belonging circumscribe what it means to be a viable subject in the context of that community. They also enable us to look at the potentially violent effects of failure to become recognizable, as well as opening up for an understanding of non-intelligibility as potentially disruptive to social norms, or even as an active strategy of resistance to said norm.

Constructing subjectivity through intelligibility and recognition

One of the most widely known and most frequently popularized discussions of the constitution of subjectivity through intelligibility has to be Butler's notion of gender as performative and guided by the heterosexual matrix, that 'grid of cultural intelligibility through which bodies, genders and desires are naturalized' (Butler, 1990, p 151). By showing how normative presumptions about the linear coherence and continuity of sex, gender and desire can be thought of as grids of intelligibility that delimit 'the very field of description that we have for the human' (Butler, 1990, p 17), Butler builds and expands upon a Foucauldian understanding of the power/knowledge nexus as providing the conditions of possibility for the social as well as the individual through grids of intelligibility (Foucault, 1978). Butler's analysis of sex/gender as performative in *Gender Trouble* (Butler, 1990) is part of their ongoing theoretical engagement with questions regarding the conditions that create and sustain 'liveable lives', the norms that determine which lives will qualify as such and the violence perpetrated upon those who fail to perform their humanness 'intelligibly' (Butler, 1990, 2004, 2010, 2011, 2015).

Butler argues that '[g]ender … figures as a precondition for the production and maintenance of legible humanity' (Butler, 2004, p 11) because its norms establish what will and will not be intelligibly human, what will and will not be considered 'real'. However, this does not only apply to norms of sex and gender but to 'all kinds of bodies whose lives are not considered to be "lives" and whose materiality is not understood to "matter"' (Meijer and Prins, 1998, p 281). They point to 'ontological field[s] in which bodies may be given legitimate expression', maintained by norms that 'establish what will and will not be intelligibly human, what will and will not be considered to be "real"' (Butler, 1999, p xxiii). It is this engagement with the performative aspect of subjectivity through intelligibility (rather than its often-cited focus on gender and sexuality) that has the most bearing upon the theoretical framework of this book.

How, then, should we understand these grids of intelligibility to work in practice? As Lauren Wilcox has pointed out, Butler's work on performativity, subjectivity and 'liveable lives' is about practices and embodiment as much as discourses. This aspect sometimes gets ignored, particularly when it comes to critiques of their theories being insufficiently 'hands-on' to be politically effective or useful (Wilcox, 2017). I will give an account of the implications of 'successful' performances of subjectivity/identity first, before looking at the violent as well as the transformative potential of 'failed' performances. As is the case with the communities of belonging discussed earlier, the 'coherence' and 'continuity' of the 'subject' that I discuss here are socially constituted and maintained forms of intelligibility rather than inherent features of personhood. The internal coherence of the subject, our self-identification with an 'I', depends on culturally intelligible notions of identity. As social beings, we are relying on others being able to see, name, recognize us before we can see, name, recognize ourselves. Or, as Butler puts it, '[I] must first be imagined from somewhere else before I can begin to imagine myself. … I cannot be who I am without drawing upon the sociality of norms that precede and exceed me' (Butler, 2005, p 68).

We strive to incorporate the norms that describe the field of the intelligible because we fear the 'being undone' (Butler, 2004) that happens to those who no longer incorporate the norm in such a way that it makes them fully recognizable as part of a social community, and thus as a valid individual. 'Our very sense of personhood is linked to the desire for recognition [which] places us … in a realm of social norms which we do not fully choose, but which provide the horizon and the resource for any sense of choice that we have' (Butler, 2005, pp 69–70). Here, we already get an indication that the normative aspect of performativity is important, but it should not be overestimated. Not only are social norms pointed out as both horizon *and* resource; the notion of performativity through which Butler approaches them is also conceptualized as a regulated process of repetition (with the potential for interruption), rather than a defining founding act (Butler, 1990, p 145). I will return to this potential for instability and change when discussing the transformative potential of misrecognition later in the chapter.

Grids of intelligibility and the social norms of recognition they legitimize rely on repetition and social rituals, 'at once a reenactment and reexperiencing of a set of meanings already socially established' (Butler, 1988, p 526). In other words, the performances in social interactions that lie at the bottom of our recognizing-one-another (and thus recognizing-ourselves) are both following established grids of intelligibility (I expect you to behave in a certain way based on who I think you are, and the situation we are in) and re-inscribing them (you fulfil my expectations by behaving the way I predicted, thus reinforcing those expectations). By extension, that means we exist 'not only by virtue of being recognized, but in a prior sense, by being recognizable' (Butler, 1997, p 5) – if I do not know what to expect or where to place you, I cannot meet you as a full human subject.

This ability to become recognizable as a fully human subject is central in a context where LGBTQ rights are explicitly incorporated into human rights discourses, with various implications for those whose intelligibility is not as easily maintained. Butler argues that if 'we believe all human subjects deserve equal recognition, we presume that all human subjects are equally recognisable', a presumption that is immediately challenged by the fact that 'the compulsory demand to appear in one way rather than another functions as a precondition of appearing at all' (Butler, 2015, p 34). Additionally, our desire to live up to the social norms by which we become intelligible/recognizable is also part of how certain normative grids of intelligibility become ratified and reproduced, thus further constraining the limits of the recognizable in a given context.

Despite this focus on how following the norms that secure recognition reproduces said norms, Butler does not deny the beneficial value and allure of recognition. They acknowledge that in liberal societies, recognition is 'that which we cannot not want' (Butler and Athanasiou, 2013, p 76), not only because to be deprived of recognitions threatens our social ability to exist but also because (much like discursive boundary making discussed earlier) recognition can materialize in legal-political terms. On a practical level, this can set the boundaries for being treated/produced as a criminal, to become the object of police violence (rather than being protected by the law), to have one's claims of injury refused as well as one's intimate/kinship relationships denied, to be stigmatized and disenfranchised while simultaneously becoming the object of fascination, fetishization and consumer pleasure (Butler, 2015, p 2).

Grids of intelligibility, therefore, is not only a concept for the analysis of how the constitution of subjectivity/identity works performatively; the question of who can become a recognizable subject is also about whose life is worth protecting, and, when lost, whose life is considered worthy of mourning (Butler, 2010). Applied to the empirical context of this book, this means that for example the protection promised by Sjunnesson and the Sweden Democrats in 2016 extends only to those recognizable as LGBTQ people according to certain grids of intelligibility. As I discuss in Chapter 6, the populist right conceptualizes sexuality as something private and non-political, aiming its protective rhetoric particularly at those LGBTQ people who live 'respectable' lives without challenging or upsetting heteronormative social institutions. Particularly racialized, but to some extent even White LGBTQ people fit into these narratives only as victims, oppressed by the dangerous racialized Other.

Non-intelligibility and normative violence

While the term recognition appears throughout Butler's more recent work, it always inevitably seems to echo with the promise of identity categories entering the legal-political realm. This is potentially due to the ways in which it has been used by other authors, for example in the discussion of sexual rights as human rights (Richardson, 2017; Bosia, 2020; Rahman, 2020; Langlois, 2022). I cover some of that ground in Chapter 2. If we focus more specifically on the notion of intelligibility, this opens up for an analysis beyond questions of rights-bearing/rightless subjects and towards engagements with who can occupy the space of being human. Normative intelligibility is deeply linked to survival, with those who have limited access to intelligibility within a certain context not only being deprived of creating an identity for themselves but having their possibilities for 'liveable lives' forcefully and often violently foreclosed. Dhawan draws on Mills' discussion of Butler's work when she argues that there are two kinds of normative violence. She identifies 'occasional and incidental violence that relates to the particular manifestation of the norm' as well as 'violence internal to norms by virtue of their constitutive "world-making" and "reality-conferring capacity"' (Mills, 2007, p 137, cited in Dhawan, 2013, p 197).

While the first instance of violence is 'occasional and incidental' and can be easily exemplified by citing the most recent instances of homo- or transphobic hate crimes, the violence that normative intelligibility exudes by virtue of its 'world-making' and 'reality-conferring capacity' is more subtle. To be subjected to physical or psychological violence because one does not comply with normative expectations regarding gender or sexuality is to be oppressed, and '[t]o be oppressed means that you already exist as a subject of some kind, you are there as the visible and oppressed other for the master subject … To be oppressed you must first become intelligible' (Butler, 2005, p 65). However, 'to be unreal is something else again. To find that you are fundamentally unintelligible (indeed, that the laws of culture and of language find you to be an impossibility) is to find that one has not yet achieved access to the human' (Butler, 2005, p 65).

As I discuss particularly in Chapter 8, the experience of unintelligibility – to others as well as to themselves – is one that many LGBTQ people racialized as non-White and/or Muslims are familiar with. There are also numerous instances of LGBTQ-phobic leaders, when pressed on their anti-LGBTQ policies, claiming that there are no LGBTQ people in a certain country or area (such as Ahmadinejad in Iran or Kadyrov in Chechnya), and thus no oppression of LGBTQ people exists (Elsner, 2019; Scicchitano, 2019; Brock and Edenborg, 2020). Now, finding yourself to be fundamentally unintelligible within a certain social context, a community of belonging, a process of boundary making – is that the experience of ultimate violence, or ultimate freedom? In the next section, I look at the potential for disruption and change that lies on the boundaries and outside the reach of grids of intelligibility, offering particular space for the manoeuvring and renegotiation of social norms to those occupying liminal and precarious positionalities.

Non-intelligibility and the possibility for re-articulation

The notion of normative violence shows how grids of intelligibility can both be ontologically violent and coercively or punitively enforced. However, this should not be interpreted as these grids being absolute and non-negotiable. As normative grids of intelligibility rely on performative repetition for their naturalization, the signification of the subject that becomes recognizable within and through these grids of intelligibility is not a *founding act*. Instead, it is a regulated process of repetition, including the constant potential for failure of that process. This, in turn, harbours the potential for dis/re-articulation of the norms that regulate the ways in which subjects appear as intelligible. Change or agency (understood in a Butlerian sense) is located within the possibility of variation on any given repetition of any given norm. While we are always dependent upon norms that enable our intelligibility, we can never fully be reduced to these norms. This is because '[n]ormative orders are always vulnerable to disruption, always haunted by that which they exclude' (Dhawan, 2013, p 198). The possibility of subversion is thus embedded in the performative nature of meaning-making (or 'sense-making') practices, discursive or otherwise. Those who are best placed to destabilize normative intelligibility are those who live at the junction of the intelligible/unintelligible. If 'I feel that without recognisability I cannot live, but I also feel that the terms by which I am recognised make my life unliveable' (Butler, 2004, p 4), then this is frequently the place from which critique emerges. Critique is here understood as an interrogation of the terms by which one's life is constrained in order to open up the possibility of different modes of living. This happens also because '[t]he normative force of performativity – its power to establish what qualifies as "being" – works not only through reiteration, but through exclusion' and 'those exclusions haunt signification as its abject borders or as that which is strictly foreclosed: the unliveable, the nonnarrativizable, the traumatic' (Butler, 2011, p 188). In other words, the constitutive outside which is excluded and rendered invisible, unrecognizable by normative grids of intelligibility, remains present 'as a haunting possibility, a promise and a threat' (Edenborg, 2016, p 20), reinforcing the distinctions that make some people viable subjects and others not, while simultaneously disturbing and complicating them. Here, the notion of haunting – already discussed in relation to the Self/Other distinction underlying processes of boundary making around communities of belonging – reappears, pointing once more to the instability inherent in attempts at fixating the meaning of collective or individual identities.

While Butler's earlier discussions of how the instability of performativity allows for resignification have often focused on discursive performances, recent work on the performative aspects of assembling discusses how this haunting possibility can become a very tangible presence when the non-intelligible make an embodied appearance, for example in public spaces: 'To walk is to say that this is a public space in which transgendered people walk, that this is a public space where [trans] people … are free to move without threat of violence' (Butler, 2015, p 52). The very existence, persistence and possibly even proliferation in the face of normative violence of those who fail to conform to norms of cultural intelligibility provide us with opportunities to show the limits of those norms, and to open up alternative grids of intelligibility. Butler argues that 'when the unreal lay claim to reality, or enter into its domain, something other than a simple assimilation into prevailing norms can and does take place' (Butler, 2015, p 62). Instead, the norms become open to resignification. Contestations of normative intelligibility are therefore always already present in those who are not-quite-intelligible or not-at-all intelligible. Their physical existence constitutes occasions where a particular nexus of power and knowledge 'meets its breaking point, the moments of its discontinuities, and the sites where it fails to constitute the intelligibility it promises' (Butler, 2004, p 216). The existence of organizations founded by and for LGBTQ people racialized as non-White and/or Muslim can be considered one such breaking point, crucially challenging assumptions about those identities being mutually exclusive (Rahman, 2020).

In their work on the 'queer art of failure', Halberstam argues that unintelligibility, that is, the failure to be recognized/recognizable by prevailing power structures, is also an important source of autonomy and active resistance to disciplinary and normative-hegemonic discourses (Halberstam, 2011). We should therefore not assume that everybody will always desire to be recognized by other people or institutions, if misrecognition is indeed a way to avoid the 'regime of power that constitutes the terms through which the recognisable subject emerges' (McQueen, 2015, p 122). The refusal to comply with normative grids of intelligibility that form the boundaries of recognition can therefore be seen as a strategy adopted by individuals and groups to navigate different contexts and relations in their lives that function according to different grids of intelligibility, an aspect I discuss further in Chapter 8. If we include this aspect of strategically avoiding or refusing intelligibility into our analysis of how people manoeuvre various meaning-making contexts, it gives us a better understanding of how notions of intelligibility and recognition are complex practices that people use as they navigate different social and national spaces.

Making sense of: grids of intelligibility

Grids of intelligibility are an integral part of boundary-making processes: collective processes of boundary making have an impact on the ways in which we construct our individual identities by making certain subjectivities and positionalities more or less feasible, recognizable, visible, *intelligible* within the context of a certain collective. Boundary making and the politics of belonging therefore enable various grids of intelligibility to determine what it means to be (or not to be) a viable subject in the context of that particular community of belonging and the identity narratives that maintain its coherence.

Grids of intelligibility enable and constrain subjectivity/identity formation: drawing on a Butlerian notion of subjectivity, grids of intelligibility are a way in which we can make sense of our own identity and positionality by way of becoming recognizable to others. In other words, we become recognizable through socially constituted and maintained forms of intelligibility – we are reliant on others being able to see, name, recognize us before we can see, name, recognize ourselves. Culturally specific grids of intelligibility enable these processes of recognition, signification and subjectification.

Grids of intelligibility harbour the potential for violence: since our sense of subjectivity and identity is connected to the desire/need for recognition from our social surroundings, grids of intelligibility are normative in their way of delimiting the field of possibility for how we recognize and describe ourselves and others. Failure to meet this normative intelligibility might entail violent repercussions, either by way of physical punishment or through the state of 'non-humanness' (and therefore social non-existence) that is accorded to those who are non-intelligible according to dominant grids of intelligibility.

Grids of intelligibility are never stable: the reproduction of grids of intelligibility relies on the continuous performative repetition of certain acts of subjectification, which gives these acts their feeling of naturalness and thus their normative (and potentially violent) character. However, these repetitions are also the point at which normative intelligibility is most unstable and most vulnerable to disruption and re-articulation. Because subjectivity signified through normative intelligibility relies on the existence of a constitutive Other, there remains a potential for those on the borders and the outside of intelligibility to make their entry into its realm, either as a haunting presence or through discursive and embodied appearances. Additionally, non-intelligibility can be used as an active strategy of resistance, to avoid, challenge or re-signify the controlling power that comes with normative grids of intelligibility.

4

Theoretical Explorations II: Racialization

Chapter 3 discussed how processes of boundary making and grids of intelligibility rely on the construction of Self vis-á-vis an externalized Other while at the same time delineating the 'field of the recognisable' (Butler, 2015, p 34) with regard to who is intelligibly human (or, in the specific case of this book, intelligibly LGBTQ). I have also addressed the question of what happens to those who fail to perform their humanness in intelligible ways, looking at the potential for violence as well as transformation inherent in the performative character of grids of intelligibility. In this chapter, I will look more closely at one specific aspect that has a long history as a marker of Otherness: race, or the social ascription of race to certain bodies. In other words, this chapter attempts to provide possible answers to the question: 'Which populations have qualified as the "human" and which have not: what is the history of this category?' (Butler, 2005, p 76). It does so by drawing on works from the fields of Black feminist studies, critical race studies and post/decolonial studies. All of these have been influential in conceptualizing how notions of race have been a central category for hierarchically differentiating people and communities, as well as of the implications these hierarchies have had, both historically and in contemporary contexts. All of them focus on the social practice of racialization, showing that 'race' is a socially constructed category, a process constantly at work in social relations.

Racialization conceptualized

Weheliye argues that '[t]he idea of racializing assemblages ... construes race not as a biological or cultural classification but as a set of sociopolitical processes that discipline humanity into full humans, not-quite-humans, and nonhumans' (Weheliye, 2014, p 4). Molina points to the grammatical form 'racialization' (*rasifiering* in Swedish), which indicates action, process, creation – racialization is something that is done (2005, p 96). Neither 'race' nor 'racism' have any kind of essential ontological value without looking at the practices and norms that turn ideas about race into effective and pseudo-natural tools for hierarchically differentiating individuals and groups (Molina, 2005). Race should therefore always be considered a social rather than a biological construct: 'Though racializations always pretend to name natural, unchanging, obvious facts, they are always ambiguous, shifting, and unstable' (El-Tayeb, 2011, p xiii). It is worth pointing out again here that racialization processes as conceptualized in the context of this book include the ascription of Otherness based on cultural customs, religion or migration, discussed later in this chapter under the term 'cultural racism'. In Western European contexts, this has particularly affected Muslim communities, or those who are racially othered as Muslims based on their names and/or their own or previous generations' countries of origin (Tudor, 2017).

While the racist hierarchies that feature in processes of boundary making historically have been built on essentialist notions of 'natural' differences between groups based on skin colour, ethnic, linguistic, religious or cultural markers, analyses of racialization processes show that race and racism are very much changing and context related. They are 'flexible social mechanism[s] for producing an internal boundary between what is considered proper and valuable, on the one hand, and foreign and inferior, on the other' (Adelson, 2005, p 8). This is related to processes of domination, with some bodies racialized as superior, others as inferior (Grosfoguel et al, 2015), but also to the creation of constitutive outsides (Tudor, 2018). By stabilizing internal notions of normalcy, racialized Others 'are crucial to the assertion of the power of sameness' (Braidotti, 2002, p 158), and by not belonging, they 'emphasize the significance of belonging' (Collins, 2009, p 77). Racialization therefore frequently features as part of boundary-making processes around communities of belonging, spilling over into the normative grids of intelligibility enabled by these processes. In this book's empirical material, this becomes particularly clear in relation to Pride Järva and the activist Instagram account, where both boundary-making processes and grids of intelligibility appear as thoroughly racialized (see Chapters 6 and 8).

Molina argues that racialization works in two complementary ways: a society is racialized, that is, it is differentiated hierarchically based on notions of race, and individuals are racialized within this society. Societal processes of racialization are thus predicated upon the existence of racialized individuals, while racialized individuals become intelligible as such only within a society where notions about race are constitutive elements of social institutions, customs, norms and everyday life (Molina, 2005). Wilson Gilmore formulates this mutually reinforcing process more drastically in relation to racialized non/intelligibility as a process of dehumanization: 'Racism is the ordinary means through which dehumanization achieves normality, while, at the same time, the practice of dehumanizing people produces racial categories' (Wilson Gilmore, 2007, p 243, cited in Weheliye, 2014, p 72). Weheliye, finally, describes the all-encompassing social relevance of race, racialization and racial identities as 'ongoing sets of political relations that require, through constant perpetuation via institutions, discourses, practices, desires, infrastructures, languages, technologies, sciences, economies, dreams, and cultural artifacts, the barring of nonwhite subjects from the category of the human as it is performed in the modern west' (Weheliye, 2014, p 3). Following these conceptualizations, racialization helps us to analyse how and to what effects certain historically specific and contextual notions of race are connected to particular processes of boundary making and corresponding normative grids of intelligibility.

Cultural racism, colour-blindness and political racelessness

From a historical perspective, research has identified different ways in which processes of racialization have occurred, as well as the different forms of racism that accompany them. The continuities from colonial racism via biological racism to today's cultural racism show that processes of racialization and racist ideologies have been continuous parts of social organization in Western European countries, justifying both colonial and domestic exploitation (Balibar and Wallerstein, 1991; Gilroy, 1993; Essed, 1996; Hesse, 2004; Laskar, 2007; Moffette and Vadasaria, 2016). The racialization processes I consider most relevant to analysing contemporary processes of boundary making around race–sex–gender as well as the grids of intelligibility they enable are based on what is referred to as 'cultural racism' (Goldberg, 2006; Martinsson et al, 2016).

In this context, connections to biology as a basis for hierarchical differentiation of individuals and groups are denied, and any references to the word 'race' are explicitly avoided. Instead, racialization processes are based on categories such as culture, religion, migration or ethnicity (Lentin, 2011). This is in line with Yuval-Davis's previously discussed understanding of how shared ethical and political values become a measurement of belonging in political processes of boundary making (Yuval-Davis et al, 2018). The discrimination, xenophobia and exclusion that accompany these racialization processes flow from 'cultural specifications of national identity', which are more 'tacitly or covertly racialised' (Gilroy, 2006, p 2). This legitimizes, among other things, racist representations of migration (from non-Western countries) as a threat to Western societies and their culture, including notions of 'multiculturalism' as a 'failed project' (Lentin, 2011, pp 2–3).

El-Tayeb discusses how religion (and in this context, she argues that 'religion' almost always means Islam) also becomes closely intertwined with processes of racialization, turning into an ethno-cultural signifier: 'Race and religion thus function as central but largely invisible factors in European concepts of identity' (2008, p 652). Race (in the sense of having a body that is racialized as non-White) and religion (as ethno-cultural signifier of Otherness) appear as the two most frequently employed aspects used to differentiate those who automatically belong within constructions of Swedishness in relation to LGBTQ rights from those who have to prove they are the 'right' kind of queer. This has led to my consistent use of the term 'racialized as non-White and/or Muslim'. And while some might argue that the term 'racialized as non-White' might be sufficient to cover both aspects, I still think there is a difference to be maintained. The ways in which they are used in current debates on LGBTQ rights are often similar, but they draw on slightly different registers of stereotypes and historical conceptualizations. They also affect different kinds of Otherness. One example of this is how migrants from certain Balkan regions might be included in notions of European Whiteness despite their being Muslim. Their Whiteness is contingent, though, and lasts only as long as they are understood to be Muslims in a way that can be integrated into notions of tolerant and progressive Europeanness (Rexhepi, 2018; Baker, 2021).

While similar at the core, various culturally racist narratives 'shift in both the target (Jews, Muslims, blacks, migrants) and the content of the narrative (dangerous, a burden to the welfare state, patriarchal, impossible to assimilate, etc.)' (Mulinari and Neergaard, 2013, p 49). These narratives also identify the roots of inequalities within discriminated communities, thus using stereotypically racist cultural features to explain these communities' social situation (Grosfoguel et al, 2015). The use of terms such as 'culture' or 'ethnicity' attempts to conceal the reproduction of racism as well as the social inequalities created by these processes of cultural racialization. 'By avoiding the word "race", cultural racism claims to be non-racist' (Grosfoguel et al, 2015, p 645), which is but the last move in a long process of denying racializing ideologies and practices (Molina, 2005). These ideologies of colour-blindness (Osanami Törngren, 2022) or 'political racelessness' (Goldberg, 2006) are ways in which contemporary processes of racialization deny their own racism. Instead, they create 'a form of racialization that can be defined as specifically European both in its enforced silence and its explicit categorization as not European of all those who violate Europe's implicit, but normative whiteness, allowing to forever consider the "race question" as externally (and by implication temporarily) imposed' (El-Tayeb, 2011, p xxviii).

This, El-Tayeb argues, creates an image of a self-contained, homogeneous Western Europe, in which discourses around racialized hierarchies are hidden under notions of 'cultural difference', while race and religion increasingly converge as identifiers of permanently externalized minorities. However, the absence of discourses on race does of course not signify the absence of racialization (or racism). Rather, it means that the experience of being racialized as non-White and/or Muslim, and experiences of racism related to this racialization, become invisible and thus even more difficult to address, politically or otherwise. The empirical chapters of this book show how discrimination along lines of race as well as sexuality and gender is disguised from view and externalized from the Swedish context through narratives about Sweden as an exceptionally gender-equal, LGBTQ-friendly and anti-racist country (for a more detailed overview of this literature, see Chapter 2).

Scholars of racialization argue that this has serious implications for those (particularly Northern) Europeans racialized as non-White and/or Muslim. They are and remain externalized through processes of racialization as long as their historical presence within Western and Northern European countries is not part of these countries' national histories. Therefore, as El-Tayeb writes, every meeting with the non-White is and will continue to be the 'first meeting' (El-Tayeb, 2011, p xxv). The way in which minorities are talked about as second-, third-, even fourth-generation immigrants shows that racialization in Western European contexts includes the ascription of migration to certain bodies racialized as non-White – they are constructed as 'never at home' in these societies (Tudor, 2017), a discourse which is xenophobic, racist and exclusionary in character (Gilroy, 2006) and which both reflects and (re)produces notions that 'there are only migrants, no minorities' in Western Europe (El-Tayeb et al, 2015).

This not only erases the lives of communities who migrated several generations ago; in the Scandinavian context, it also crucially affects the positionality of colonized indigenous populations. Swedish (post) coloniality as lived and experienced by the indigenous Sámi population, one of the main internal racialized Others throughout Swedish history, is frequently overlooked or ignored (for exceptions, see Keskinen et al, 2009; Loftsdóttir and Jensen, 2012; Naum and Nordin, 2013; Andersen et al, 2015; Knobblock, 2021). Even the empirical scope of this book focuses mostly on racialization processes connected to migration (experienced or ascribed) into Sweden, very much in line with the discursive externalization of the racialized Other from both Sweden and notions of Swedishness.

For anybody who actually newly arrives into these contexts, it means there already exists a history of racialization and racial hierarchies linked to existing people and communities. They arrive, therefore, in a 'space of power relations already informed and constituted by coloniality' (Grosfoguel et al, 2015, p 641), which will in turn impact the way in which they will be made sense of and make sense of themselves in relation to racialized grids of intelligibility. Drawing on Fanon, Bacchetta points towards 'the damage of gender, racism, slavery, colonialism, of heteronormativity and even homonormativity, of immigration, war' as being 'such that those who are Othered in relation to the dominant order, who are actually formed within it as subjects, do not automatically consider themselves as full subjects and are not considered as full subjects' (Bacchetta, 2010, p 182). This inability to become intelligible to oneself (as for example both racialized *and* LGBTQ) due to existing normative grids of intelligibility foreclosing one's subjectivity has already been discussed in the previous section. However, understanding it through contemporary processes of cultural racialization is crucial in relation to the empirical context of this book, because it puts both the boundary-making processes and the grids of intelligibility enabled by them into a colonial-historical perspective of racialized Othering.

(Not) being White as (not) being human

The acknowledgement that racialization is something that happens in relation to all bodies and not only those who are racialized as non-White is central to the concept of racialization. Notions of Whiteness are also, and crucially so, produced through processes of racialization. Being 'White' is something we become and by virtue of which we are positioned within a social hierarchy that is constantly (re)produced through practices that normalize Whiteness and the privileges that come with it, while Othering those who are constructed as non-White. Weheliye argues that 'whiteness designates … a series of hierarchical power structures that apportion and delimit which members of the Homo sapiens species can lay claim to full human status' (Weheliye, 2014, p 19).

Svensson separates 'marked racialization' as an objectifying process applied to those bodies racialized as non-White, and unmarked racialization applying to those who are 'Whiteified [my translation]' (Svensson, 2015). This unmarked racialization means that race is a construct most frequently applied to those racialized as non-White, while 'Whiteness' functions as the norm of what it means to be 'human' (Dyer, 2005, p 10). Whiteness's claim to power in many contexts is therefore one of speaking for the 'commonality of humanity' (Dyer, 2005, p 10). Those racialized as non-White, on the other hand, can only ever represent their 'race' and are therefore frequently made intelligible first and foremost by being racialized as non-White (rather than as people with various genders, sexual identities, class backgrounds). Importantly, however, processes of ascribing Whiteness are also contextual (or contingent) – moving from a comfortable position of unquestionable Whiteness in one's home country into a more insecure one of liminal Whiteness is an experience shared by Eastern Europeans migrating westwards, for example (Rexhepi, 2016; Krivonos, 2020; Baker, 2021; Sime et al, 2022). This contingency is closely connected to notions about Eastern and Central Europe as traditionalist and conservative, and by extension heterosexist as well as homo- and transphobic. As discussed elsewhere in this book, that differentiation is used both by those who consider themselves defenders of said 'traditional values' and those who argue that countries like Poland or Hungary need to 'catch up' (Kulpa, 2014; Kahlina, 2015; Brock and Edenborg, 2020; Korolczuk, 2020b; Polkov, 2023).

As postcolonial scholars have pointed out, the position of Whiteness as the definition of what it means to be human has been created and is maintained through processes of objectification by way of binary thinking, where each term gains meaning only in relation to an opposite counterpart (Collins, 2009). Drawing on Wynter, Weheliye states that when 'the white colonial subject encounters herself of himself as the "fullness and genericity of being human" … he or she only does so in relation to the deficiency of the black subject and indigenous' (Wynter, 2001, p 40, cited in Weheliye, 2014, p 26). On the other hand, Fanon writes that 'not only must the black man be black; he must be black in relation to the white man' (Fanon, 1967, p 90, cited in Weheliye, 2014, p 26). Other well-established binaries beyond White/Black in this context are reason/emotion, mind/body, culture/nature and subject/object, often also related to the division between male/female (Fanon, 1967; Halpin, 1989; Hall, 1997b; Collins, 2009). More recently, secular/religious has appeared as another such binary, yet again aimed at the Othering of Muslims in Western European contexts (Rahman, 2015). Whiteness as a grid of intelligibility for 'humanness' is thus created by objectifying those racialized as non-White as the oppositional Other, separating the 'knowing self' from the 'known object' (Richards, 1980, quoted in Collins, 2009, p 78).

Since racialization processes most often occur through the marking of bodies, with some bodies racialized as superior, others as inferior, Ahmed's 'phenomenology of whiteness' (2007a) is useful in order to further conceptualize what it means to occupy a body that is read as not living up to normative grids of intelligibility (for example, regarding what it means to be recognizably LGBTQ in a Swedish context). Ahmed describes Whiteness as 'an ongoing and unfinished history, which orientates bodies in specific directions, affecting how they "take up" space' (2007a, p 159). If being White is the norm for what it means to be human, then the 'body-at-home' in this world is one that can comfortably 'inhabit whiteness', comfortably 'extend into spaces that have already taken [its] space' (Ahmed, 2007a, p 158). On the other hand, those who cannot inhabit Whiteness become 'bodies out of space' (Puwar, 2004), bodies who stand out, and by their standing out confirm the normative Whiteness of these spaces (Puwar, 2004; Ahmed, 2007b).

Weheliye points to this as 'the visual modalities in which dehumanization is practiced and lived' (Weheliye, 2014, p 6). Whiteness is invisible, while non-Whiteness is very much visible. Standing out also means being questioned: 'Who are you? Why are you here? What are you doing?' These questions might not be actual questions; they can also be raised eyebrows, or the silencing of a room when you enter. The body racialized as non-White is made intelligible as not belonging. As research (including this book) shows, this non-belonging has serious implications for the ways in which lives racialized as non-White play out in Western societies. So while race is a social construction, racialization is also – and always has been – a material process with globally dispersed consequences (Molina, 2005, p 102), much like boundary-making processes and the normative grids of intelligibility enabled by them. The implications of these processes are most clearly visible in the empirical material on young people's experiences of growing up in Sweden as racialized as non-White and/or Muslim as well as being LGBTQ.

However, as discussed previously, the position of not being a full human subject might in fact mean more than just being forced to align your identity construction with existing normative grids of intelligibility. Both Butler and Weheliye (albeit coming from slightly different directions) have argued that those parts of humanity who have been radically deprived of the status of 'full humans' have the most to offer when it comes to challenging existing notions of who the human is and should be (Butler, 2004; Weheliye, 2014). Bacchetta has pointed out that 'the most hyper-subaltern and hyper-critical LTQ+POC subjects' and 'some of the most innovative and effective modalities of resistance' (Bacchetta, 2017, p 156) might remain altogether invisible, because they remain outside dominant grids of intelligibility. This is in line with Butler's argument that those who are best placed to challenge and disrupt normative grids of intelligibility are those living their lives on its edges or just beyond the boundaries of recognizability. Also with regard to racialization as a social process of delimiting 'the human', extreme non-intelligibility harbours the potential for violence, as well as creates room for manoeuvring, for resistance and for resignification. The following section therefore explores the queer potential of occupying positions of racialized difference.

The queer potential of racialized difference

As this book explores both theoretically and empirically, processes of racialization have a long tradition as a method for the production of respectable and innocent genders and sexualities considered worthy of visibility, recognition and protection. They are closely linked to colonial thought and policy making. Using the inclusion of certain kinds of LGBTQ people in order to demarcate a dangerous, threatening or otherwise problematic Other is predicated upon an understanding of progress and modernity inspired by European Enlightenment thinking, within which the acknowledgement of women's rights and LGBTQ rights becomes a measurement of 'how far' a country, nation or community has 'progressed'. These temporal-developmental differentiations between 'the Self' and 'the Other' (and the various implications of being seen as one or the other) are maintained by a dialectic of respectability that relies crucially on sexuality and gender identity as always already also racialized.

'Race as a mode of governing and knowing' (Moffette and Vadasaria, 2016, p 294), performed through the self–other dialectic described previously, entails that there are long-established grids of intelligibility for the ways in which populations or individuals racialized as non-White are read as threatening and violent (Moffette and Vadasaria, 2016, pp 293–5) which are crucial to our understanding of much of the rhetoric employed in contemporary 'exclusive inclusions' around LGBTQ rights and issues. They build on 'interconnected genealogies of race' (Moffette and Vadasaria, 2016, p 294) and the longstanding colonial history of race as 'an administrative and anthropological category' (Hesse, 2004, p 13, quoted in Moffette and Vadasaria, 2016), even if they increasingly take the form of 'cultural' rather than biological racism.

The racial grammar that demarcates difference through this self–other dialectic has enabled various figurations of 'the Other', including the savage, the primitive, the colonized (Rao, 2020) and the victim (Tschalaer, 2021), but also the unwanted im/migrant (Luibhéid, 2008) and the terrorist (Puar, 2007). All of these rely in one way or another on civilizational discourses born within the context of modern colonialism, and all of these have made possible specific (more or less violent) practices of intervention and population management. 'The hateful Other' who threatens (White) queers (Haritaworn, 2015) is just the latest incarnation in this long line.

While scholars have acknowledged the ways in which these various figurations have also been sexualized and gendered as the weird, the deviant, the morally dangerous (Laskar, 2015a, 2015b), thus calling attention to how the policing of racialized subjects and the policing of queer subjects have gone hand in hand, queer theory has not always been successful at addressing the fact that there is no 'unracialized' sexuality/gender and that sexualized/gendered difference is *always* also racialized. I argue that awareness of the ways that bodies racialized as non-White have been and are read and treated as always potentially threatening is crucial for our understanding of how certain individuals are more susceptible to the dangers of not being included in the 'gay-rights-as-human-rights' discourses (discussed in more detail in Chapter 2), thus being even less able to afford a position of 'not wanting rights'. Taking a queerer look at racialization can actually take us beyond the realm of the Self–Other dialectic, thus potentially adding to our ability to account for homonormative/homonationalist processes in all their complexity.

In order to do this, I draw on *Habeas Viscus* by Black studies scholar Alexander Weheliye, in which he expands upon the self–other/subject–object dialectic by investigating what he calls those racializing assemblages which 'constru[ct] race not as a biological or cultural classification but as a set of sociopolitical processes that discipline humanity into full humans, not quite humans, and nonhumans' (Weheliye, 2014, p 4) and as such play an essential role in the construction of modern subjectivity. His interest goes beyond merely analysing these hierarchical processes, as he aims for a disarticulation of 'the human from the world of Man' (Weheliye, 2014, p 32) and an unearthing of alternative ways of being human beyond modern (Western) discourses of subjecthood that require legal recognition. Falling back on Black feminist writers Hortense Spiller and Sylvia Wynter, Weheliye identifies 'the flesh' as a way of considering 'alternative versions of humanity' (Weheliye, 2014, p 10), namely those which exist outside the realm of the recognizable. This, I argue, applies to non-normative sexualities and genders along similar lines of (non)recognition as processes of racialization, something which Weheliye alludes to but does not develop.

In his account, the violence of historical relations of dominance based on processes of racialization creates a 'fleshly surplus' (Weheliye, 2014, p 2) that evades capture, where alternative ways of humanity can be identified outside the realm of the human. His *Habeas viscus* (You shall have the flesh) thus both pre- and exceeds the body referred to in *Habeas corpus*, commonly acknowledged as the law's utterance of recognition of subjecthood. Black studies, Weheliye argues, is particularly suited to 'perceive and understand a world in which subjection is but one path to humanity' because of the way in which Black cultures have been routinely excluded from access to '[m]an's language, world, future, or humanity' (Weheliye, 2014, p 135). Looking at how humanity has been 'imagined and lived by those subjects excluded from [the domain of man]' (Weheliye, 2014, p 8) thus unsettles and displaces (or, as I would put it, 'queers') the centrality of legal recognition with regard to who counts as 'human'. It connects to Butler's assertion about the performative role of non-intelligible (queer) bodies and lives physically assembling (Butler, 2015), opening up for an acknowledgement and awareness of the various lives lived beyond the realm of the recognizable. This queering of the category of 'the human' by way of Weheliye's analysis of assemblages of racialization thus has implications also for those who are 'non-human' for other reasons than their being racialized as non-White. In turn, the potential for competition between minoritized groups for legal recognition as a scarce resource becomes diffused (Weheliye, 2014, p 13), and new intersectional alliances become possible.

I argue that we can combine Weheliye's analytical and political striving for alternative modes of existence, humanity and liberation beyond the recognition of the law (based in the acknowledgement that racialized assemblages have and will continue to exclude certain populations from that recognition) with queer approaches that challenge the presumed coherence of concepts such as 'the normal' or 'the perverse' (Butler, 2009; Weber, 2016b). As discussed in previous chapters, a plural logic of the and/or exposes the inherent instability of these boundary-making moves by showing the various ways in which LGBTQ people can occupy complex positionalities in contemporary homonationalist narratives. Weheliye's work on racialization brings to our renewed attention the role racialization plays in the separation of the human from the non-human via legal recognition, and then raises the stakes by encouraging us to look beyond, for the political potential for freedom and emancipation that lies with those who have been and continue to be excluded from subjecthood. Together, these approaches not only nuance claims about the homonormative, homonationalist or homocolonialist character of certain political processes of boundary making; they also help us analyse the ways in which LGBTQ people are variously positioned to deal with these. They thus go beyond academic relevance, enabling us to direct our activist interventions in the most efficient way, a question to which I will return in the concluding chapter of this book.

Making sense of: racialization

Racialization is a process of social hierarchization: while 'race' as a category has historically been based on essentialized notions of 'natural' differences between individuals and/or groups, the ascription of race to certain bodies is in fact a social process that serves to hierarchically differentiate them. Hierarchies constructed through processes of racialization find their expression in racism, that is, the ways in which people are treated differently depending on whether they are made intelligible as White or non-White within a given context. Looking at racialization as a social process denaturalizes the category of race, showing instead the ways in which it is context related and changing.

Processes of racialization include the construction of Whiteness: racialization happens in relation to all bodies, not only those who are racialized as non-White. The ascription of Whiteness is also produced through processes of racialization, as it depends on the ascription of non-Whiteness to others. Importantly, in many contexts and due to colonial legacies, Whiteness functions as the normative grid of intelligibility with regard to what defines those who are representations of a neutral humanity in general, rather than a specifically raced human being.

Racialization works in context-specific ways: while the ascription of race brings our thoughts most frequently to the ways in which it is connected to variation in skin tone, processes of racialization have used and still use a variety of signifiers to mark the Other racialized as non-White, frequently in order to avoid the word race and the connotations it evokes. This includes various notions of culture and ethnicity, religion, but also the ascription of migration, that is, the externalization of certain people as 'not from here'.

Crucially, racialization and racial hierarchies can exist even when the word race is not used to demarcate difference.

Putting theories to work

Theory, while on occasion beautiful on its own accord, is best put to work in attempts to understand the world around us. In the following section, I give an account of how the theoretical approaches discussed in Chapters 3 and 4 help us approach the questions analysed in this book. What do the different concepts, individually and in relation with each other, contribute to an overall understanding of the different ways in which LGBTQ rights feature in contemporary constructions of Swedishness, which (subject) positions are made available within these discourses, and how do people manoeuvre these positions?

The starting point of my enquiry is the construction of various notions of Swedishness around particular ideas of what this Swedishness entails with regard to both sociocultural values and rights related to the lives of LGBTQ people. The first question explored in this book – 'How are LGBTQ rights mobilized in contemporary constructions of Swedishness?' – therefore deals with the construction of a collective Self, described in terms of national belonging and achieved via the demarcation of internal and external Others along lines of rights, social norms and values. Yuval-Davis's concept of the politics of belonging and the literature on b/ordering both contribute to our ability to disentangle these attempts at constructing various notions of Swedishness by stressing the ways in which they are social processes, constructive of the community they claim to describe as well as the value system said to define belonging within the specific context of this community. This means I approach the material with the intention to deconstruct such instances as Pride Järva or the appearance of a rainbow flag in Swedish Armed Forces' marketing campaigns, looking at how categories of racial, cultural, gendered and/or sexual difference are deployed to create various notions of (non-)belonging.

This also guides the analysis towards looking at the contested nature of these attempts at boundary making. The continued 'haunting' presence of externalized Others as conceptualized in the literature, but also the ways in which inclusion is conditioned (as is the case of LGBTQ people racialized as non-White and/or Muslim) challenge the attempts at coherence, stability and binarity that characterize the creation of collective (national) identities. The differentiation of people into Self/'inside'/included and Other/'outside'/excluded, therefore, needs to be approached as more complex and ambivalent than it seems, which guides my research towards looking for these complexities within contemporary constructions of Swedishness. These complexities are addressed with the help of concepts from the field of queer theory.

Literature that discusses the creation of subjectivity as/through intelligibility enables us to connect the construction of collective identities through politics of belonging demarcated by (among other things) sexuality, gender and race to the individual's sense of self within the context of these collectives. This is particularly relevant with regard to the question 'Which subject positions are made available in these constructions, and how are they negotiated by LGBTQ people racialized as non-White and/or Muslim?' The making of boundaries (such as the ones constructed by connecting Swedishness to LGBTQ rights) draws upon and enables specific grids of intelligibility for who is included within these boundaries, by making certain subjectivities more or less recognizable and their lives more or less liveable. The (attempted) coherence of the collective Self as promoted by politics of belonging thus crucially impacts the ways in which we can make sense not only of others but of ourselves as individuals. Grids of intelligibility are therefore an integral part of boundary-making processes. The concept enables us to look at the connection between these processes and adds an explicit discussion of the ways in which the normative aspect of intelligibility harbours the potential for the violent aspects inherent in a state of non-intelligibility.

At the same time, it helps to further conceptualize and open up the analysis towards the instability and disruption of these acts of signification and subjectification. This is particularly relevant for understanding the ways in which LGBTQ people racialized as non-White and/or Muslim experience and manoeuvre the subject positions suggested and made available to them in boundary-making processes around notions of Swedishness. As boundary making and the subjectivity circumscribed by normative intelligibility rely on the existence of constitutive Others, these Others maintain the potential for disturbing or resignifying grids of intelligibility through discursive and embodied appearances or as a 'haunting' presence. A positionality that is non-intelligible can even be seen as an active strategy of resistance against the power of normative grids of intelligibility, carving out a 'liveable life' not by compliance but by manoeuvring multiple social contexts and their ambivalent parameters of intelligibility and recognition.

Since previous research has shown that the ascription of race plays a central role with regard to boundary-making processes enabled by normative notions of sexuality and gender, this research project also investigates the question 'What role do processes of racialization play in these constructions [of Swedishness]?' An engagement with racialization as a process of social hierarchization therefore is another crucial theoretical component. It enables us to explore how the ascription of race to certain bodies serves to hierarchically differentiate them from those who are made intelligible as 'White' and therefore 'without race' or 'just human' in specific contexts. This ascription of race is a crucial part of boundary-making processes around notions of Swedishness as LGBTQ-friendliness, and the concept of racialization helps us to more clearly identify what role it plays both with regard to how these boundaries are drawn, and who is made (non-)intelligible through these boundary-making processes. Looking at racialization as a context-specific ascription of Otherness opens up the analysis for being able to include othering and discrimination of groups even when the word 'race' is replaced by various notions of 'culture' or 'ethnicity'. This is analytically particularly useful because it helps to disentangle the ways in which people who are LGBTQ *and* racialized as non-White and/or Muslim get caught in discourses on LGBTQ rights ascribed to racialized communities and groups in acts of boundary making.

However, racialization is a central concept not only due to the fact that race is used as a marker of Otherness within the specific geographical context investigated here. As discussed, racialization processes have both historically and theoretically delimited the very field of who at all is/can become 'human' (Weheliye, 2014), and thus live the 'liveable lives' (Butler, 2005) enabled by grids of intelligibility in the context of communities constructed through boundary-making processes. To approach the construction of human subjectivity through processes of racialization is to acknowledge the ways in which collective boundary making and the grids of intelligibility it enables are always already racialized. At the same time, it points the analysis once more towards the complexities of any kind of signification processes through boundary making – a reminder that there are and have always been lives lived outside the realm of that which makes one intelligibility human, intelligibly 'Self'.

5

The How To: Queer and Feminist Methodology

Feminist and queer research approaches build on the conviction that academic knowledge is both created by and creating social relations; that in fact any kind of knowledge production is part of social production in general, and that as researchers, we cannot remove ourselves from those relations of knowledge/power. We cannot, as herising puts it, 'claim epistemological or ontological innocence for we are not outside of the conditions, contexts, and positionalities of life' (herising, 2005, p 139). How we select our material and generate our data always includes a prioritization of what we think 'matters'. What matters to us is of course guided by research questions, empirical material and theoretical approaches but also by personal experiences and intersectional positionalities. On the following pages, I discuss methodological aspects such as site selection, data generation and analysis as well as the ethical challenges that come with being a queer researcher researching 'queer stuff'. I also reflect on the process of writing as part of the analysis. Writing is particularly important in qualitative research as 'qualitative work carries its meaning in its entire text' (Richardson and Adams St. Pierre, 2005, p 960). Within traditions of situated knowledge production, validity has to be created through reflexivity and transparency about how knowledge claims came about. Being clear about how and what we write at different stages is therefore an important part of that process of validation. Hopefully, this chapter will be of interest both to the seasoned researcher and those curious about how to design their own research projects.

Choosing a field, selecting sites

This book engages with three specific research sites concerned with boundary making around notions of Swedishness connected to LGBTQ rights as well as grids of intelligibility enabled by these discourses. They show contradictions and previously untold stories and thus provide unique opportunities to contribute to our understanding of these processes. Here, I briefly introduce each of them before discussing how the combination of these different sites enabled me to approach the questions that guide this project. In line with feminist and queer principles of situated knowledge production, site selection developed during the course of the research period, rather than being predetermined. Bazeley stresses the importance of allowing for 'planned flexibility' when designing qualitative research projects because of the ways in which our research needs to accommodate 'the inevitable twists and turns occasioned by real-world contingencies' (Bazeley, 2013, p 32). As a researcher, this provides the opportunity to follow different constructions of Swedishness and the ways in which they make people variously intelligible as these constructions appeared in their contemporary political context. This is both useful and important, not least with regard to the political relevance of this study. To be able to react to developments as they happen is an advantage not simply because it gives an indication of the ways in which the political context around these issues is dynamic and ever-changing but also because it enables me as a researcher to follow these dynamics and thus provide a more nuanced analysis.

Pride Järva became the first site because the populist right's outright 'appropriation' of LGBTQ issues and the resistance against it made it one of the most politicized instances of mobilization of LGBTQ rights for the sake of constructing specific notions of Swedishness at the time. It shows the aggressive Othering that accompanies this move particularly clearly, while also giving room for the fact that Sjunnesson failed to engage Swedish mainstream LGBTQ movements in his campaigns and was even met with counter-demonstrations and banned from Stockholm Pride's properties. There was thus an element of contradiction in this site that caught my attention, with two demonstrations taking place simultaneously, both of which appealed to LGBTQ rights in different ways. Since a video of the event was preserved as a YouTube upload and was therefore available on social media long after the actual event, it also attained a more long-lasting quality, maintaining and projecting its message beyond the actual occasion of the marches (see Gerbaudo, 2018 for a discussion of the relevance of social media for populist political discourses).

The second site is a collection of nationwide marketing campaigns published by the Swedish Armed Forces (SAF) every year to coincide with Stockholm Pride. In these campaigns, 'Swedish progressiveness' is frequently exemplified through equality between people of all sexual orientations and gender identities and portrayed as being under threat from LGBTQ-phobic external forces. I started to encounter the campaigns around the same time as I was conducting research on Pride Järva, and I was intrigued by the way in which they echoed the narratives presented there in many ways while at the same time seemingly avoiding the blunt racism and *obvious* Othering.

The coexistence of these two sites enables us to approach constructions of Swedishness qua LGBTQ-friendliness from what appears to be widely diverging political standpoints: on the one hand, the political far right, always critical of the Swedish government for its various failures; on the other hand, the SAF, by definition the guarantor and protector of the feminist/pro-LGBTQ policy making that many recent Swedish governments have prided themselves on (Jezierska and Towns, 2018; Rosamond and Hedling, 2022). However, the ways in which these actors employ similar discursive registers show just how readily available certain narratives around gender, sexuality and race are for the construction of political projects of belonging, even when these projects diverge in their politics.

The third research site is an Instagram account, started by activists to provide a community platform for racialized LGBTQ people. This site also tells a story of how Swedishness is constructed through notions of LGBTQ-friendliness. It does so through the words of people describing what it is like to be both LGBTQ and racialized as non-White and/or Muslim in predominantly White Swedish LGBTQ contexts. As such, it is particularly well suited for analysing grids of intelligibility around sexuality and gender in relation to race, since the stories shared on this account show how these grids constantly manifest themselves in everyday situations. They show the policing and punishing of certain racialized sexualities and gender identities as well as the creation of counter-narratives. These young people share experiences of living their lives *within* boundary-making narratives of Swedishness as made intelligible by, among many other things, the occurrence of Pride Järva or the widespread presence of SAF marketing material.

As social scientists, the world that we attend to will always, inevitably, exceed the limits of our research funding, project duration or page count. While this site selection, therefore, cannot tell us everything, it enables us to learn something about how contemporary notions of Swedishness are constructed through mobilization of sexuality, gender and race and how this enables normative grids of intelligibility, which people both manoeuvre and contest. As Richardson puts it, '[h]aving a partial, local, and historical knowledge is still knowing', and in some ways, 'knowing' becomes easier for those who recognize 'the situational limitations of the knower' because we are under no obligation to try to 'play God' (see also Haraway, 1988; Richardson and Adams St. Pierre, 2005, p 961). In order to make the process of this particular knowledge acquisition more transparent for the reader, the following section discusses the different ways in which I collected my material and generated data for analysis.

Approaching the world, generating data

The analysis of Pride Järva is centred on the speech Sjunnesson gave in 2016, which was transcribed verbatim from a video clip published on the YouTube channel of the right-wing website Avpixlat (Avpixlat, 2016). As mentioned, this speech is a highly politicized instance of homonationalist boundary making around notions of Swedishness, as it was contested by LGBTQ activists both before, during and after the event. However, it is also an entry point into more underlying right-wing discourses on LGBTQ rights, Swedishness and racialized Otherness at the time. The speech was therefore contextualized with the help of Swedish media reporting on the event as well as existing research on the Sweden Democrats' history of anti-LGBTQ policy making (see Bazeley, 2013, pp 81–2 on the importance of contextualization in qualitative data analysis). Based on Sjunnesson's engagement with the populist US website Breitbart, I also included an exploratory reading of English-speaking 'alternative' right-wing news websites that had picked up on the event. This contextualization proved crucial in the analysis, as it brought into sharp focus the instability of Sjunnesson's attempts at categorical boundary making around Swedishness in relation to LGBTQ rights.

The material for the pride-related SAF marketing campaigns was collected from a yearly poster campaign published from 2015 onwards. These campaigns usually take the form of a single image/slogan combination that is reproduced in different contexts (on billboards, public transport, social media and major national newspapers). I analysed campaign posters published between 2015 and 2022 in an attempt to follow the construction of Swedishness in relation to LGBTQ rights as portrayed by the SAF in their marketing material. Over time, these campaigns increased in publicity, not least when they started appearing as a full-page advert in major Swedish daily newspapers in 2019. In many cases, the release of the campaign has been met with a conservative right-wing backlash. In total, I analysed seven campaign posters, which were contextualized through a media analysis comparable to the one conducted for Pride Järva.

When analysing the Instagram posts, I limited myself to analysing the textual material. Despite Instagram being an app that was originally developed for the sharing of pictures, my material consists only of texts being posted in the pictures' captions. In these texts, the writers describe in their own words crucial experiences of being racialized as non-White and/or Muslim while being LGBTQ in a White Swedish context. This part of the analysis is therefore not a social media study, as it does not analyse Instagram posts as double modalities of visual and textual elements. I was primarily interested in the content that was produced *by* the account (through the writings of the administrators and the guest posters) rather than *on* the account (which would have included the comment sections below every entry). There were two main reasons for this.

First, in order for any analysis to be successful, the process of data generation has to pay attention to the feasibility of the researcher(s) actually being able to analyse the bulk of the material (Bazeley, 2013, p 48). The entries published during the period I followed were so long and numerous that they provided more than enough material for analysis. I selected almost 700 primary entries published by 86 different writers between November 2015 and December 2017, some of them several A4 pages long. These were imported into NVivo, in order to be analysed through a process of close reading and coding. In addition to the issue of avoiding the generation of excessive, unmanageable amounts of data, I was reluctant to engage with the community interaction that was happening in the comment section below the posts. This was, after all, a community with a specific purpose, directed towards a group I do not belong to, an ethical issue I discuss in more detail elsewhere in this chapter.

Discursive analysis: theory and practice

This book approaches boundary-making processes and grids of intelligibility through the analysis of various forms of texts. In this, it follows post-structuralist assumptions that language is a constitutive force which, rather than merely 'reflecting' social reality, is at the very centre of those processes of meaning making that constitute our social world (Jørgensen and Phillips, 2002). Speech acts (like Sjunnesson's speech at Pride Järva), personal writing (like the Instagram entries), but also images (like in the SAF's campaigns), are therefore instances of discursive meaning making which play a crucial role in how we understand ourselves and those (objects and people) around us.

The analysis of text-based meaning-making processes, particularly when they are referred to as 'discourses', is usually portrayed to exist in separate schools, all with their own distinct combination of ontology, epistemology and methodology (see Jørgensen and Phillips, 2002; Phillips and Hardy, 2011; Zotzmann and O'Regan, 2016; Kølvraa, 2017; Wodak and Forchtner, 2017). In this book, I use concepts from different 'schools' within the context of post-structuralism, looking for their capacity to provide me with explanatory value in relation to my material and empirical context, rather than subscribing to one particular approach for the sake of orthodoxy. In this, I am falling back on Halberstam's description of queer methodology as 'a scavenger methodology that uses different methods to collect and produce information on subjects who have been deliberately or accidentally excluded from traditional studies of human behaviour' (1998, p 13). I also subscribe to Foucault's insistence that as a researcher, it is more important to keep your eyes on the things you want to understand than to follow any proposed 'correct' way of understanding them (that is: methodology for the sake of methodology [see also Bazeley, 2013, pp 9–12; Keller, 2017]). Finally, as this project combines analysis of visual and textual material, it is also oriented towards Bleiker's pluralist approach to methods that values complexity over disciplinary boundaries (Bleiker, 2015, 2018b). This section should therefore not be understood as a pledge of allegiance to any specific *kind* of discourse analysis. In the feminist research tradition, it aims to provide validity to my findings by laying open the practicalities of how the analysis was done.

Two foundational assumptions guide this kind of post-structural analysis: the constitutive power of language through meaning-making processes (including the ways in which these are implicated in knowledge/power nexuses [Foucault, 1977]), and the constant instability of those processes of meaning making due to their being relationally constituted. One central component of post-structuralist analyses is the making of meaning through differentiation, a process in which the 'self' is brought into being by separation from a constitutive outside/Other (Derrida, 1978; Foucault, 1978; Laclau and Mouffe, 1985; Hall, 1997b). While this has its roots in the Saussarian notion of linguistic systems (de Saussure, 1974; Jørgensen and Phillips, 2002, pp 10–12), in which every sign acquires and maintains meaning in relation to other signs, post-structuralist approaches explicitly acknowledge the ways in which signs are only temporarily stabilized (Laclau and Mouffe for example speak of the temporary 'closure' of discourses [Laclau and Mouffe, 1985, p 110]).

This means that concepts such as 'Sweden' or 'Swedishness' are only ever knowable within their specific contexts of signification, as well as being open for multiple meanings. In order to approach these temporary stabilizations through difference analytically, I draw on logics of equivalence and differentiation (Kølvraa, 2017; Hall, 2021), which enables me to look for the various ways in which, for example, Swedishness is constructed both by virtue of being something and not being something else. By looking for chains of equivalence and difference (Laclau and Mouffe, 1985, pp 127–34), I gain insight into how boundary-making processes around constructions of Swedishness are discursively enacted, but also what kinds of signs are particularly prominent in these constructions.

These signs are referred to as key signifiers or nodal points, which organize discursive processes of meaning making by temporarily fixating signs around them (Laclau and Mouffe, 1985, p 112; Jørgensen and Phillips, 2002, p 50). These key signifiers are also interesting with regard to the second major aspect of this project: the notion of grids of intelligibility. The temporary stabilization of the (LGBTQ-friendly, tolerant, Swedish) Self through processes of differentiation from a constitutive Other has implications not only for the ways in which this Self is constituted discursively but also with regard to who can and cannot comfortably (or at all) occupy a position within the discursive boundaries of that Self. These processes delineate, among others, boundaries for the 'right' and 'wrong' kinds of queerness within the context of constructions of various notions of Swedishness, thus making possible/speakable (as in: accessible through established discursive formations) certain experiences while silencing others. As discussed earlier, discursive meaning-making processes are crucial to how we make sense of the world around us, but also to how we make sense of ourselves. While these acts of sense making have also been discussed in terms of identity and/or subjectivity (Hall, 1996, 1990; Edkins and Pin-Fat, 1999; Braidotti, 2002; Yuval-Davis, 2006), I approach them through the notion of grids of intelligibility (Butler, 1999). This concept is suitable for analysing precisely the complex and instable aspects of the relationality with which we make sense of ourselves and others around us. It enables us to draw on queer assumptions about meaning-making processes as unstable, complex and ambiguous. Seeing discourse as temporary closure therefore crucially involves the possibility for change with every utterance and repetition. To account for this as well as for the inherent instability of the discursive constitution of collective and individual identities through grids of intelligibility, I also rely on Butler's concept of performativity (Butler, 1999).

As discussed in Chapter 3, Butler sees the way in which we as subjects are constructed and (re)construct ourselves by repeating the very terms by which we are constituted as always also being the exact point where there is a possibility of challenging and reworking these terms through resignification (Butler, 1993, p 123). Discursive acts of boundary making are described by Butler as 'internally unstable affairs' (Butler, 1993, p 126). This means that while the boundary-making processes I identify enable certain grids of intelligibility for what constitutes 'liveable lives' within a given context (Butler, 2005), these remain unstable and open for (re-)negotiation and re-signification.

Additionally, there are certain discursive formations that are maintained either through the absence of particular signs – something becomes meaningful despite or precisely because it is not mentioned in a certain context – or because of the 'stickiness' of signs to others (Ahmed, 2004a, p 93). I follow Ahmed's understanding of how

> signs become sticky through repetition; if a word is used in a certain way, again and again, then that 'use' becomes intrinsic. ... The sign is a sticky sign as an effect of a history of articulation. ... The stickiness of the sign is also about the relations or contact between signs [and] to use a sticky sign is to evoke other words, which have become intrinsic to the sign through past forms of association. (Ahmed, 2004a, pp 90–2)

This relates back to Butler's notion of performativity, in which the 'success' of a performance (discursive or otherwise) is largely dependent on working within already established boundaries of meaning making (1990). There is therefore a need to remain aware of silences, absences and implied associations when analysing discursive boundary-making and meaning-making processes through grids of intelligibility.

While discourse is frequently understood to be referring to text as produced in speech or writing, they are just two of numerous signifying practices. Visual material played a central role in analysing the SAF's campaigns. Scholars like Bleiker and Hansen consider images and visual artefacts to also 'do things' discursively in meaning-making processes (Hansen, 2015, 2018; Bleiker, 2018a, p 3). Through processes of (re)presentation and (in)visibility, they create conditions of (im)possibility, shaping the boundaries of communities and identities and affecting how we make sense of ourselves and others (Hall, 1997a; Altermark and Edenborg, 2018). Analyses of hegemonic gazes or stereotypical visualization of minorities show the power that comes with the normalization of certain regimes of representation (Hall, 1997a). As images appeal to our emotions, their affective dimension can potentially enhance an image's message and discursive impact in comparison to similar messages being conveyed in text-based discourses (Hansen, 2015; Hansen et al, 2021). In relation to my material, I therefore combine the analysis of text- and image-based meaning-making processes under the umbrella of post-structural engagements with how we make sense of the world discursively.

As this study contains three different empirical sites that generated different kinds of data for analysis, the practical process of data analysis has varied from site to site. The following sections gives brief examples of what the analytical process for each of the sites looked like, hopefully providing an instructive insight into how we can make sense of meaning-making processes in multiple ways.

Sweden and its hateful Others – analysing Pride Järva

When analysing Pride Järva, I was dealing with a comparatively limited amount of material. This allowed for a close reading of Sjunnesson's statements, while also giving an indication of how he explicitly and implicitly drew on already circulating discourses.

I initially identified Sweden as the key signifier around which the speech was organized. Since Sjunnesson's speech is full of discursive boundary-making moves around various notions of Swedishness, I then conducted my analysis mainly with the help of chains of equivalence, by looking for statements that combine other signs with Sweden/Swedishness by ascribing either sameness or difference. For example, I identified chains that differentiate the particular area of Stockholm that he is in (Järva) from the rest of Sweden. Järva and its inhabitants are ascribed 'intolerance': they "do not respect Swedish [anti-discrimination] legislation", and they "do not see themselves as being a part of Sweden". On the other hand, "Sweden" as he describes it is a country where "we accept people no matter their sexual orientation", where "women walk safely at night" and where "girls can kiss girls, and boys can kiss boys". By maintaining this focus on the ascription of difference, it was possible to follow these differentiations throughout his speech.

I also looked at how difference was discursively created by implication, as Sjunnesson lets the audience of his speech draw their own conclusions. This occurs when he talks about "a transexual called Jack", who he claims was physically abused in the Järva area. Since he has spent five minutes establishing the inhabitants of that area as violent homophobes, the mentioning of that attack implied that the attackers were those 'Others' who lived there. I therefore extended my chains of equivalence/difference to implied or 'sticky' signs (Ahmed, 2004c, pp 89–92). These were important with regard to the 'internal' coherence of Sjunnesson's speech (when he drew on something he had established earlier on), but also with regard to the wider contextualization through other texts (showing me when he drew on more widely established understandings of racialized immigrants as dangerous or threatening, for example).

Follow the rainbow flag – analysing SAF campaigns

The analysis of this site relied more on images in combination with text. As discussed, these images are also *discursive*, that is, they are analysed as a combination of signs within meaning-making processes that are part of discursive boundary making and grids of intelligibility. This means they need to be carefully contextualized and read in relation to the other signs (Weber, 2008; Hansen, 2011b; Adler-Nissen et al, 2020). A rainbow flag on a military campaign poster might still consist of colourful blocks stacked on top of each other, but just like signs appearing in writing or speech, its meaning is crucially affected by the context of its appearance. This is particularly important with regard to signs with well-established symbolic meaning such as the rainbow flag, constituting a global symbol for LGBTQ movements (see for example Alm and Martinsson, 2016 and Wasshede, 2021 for discussions of how the meaning of the rainbow flag shifts in relation to context).

I draw on Ahmed's notion of non-performativity (Ahmed, 2006) to assess the ways in which symbols such as the rainbow flag can become outward stand-ins for the political change they are promising about an organization (or a nation), rather than actual change happening. While present and visible on the outside, they become 'non-performative' with regard to the cause they are a symbol of, externalizing issues such as racial, sexual or gender discrimination. Following Ahmed's encouragement to 'follow' signs around different contexts (2006, p 105), I continually asked myself, 'What does a certain image do as part of a specific campaign, on a website, a billboard, or a newspaper advertisement?' This included the possibility of it not doing anything at all, or, rather, hiding that nothing was being done.

Key signifiers and chains of equivalence were once more the main tools used in the analysis, by combining the campaign images with an interpretation of the accompanying captions (see Bleiker 2015, 2019 on the need for pluralistic methods when analysing visual material). This means I looked at the images and texts separately as well as combining them in analysis.

The rainbow flag is the central visual key signifier that I followed around the different campaigns to see what it was 'doing' in particular contexts of meaning making. While the rainbow is used throughout as the re-appearing visual marker of LGBTQ rights and identities, it became clear that elements like camouflage patterns, military uniforms and increasingly also combat equipment are present to 'ground' the rainbow representation within a well-established military iconography.

The analysis of the campaign messages reinforced this interpretation. The reappearing nodal points around which the captions were oriented concerned the 'right to be who you are' and the 'duty to defend [this right]'. By analysing chains of equivalence, I identified 'the right to be who you are' as an issue of equality and non-discrimination in the earlier campaigns, while the later campaigns focus more on this right being under threat and therefore in need of defence by the SAF.

By looking at how these campaigns visually portray LGBTQ people, I also identified the double position of LGBTQ-rights-holders as 'normal' Swedish citizens in need of protection from a dangerous Other and as the LGBTQ soldier who 'does' the protecting. This double positioning of LGBTQ people in the material indicated that even seemingly clear-cut Self/Other distinctions can defy binary logics of either/or and instead work within what Weber calls the plural logic of and/or (Weber, 2016b). The way in which LGBTQ people were multiply positioned in these constructions of Swedishness by being both the symbol for aspects of Swedishness that needed protecting (that is, the pro-LGBTQ value system) and their protectors indicates once more the potentially ambiguous and unstable ways in which the boundary making around collective identities works through the enabling of grids of intelligibility.

Othering and intelligibility – analysing Instagram entries

The analysis of the Instagram account was more explicitly concerned with grids of intelligibility for LGBTQ people racialized as non-White and/or Muslim. Here, I identified instances where writers shared experiences of being made intelligible (by others or themselves) through boundary-making processes and then looked at these experiences as a way of analysing which grids of intelligibility could be considered most prevalent across the group of writers posting on the account. Through an understanding of how LGBTQ people racialized as non-White and/or Muslim themselves experienced their being positioned within the discursive construction of LGBTQ-friendly Swedishness and homophobic racialized Otherness, I could get a better view of how processes of boundary making dis/enable certain ways of 'being queer' (as well as being enabled by them). Reflecting on the ways in which my own Whiteness might impact the questions I ask and the conclusions I draw, I also decided to limit my analysis to those parts of the material explicitly dealing with the experiences of LGBTQ people racialized as non-White and/or Muslim in the context of White LGBTQ communities. Expectations about gender and sexuality of course exist beyond these specific contexts, and the writers are exposed to and engage with a variety of those. While the writers touch upon these other experiences in their posts, they are not the focus of this analysis.

Since data collection generated a large amount of material, I used the qualitative data analysis software NVivo in order to organize and code the material. I did several rounds of close readings of these entries (Bazeley, 2013, p 126), coding them during each round. While the use of qualitative data analysis software has been criticized by qualitative researchers for distancing researchers from their data and the danger of people relying on computer-assisted quick-fix solutions rather than analytical rigour (see Bazeley, 2013, pp 136–45 for a discussion of the benefits and problems of qualitative data analysis software), in this case the software actually enabled me to get closer to the material. It helped me not only to keep track of the data despite the large amount of text; it also enabled me to maintain complete and intact source texts. This was particularly important, as I wanted to give as much space as possible in the final analysis to the writers' own voices by using long quotes (see Chapter 8).

Writing as analytical work

To complete the methodological discussion, I take a look at a central aspect of academic life whose importance for analytical work is frequently overlooked and the mastery of which is often taken for granted. *Writing* is of course the most common – if not always the most effective – way to publish and thereby to communicate our research to others, but its relevance as an analytical tool should not be underestimated. This section discusses writing as an important part of research work, looking at the relevance of writing for the analytical process.

Writing might not be included as an analytical method in many standard textbooks on qualitative research methodology, but there are those who discuss 'writing as a method of inquiry' (Richardson and Adams St. Pierre, 2005). This approach is particularly common among feminist, queer and post/decolonial researchers occupied with demystifying the process of knowledge production, thus challenging the privileged role of the researcher as the producer of 'objective truths' (Brown and Strega, 2005; Ackerly et al, 2006; Collins, 2009; Browne and Nash, 2016). Instead, they see writing as a kind of enquiry, a form of data collection and as a sense-making tool (Colyar, 2009). Rather than starting to write once we know what we want to say, with all our arguments thought-out and organized, these authors encourage us to use writing as part of the meaning-making process, both 'a symbolic system which articulates what we know, but ... also a tool whereby we come to these understandings' (Colyar, 2009, p 422).

Two ways of looking at the role writing plays in analysis particularly inspire me: in her work on queer partner migration, Ahlstedt calls writing 'a way of collecting more data, but from one's own head' (Ahlstedt, 2016, p 143), and Adams St. Pierre describes expository writing as 'tracing of a thought already thought' (Richardson and Adams St. Pierre, 2005, p 967). This acknowledgement of writing as a process, which almost in a physical, embodied way connects what is in front of you (your empirical material, your background literature, your theoretical framework) with what might be inside of you (the way in which your brain connects these) requires that we account for how we write when discussing our method and analysis.

Writing has been part of my analytical work in a number of different ways. First, I approach existing literature and theoretical frameworks by writing about them. Particularly with regard to more complex theoretical literature, writing about, and thereby rephrasing complex academic lingo in my own words, helps me not only make sense of a certain approach; it also allows me to see whether I can 'make it my own' by making sure that it allows me to understand the issues and questions I want to understand. Secondly, I write throughout the analysis of empirical material. As I approach a new body of material, I also start writing annotations. These annotations exist next to and apart from the actual in-text coding of the material, and they relate more to overarching themes, including references to existing literature and theoretical concepts. As the coding progresses and becomes more intricate, so do the annotations, which are living documents and, in many ways, constitute a conversation with myself. Here, arguments are tested, connections are made and insights are reached, because they are less constrained by the more rigid expectations of 'formal' analytical methodology. They can thus draw on the full archive of previous analyses and literature that exists at the back of my mind.

Finally, I write about the writing. Colyar explains this process beautifully in her article 'Becoming writing, becoming writers', where she discusses 'nonintroductions' and 'false beginnings' (Colyar, 2009, p 421) as a way of getting a text underway, explaining to herself what it is she wants to say and what she needs to do in order to say it. Writing about writing frequently is the final step in the analytical process. Here, the conversation moves from being between me and myself to an attempt to communicate with others, forcing me to make transparent those aspects of my analysis that allow a reader to follow my argument. By doing so, seemingly unimportant details might suddenly gain greater relevance, whereas others might retract into the background. One example of this is Pride Järva, where I realized fairly late in the process that the analysis required a careful contextualization for an international audience, leading me to re-consider the role of (local) queer activism as an antagonist in Sjunnesson's speech.

Writing is a social activity, an attempt to communicate (to myself or others) the content of my analysis as well as the ways in which it came about. The conversational aspect, the expository writing as a tracing of a thought already thought (or unearthing of thoughts previously unthought) is crucial to analysis, because it helps to 'connect the dots' of empirical findings. Making this process explicit and thereby asserting that '[w]riting is qualitative methodology' (Colyar, 2009, p 433) can not only increase confidence in one's own analysis; it also serves as a way of honouring queer and feminist commitments to the situatedness of knowledge.

Ethics and positionality

Feminist, queer and postcolonial researchers across disciplines practise self-reflexivity as a way to contextualize research. They critically reflect on how positionalities and experiences influence the questions we ask and the findings we arrive at, as well as how we interact with those we meet on the way (Haraway, 1988; Collins, 2009; hooks, 1989; Brown and Strega, 2005; Ackerly et al, 2006; Browne and Nash, 2016). This happens not based on the assumption that it is possible (or desirable) to name our own baggage in some kind of academic-methodological disclaimer and then move on. Rather, it is a way of creating accountability, acknowledging our own investments in our research as well as the fact that *any* kind of research(er) is always already implicated in existing 'conditions, contexts, and positionalities of life and living' (herising, 2005, p 139). Throughout the book, but particularly in this section, I aspire to do so by making myself, my questions and reflections, visible to the reader. Over the course of this project, I have struggled with a number of challenges related to my positionality as a researcher and queer activist, as well as to ongoing political debates regarding the position of LGBTQ people in Swedish society, particularly those racialized as non-White and/or Muslim. I will briefly try to unpack some of these here.

First, how do we critically engage with homonationalist narratives without having to disavow the legal and social progress that undeniably is being made as the result of LGBTQ activism, or playing into the hands of anti-LGBTQ actors? Specifically, how do we do so in a time when some of that progress is actively being rolled back by anti-gender politics? My critical analysis of the mobilization of LGBTQ rights in national(ist) military campaigns, for example, could (albeit from a very different perspective) add to the chorus of critical voices that the campaigns had been met with from right-wing homo-, bi- and transphobes who saw their hetero-sexist conceptualizations of Swedishness threatened. Notwithstanding their message, these campaigns were after all also the outcome of heavily criticized pro-LGBTQ activist work that had been done internally by military personnel. This work becomes invisible if the analysis focuses solely on critiquing the ways in which LGBTQ people (as rights-holders and/or soldiers) are mobilized as symbols of a nation in need of military protection. It is therefore necessary to also acknowledge that these kinds of campaigns in complex and contradictory ways do hold some potential of destabilizing an inherently patriarchal and heteronormative institution.

For me, this complexity remains one of the main challenges with regard to researching the ways in which LGBTQ rights and identities have become nationalist boundary makers. To simply identify the villains in mainstream LGBTQ politics in order to then quickly distance oneself from them and instead continue the search for the truly radical queer subject continuing the fight in a truly radical queer movement (Kosnick, 2015, p 694) can therefore not be the solution. This approach simplifies the complexity of how different LGBTQ people are positioned in contemporary processes of boundary making. As researchers, we have the analytical tools at our disposal to engage with these questions instead of shutting them down, by continuing to work intersectionally and relating back to global archives of queer and feminist thought (Dhawan, 2013; see Collins, 2015; Weber, 2016a; Rao, 2020). Rather than creating corrective accounts of 'bad' and 'good' LGBTQ activism, we need to continue to deconstruct complex power relations. Focusing too much on 'homonationalism' as a politics can give the misleading impression that 'there exists a non-complicit, "authentically queer" performance of LGBTQ identity' (Bulmer, 2013, p 148). When revisiting the concept, Puar herself stressed that homonationalism is 'not a descriptor, not an adjective' but primarily an analytic tool that helps to critically take apart convergences of state practices, transnational queer commodity culture, human rights discourses and wider global phenomena which make it attractive for states to embrace (and reject) LGBTQ rights at certain points in time (Puar, 2022, p 2).

A second challenge concerns how we can make sure that we are being outspoken against sexist, racist and otherwise oppressive structures and norms both within majority and minority contexts. How do we avoid one critique erasing another? While this project focuses on a critique of homonationalism and Swedish gender exceptionalism, those are of course far from the only or even the most prevalent concerns when it comes to oppression along lines of race, sexuality and gender identity. In order to do justice to the complex ways in which racism, sexism, homo-, bi- and transphobia in different ways form structures of oppression everywhere in society, we need to analyse these specific forms of oppression as well as how their various forms interlock. Again, the resurgence of anti-gender attitudes and policy making in countries previously assumed to be working towards the achievement of liveable lives for all queers makes this painfully apparent, as does the fate of sexual and gender minorities in armed conflicts partially legitimized through the protection of LGBTQ rights or traditional values.

Dhawan argues that 'the necessity of anti-imperialist and antiracist critique within queer politics must be accompanied by a critique of "reproductive heteronormativity" within postcolonial contexts' (2013, p 195), and that it is 'important to note that securitization and sexuality, danger and threat, family and nation ... are equally deployed in non-Western contexts, not as mere parrots of the West, but with their own coercive agendas' (2013, p 212), something which Rao echoes in his work on the many mutations of queerness and anti-queer sentiments across postcolonial contexts (Rao, 2020). Being occupied with criticizing one form of violence does therefore not absolve us from taking issue with another. While this book focuses on normative notions of gender and sexuality in predominantly White LGBTQ contexts, this does not mean that similar grids of intelligibility do not exist in other contexts, including postcolonial and diasporic ones. It is therefore crucial to maintain a critique of the multiple sources that enable normative grids of intelligibility along lines of race, gender and sexuality.

The third challenge concerns my own positionality as both a White researcher and an activist in relation to this project: how can I engage with LGBTQ activism in a way that will further anti-racist work and the decolonization of queer movements? In other words, how can the researcher become an effective ally? I had to find ways to investigate the racializing aspects of contemporary constructions of Swedishness without becoming yet another White person who diverts resources from anti-racist activist communities by demanding to be educated, something that has frequently been pointed out as a problem by anti-racist groups (Lorde, 1984; Ahmed, 2004b; Srivastava, 2006).

Focusing on the stories told by LGBTQ people racialized as non-White and/or Muslim on the Instagram account provided a window into their experiences without having to take up much of their time or energy. As the account's privacy setting is 'open', the account provided a virtual space that is predominantly for LGBTQ people who are racialized without being completely separatist. Additionally, the administrators encouraged the audience at a public event I attended to widely share the account, as one of the reasons for its existence was to raise awareness about the experiences of racialized LGBTQ people beyond the limited group who already followed the account and recognized themselves in the stories shared. Once I had familiarized myself with the material, I also decided to limit my analysis to those parts of the material explicitly dealing with the experiences of LGBTQ people racialized as non-White and/or Muslim in the context of *White* LGBTQ communities. I would thus contribute with knowledge about majority spaces I was myself familiar with, rather than focusing on context I had little insight into. I finally decided not to engage with the community interaction going in the comment section below the individual posts, as this community-building aspect was clearly directed towards racialized LGBTQ people rather than being part of the effort to 'raise awareness'.

This has hopefully helped me to focus my capacity as a researcher on issues I am well placed to critically investigate. It has enabled me to analyse in depth how LGBTQ emancipation discourses are deployed to spread Islamophobia and racism, how LGBTQ rights and identities are used in the creation of nationalist imaginaries complicit with contemporary forms of cultural racism and how these boundary-making processes enable grids of intelligibility for (non-)belonging, positioning some people as privileged others and others as unwanted outsiders. Developing critical knowledge about the ways in which flying the rainbow flag does not necessarily advance the creation of 'liveable lives' for LGBTQ people, and certainly not for all of them, allows me as an activist and a part of the Swedish LGBTQ community to add to the ever-growing archive of our own history. Using my resources as a researcher to distribute that knowledge by way of publication, in teaching and through public speaking means it will continue to grow beyond LGBTQ circles. After all, '[t]he point [in queer and feminist research] is not just to read the webs of knowledge production; the point is to reconfigure what counts as knowledge. ... The point is, in short, to make a difference – however modestly, however partially' (Haraway, 1994, p 61).

6

Pride Järva: LGBTQ People in Right-Wing Nationalist Discourses

The grainy YouTube video shows a middle-aged White man standing in a market square, addressing people from a makeshift stage. Over white trousers, he is wearing a bullet-proof vest and a red baseball cap reading 'TRUMP 2016'. A small group of demonstrators becomes visible. They are waving rainbow flags, Swedish national flags and signs saying 'HBTQ [*sic*] rights everywhere' and '#NoOrlando'. The latter refers to the 2016 shooting at Pulse, an LGBTQ nightclub in Orlando, when a shooter called Mateen Omar killed 48 people, claiming to act on behalf of ISIS [Meyer, 2020]). Behind the demonstrators, uniformed police are patrolling among people doing their shopping. This is Pride Järva 2016, a march organized by right-wing publicist Jan Sjunnesson in Rinkeby, a northern suburb of Stockholm. A party member of the nationalist-populist Sweden Democrats (SD) and at the time staff writer for far-right website Avpixlat, he tells his listeners that while Sweden is inherently tolerant of gay people, this tolerance and the people upon which it is extended are threatened by the increasing influx of homophobic immigrants from Muslim countries. And since established LGBTQ organizations are too "politically correct" to take up this issue, it is up to him and likeminded people to speak up and to protect Swedish values, Swedish laws and the rights of gay people in Sweden. While he speaks, the police prevent a group of protesters from entering the square. The activists are shouting "Not in our names!" and "No racists in our streets!"

 This chapter discusses the event Pride Järva, and in particular a speech delivered by Sjunnesson on the occasion of Pride Järva 2016. While earlier studies on homonationalism in Europe have often focused on ways in which LGBTQ rights organizations have used racialized Othering to advance their issues into the political mainstream, I argue that Pride Järva is indicative of the specific ways in which right-wing political actors actively exploit LGBTQ issues and established homonationalist narratives in their nationalist boundary-making in order to exclude racialized Others. They use LGBTQ rights to construct and reproduce notions of tolerant and progressive Europeanness (here in the form of Swedishness) vis-à-vis a threatening Islamic and racialized Other who is 'imported' (as Sjunnesson puts it) into Western European countries. They employ and reproduce some of the same homonationalist discourses as certain LGBTQ organizations, activists and politicians, but they also differ from them in that these right-wing actors themselves have been (and are) actively and consistently opposing the expansion of LGBTQ rights and continue to stigmatize LGBTQ people as internal non-heteronormative, non-cisnormative Others. Instead, they attempt to enlist LGBTQ rights and the activists fighting for them for their own xenophobic, racist and nationalist projects of racialized Othering without actual engagement in LGBTQ rights. This has implications not only for constructions of who belongs and does not belong within boundaries of Swedishness; it also draws upon as well as reinforces specific notions of who is and who is not intelligible as 'the right kind of queer' within these boundaries.

Sjunnesson's speech at Pride Järva is part of wider discourses constructing and reproducing Swedish – and by extension European – selves and others along lines of gender and sexuality. He clearly draws on and reproduces existing narratives that are recurrent and widespread beyond the political right. In fact, their recurrence is to some extent what makes Pride Järva possible at all. As I discuss elsewhere in this book, central among these narratives are notions of Sweden as a particularly progressive country with regard to gender equality and LGBTQ rights (described as Swedish gender exceptionalism [Alm et al, 2021]), descriptions of homophobic hate crimes with racialized/Muslim perpetrators (Klatran, 2021) as well as so-called rescue narratives (Hiller, 2022), all of which can be found in statements by politicians and activists beyond the right-wing part of the political spectrum. I argue that Sjunnesson builds on and extends them by adding a protector narrative particular to right-wing political actors, revolving around the notion of leftist political correctness silencing LGBTQ concerns about immigrant homophobia. This alleged failure of Swedish LGBTQ organizations to protect Swedish LGBTQ people is portrayed as making it necessary for the populist right to step in and to stand up for Swedish values and laws as represented by LGBTQ rights. As the chapter shows, this position as the truth-speaking protector of gays fits badly with Sjunnesson's language and politics. It also demands a domesticated, depoliticized and defenceless LGBTQ community at ease with living private lives tolerated by a heteronormative majority under the protection of an otherwise homo- and transphobic right, and with no interest in opposing the violent exclusion of other minorities. So even if Sjunnesson shares some of his rhetoric with other homonationalist actors, his (dis-)engagement with LGBTQ issues and activists sets him apart.

After a brief discussion of existing literature on European right-wing homonationalism, this chapter looks more closely at the Swedish context, particularly SD's conceptualization of LGBTQ people as docile internal others. Based on reporting around the event, I discuss the evolution of and resistance to Pride Järva and analyse Sjunnesson's speech in Rinkeby in 2016, focusing on the various ways in which he uses LGBTQ rights to construct threatening non-Swedish Others, portraying himself and his political associates as truth-telling protectors of LGBTQ people.

'Right' and 'wrong' kinds of Others

As discussed elsewhere in this book, racialized notions of gender and sexuality have throughout history been used to distinguish between acceptable and unacceptable ways of being European, demarcating the normal and the deviant, the desirable and the undesirable, the insider and the outsider. While homosexuals have previously been one of the cultural Others on the borders of Western European societies, they are now in many ways actively incorporated as markers against racialized non-Western (often Islamic) others. This European brand of homonationalism has frequently been built on narratives around threat and protection, making it easy to integrate into the rhetoric of the populist far right. As certain members of the LGBTQ community achieve symbolic entry into citizenship and nationhood, they provide living examples for the self-definition of Western European countries as sexually progressive and morally superior, and their sexual liberation is used to create a temporal segregation between 'European modernity' and more traditional (read: conservative, patriarchal) racialized and Muslim communities. Difference becomes carefully managed, 'the homosexual other is white, the racial other is straight' (Puar, 2007, p 32), and the homosexual Other is no longer a threat but instead the victim of a threatening racial Other. Some (frequently: White, able-bodied, well-earning and gender-conforming) LGBTQ people go from being the wrong to being the right kind of Other.

The more various political actors proclaim themselves protectors of LGBTQ rights, the easier it is for these rights – and the activists fighting for them – to be instrumentalized in campaigns that lead to the vilification, oppression and policing of externalized, bad Others. Crucially, only certain kinds of queers are considered fit to be included in nationalist narratives. This becomes particularly clear from the way in which the populist right in Sweden has variously conceptualized LGBTQ identities in recent decades. As this chapter will show, they demand a demobilized, depoliticized LGBTQ community, not contesting heteronormative institutions but upholding them by aiming for inclusion within them (compare Duggan, 2002, p 180); and more interested in living an undisturbed private life as part of the heteronormative nation than in furthering queer and anti-racist politics or opposing state-sanctioned violence against other minorities. Their inclusion of the LGBTQ Other into the nation is therefore always conditional, depending on their Otherness not fundamentally disturbing heterosexual and cis-gender norms.

Homonationalism, gender exceptionalism and the Swedish far right

Notions of threat and protection are central to processes of inclusive othering. As discussed in Chapter 2, the folding of LGBTQ people into the 'us' in this 'us–them' rhetoric (Puar, 2006, p 70) enables Western European countries to project themselves as safe for LGBTQ people in comparison to countries in the Middle East, Northern Africa and Eastern Europe. This rhetoric frequently includes communities within European societies who are assumed to live by the values of those countries due to their migrant roots. As touched upon in previous chapters, discourses around migrants' cultural values and sexual rights in Europe have framed Muslim and racialized women and LGBTQ people as faceless victims who have to be liberated from the oppressive patriarchal structures said to exist in migrant 'ghettos' in Western Europe's larger cities (El-Tayeb, 2012, p 80). Not only right-wing actors but also LGBTQ and women's rights organizations have been part of perpetuating these dominant themes around racialized and Muslim communities and sexual rights in the European context (Hiller, 2022; Klatran, 2021; Tudor and Ticktin, 2021). They have been criticized by queer-of-colour organizations for speaking about migrants and racialized Europeans rather than with them and for cashing in on growing anti-Muslim sentiments in the process of moving LGBTQ rights into the focus of a wider public (El-Tayeb et al, 2015). They are, Haritaworn argues, actively scripting 'the drama of the hateful Other, who must be educated into the cosmopolitan community' (Haritaworn, 2010, p 73).

Puar states that '[l]ike modernity, homonationalism can be resisted and re-signified, but not opted out of: we are all conditioned by it and through it' (Puar, 2013, p 336). This chapter argues that it is against this discursive omnipresence of homonationalist language that right-wing political actors in Sweden have been able to selectively take up, build upon and employ their own version of the narratives referred to earlier, despite standing in open opposition to the expansion of LGBTQ rights and despite their continued internal Othering of LGBTQ people. In contrast to rescue narratives concerned with the emancipation of racialized LGBTQ people, these actors focus on White Swedish LGBTQ people who are threatened by the homophobic attitudes racialized communities are assumed to have. In their narratives, homophobia and transphobia are no longer part of oppressive power structures of Western societies; instead they become cultural problems, connected to specific minority groups that live within, yet separate from these societies. Much like in the other empirical sites discussed in this book, the ongoing structural discrimination of LGBTQ people in Sweden disappears behind these overarching narratives of threat and protection.

Sweden, as the location of Pride Järva, is particularly interesting with regard to this characterization of homophobic threats because of widespread notions regarding Swedish exceptionalism when it comes to gender equality (Martinsson et al, 2016). These notions, as discussed in previous chapters, predate, but also strongly overlap with and reinforce, homonationalist narratives. In line with Haritaworn, I argue that these wider notions of Europeanness or Swedishness constructed along lines of progress, secularism and rationality ignore 'a criminalizing, pathologizing, and deeply oppressive past' (Haritaworn, 2012, p 76) when it comes to LGBTQ experiences. This is certainly true with regard to Sweden's right-wing populist party, the SD. With roots in the Swedish neo-Nazi movement, the party first entered the Swedish parliament in 2010 and established itself as the third-largest party in 2014. The SD finally became a shadow member of the Swedish government when they agreed to prop up a conservative coalition unable to gather its own parliamentary majority after the 2022 elections. While Sjunnesson was never an appointed spokesperson for SD, and Pride Järva not officially a party event, he was an active party member and previous editor-in-chief for the party's newspaper. SD's rhetoric underlies many of his statements related to Pride Järva. Promoting what they themselves call immigration-critical politics, the party has frequently been characterized as racist, xenophobic and Islamophobic, as well as strongly conservative, projecting a heterosexist ideal of the nuclear family as the core unit of the nation (Towns et al, 2014; Sager and Mulinari, 2018; Norocel et al, 2022). As such, they have also consistently campaigned and voted against the expansion of LGBTQ rights. Publications from the party's earlier years (1980s–early 2000s) refer to (male) homosexuality as an illness and a threat to society (Westerlund, 2015, pp 10–15). More recent statements see LGBTQ people as sexual deviants, not necessarily to be persecuted, but not to be allowed to marry or have children either (Westerlund, 2015, pp 30–5). Between the mid-2000s and the elections that finally brought the party into positions of powerful political influence in 2022, LGBTQ issues have almost exclusively been discussed with reference to violent homophobia and sexism as an integral part of Islam (Westerlund, 2015, p 36). During the 2010 election campaign, party leader Jimmie Åkesson even tried to publicly frame SD as LGBTQ-friendly, explicitly referencing 'increasing mass immigration and islamisation' (Åkesson and Herrstedt, 2010). This discursive connection between LGBTQ rights and immigration is very close to a more frequently used tendency by party representatives to frame questions of gender equality in relation to threats from external (racialized) others (Edenborg, 2020a; Norocel et al, 2022). While my analysis in this chapter focuses on public statements made by the party's representatives in major Swedish news outlets, various online forums as well as the comments below some of these statements show the party's supporters to be deeply homo- and transphobic and equally deeply troubled by their party publicly embracing LGBTQ issues. Engaging with those discourses exceeds the reach of this chapter, but they are important to bear in mind when considering the party's official stance on LGBTQ rights throughout the first decade of the 21st century. Recent developments have shown that SD's homonationalist statements have since been replaced by open opposition to LGBTQ rights (Lagerman, 2023a).

LGBTQ voices from within the party, as far as they appear in public, mirror the official party line. Apart from alerting to the dangers of Islamization, a group called 'SD-HBT' have argued that pride parades are showcasing LGBTQ people like circus animals (Thunell et al, 2014b; HBT is the Swedish abbreviation of homosexual, bisexual and transsexual) and that sex education at pride events only reinforces prejudices about LGBTQ people being promiscuous and obsessed with their sexuality (Thunell et al, 2014a). In their eyes, LGBTQ people being overly affectionate (or even sexual) in public are begging for trouble. They consider sexual orientation and gender identity private issues to be kept outside the political sphere and refuse to use the term queer – rather than challenging norms, society should try to live in symbiosis (Thunell et al, 2014). They promote a notion of LGBTQ people as sexual deviants, to be tolerated if they behave, and argue at most for a privatized and depoliticized LGBTQ other, looking for inclusion and integration into the norm. In 2023, spokespeople for LGBTQ people within SD stressed that there needs to be space for those who are 'LGBTQ, but not left-wing', after the party was once more excluded from participation at Stockholm Pride on the basis of their racist and anti-LGBTQ policies (Rubbestad and Broman, 2023).

At the same time, their political actions since entering the parliament in 2010 have shown that actually working towards inclusion of LGBTQ people is not high on the SD's agenda. Particularly at local levels, politicians from SD have time and again interfered with pride-related events (such as the raising of the rainbow flag on public buildings) and have actively worked against the extension of LGBTQ rights (RFSU, 2020; Lagerman, 2023a). This has only accelerated after their election success in 2022, when SD gained just over 20 per cent of the votes and became a shadow member of the Swedish government. One recent discussion about LGBTQ issues driven by the populist right concerns so-called 'drag queen story hours', a feature in local libraries that involves drag artists reading fairy tales to children.

After local SD politicians intervened, some of these events were cancelled, while others had to be held with security in place after threats were made to libraries (Thorén, 2022). Overall, right-wing threats against LGBTQ events and organizations in Sweden have noticeably increased since the mid-2010s (Lagerman, 2023b; Linander et al, 2023).

The making of Pride Järva

Pride Järva took place for the first time in July 2015, during the same week as Stockholm Pride. On social media, Sjunnesson announced he was planning a march from Tensta to Husby, two of Stockholm's suburbs where many immigrants and racialized Swedes live. A heated media discussion followed. Among other critical commentators, anti-racist think tank Inte rasist men … pointed out that Sjunnesson had close connections to SD, and that this parade was probably created to reproduce notions of the racialized suburbs as inherently homophobic, intolerant and in need of 'enlightenment' (Johansson, 2015). Sweden's main LGBTQ organization, The Swedish Federation for Lesbian, Gay, Bisexual, Transgender, Queer and Intersex Rights (RFSL), and the organizers of Stockholm Pride, distanced themselves in a public statement from Pride Järva, stressing that anti-racism was an important part of their work, while Sjunnesson had 'made himself known as a person who spreads hate against Muslims … and does not back up LGBTQ rights' (RFSL, 2015). Queer and anti-racist activists from Stockholm's suburbs rallied to organize a protest on Järva field stating that "[w]hen racists and Islamophobes want to use LBGT-peoples' struggle as a battering ram against Muslims we need to say NO and put our foot down". "This is a common strategy" said organizer Emelie Mårtensson,

> 'putting two oppressed groups up against each other and saying that we only can take care of one. It shifts the focus from the fight between oppressed and oppressor to conflicts between oppressed groups. … They paint a caricature image of the suburbs regarding women's and queer lives. Their image of the suburbs is wrong.' (Irani, 2015)

Sjunnesson replied by accusing RFSL and the 'political left' of being cowards who ignore the fate of LGBTQ people in the suburbs. Avpixlat's editor-in-chief Mats Dagerlind came to his support, writing under the pseudonym 'Matilda Dagerlind' (an ill-conceived joke about transgender identities, accompanied by a picture of himself wearing a rainbow flag as a headscarf). He called RFSL and Stockholm Pride politically correct hypocrites who rather than standing up for their rights on the 'barricades' in the suburbs spend their time in the city centre, dancing, drinking 'pink champagne' and ranting against 'honourable attempts' to make the suburbs safer for LGBTQ people (Dagerlind, 2015). The word barricades and their placement in the suburbs marks clearly where Dagerlind situates the boundaries between safe and unsafe spaces for LGBTQ people in Sweden (and that such clear boundaries exist, along lines of cultural difference). Sjunnesson later echoed this in his speech at Pride Järva 2016. Pride Järva 2015 consisted of Sjunnesson and about twenty participants marching from Tensta to Husby, where they were met by up to 200 queer and anti-racist protesters. A sizeable police force and numerous national and international journalists accompanied the march.

Pride Järva 2016 followed similar patterns. When the march was announced to once again coincide with Stockholm's annual pride-week, RFSL and Stockholm Pride immediately released a statement, saying that 'you cannot work against any discrimination with any form of credibility if you at the same time endorse or reproduce other kinds of discrimination' (Pride, 2016). They also pointed out that 'many LGBTQ individuals have themselves experienced threats and violence by the groups that the organizers behind Pride Järva belong to' (Stockholm Pride, 2016). A group called Queers against Fascism and Racism organized a demonstration to follow the march, stating that Pride Järva was not going to "spread their racism, hate-speech and Islamophobia" without being challenged by activists – 'We are here to show that they cannot use us as a battering ram for their fascist propaganda' (Göteborgs Posten, 2016). However, the public debate prior to the march lacked some of the previous year's urgency, with mainstream media responses dominated by reporting on the event itself, rather than opinion pieces.

Sjunnesson tried to put Pride Järva 2016 into an international context by connecting it to similar events. He claimed that the march was inspired by Ahmed Marcouch, a Moroccan-born Dutch social-democrat. As the head of the district council for Slotervaart, an Amsterdam borough with a large immigrant population, Marcouch had succeeded in moving the start of the 2009 Amsterdam Pride to Slotervaart in an attempt at introducing 'Dutch values' to migrant-dominated parts of Amsterdam (Buruma, 2009). Sjunnesson also invited Milo Yiannopoulos to speak at Pride Järva 2016. Openly gay and at the time employed by alternative-right online media Breitbart News, Yiannopoulos had been drawing large crowds (and violent protests) as the face of the 'Gays for Trump' campaign (Quensel and Vergara, 2016). Yiannopoulos initially said he was "going to lead a pride march through a Muslim ghetto in Sweden" (Breitbart News, 2016a) but eventually took back his commitment, allegedly after a Breitbart News security team had considered the 'Muslim ghetto' too dangerous (Breitbart News, 2016b). Despite Yiannopoulos's failure to turn up, the event and the situation in Sweden were discussed in several English-language online media outlets marketing themselves as alternative news sources (Infowars, 2016; RuptlyTV,

2016; TheRebel, 2016). Pride Järva should therefore also be seen in the wider context of right-wing homonationalist projects beyond the Swedish context, with Sjunnesson actively attempting to establish himself internationally as the immigration-critical interpreter of Swedish LGBTQ concerns.

Looking at the actors behind and resistance to Pride Järva makes clear that this event goes beyond the scope of many instances of homonationalist rhetoric analysed in the existing literature. The organizer is unattached to LGBTQ causes and instead closely aligned with a political party known for its resistance to LGBTQ rights and the homo- and transphobic attitudes of its members and supporters. In this, he differs from LGBTQ activists using very similar rhetoric, such as Peter Tatchell in the UK (Erdem et al, 2008). Pride Järva is met not only with protests from anti-racist, queer-of-colour coalitions (as has been the case with mainstream LGBTQ organizations using homonationalist language) but also from the predominantly White Swedish LGBTQ establishment (RFSL and Stockholm Pride). Sjunnesson himself makes no attempt to integrate his event into existing LGBTQ/pride structures, possibly because he knows his reputation prevents his access to these spaces. Instead, he revels in and uses the resistance from LGBTQ activists as proof that his position as truth-speaking protector of LGBTQ people is justified. Pride Järva therefore gives us the opportunity to analyse how right-wing actors look at and try to use LGBTQ rights and LGBTQ activists as tools for their own agenda of racialized exclusion, despite their obvious disassociation from the LGBTQ community – the way in which this is made possible by the prevalence of homonationalist narratives in Western European contexts, but also the way in which it fails due to the resistance of queer and anti-racist activists.

Pride Järva 2016 consisted of around 30 marchers, followed by roughly the same number of vocal protesters, and police. At Rinkeby square, they stopped to listen to a short speech by Sjunnesson. This speech calls for a closer analysis because it draws on and connects many of the existing narratives in which LGBTQ rights are used to mark the boundaries of belonging to acceptable notions of Swedishness as well as the grids of intelligibility they draw upon and reproduce.

Swedishness and the boundaries of being gay in public

Sjunnesson starts by explaining why he is organizing Pride Järva in Rinkeby. Even if it sometimes might appear otherwise, he says, Rinkeby is part of Sweden, and Pride Järva is a demonstration calling forthe same laws and legal rights to apply everywhere in Sweden:

> 'In Sweden, you respect people regardless of their sexual identity. In Sweden, women and girls should be able to walk safely at night. In

Sweden, girls and boys are allowed to drink coffee with whomever they want during the day, and maybe even during the evening. In Sweden, girls are allowed to kiss [*pussa*] girls, and boys are allowed to kiss boys.'

'[Rinkeby] is a part of Sweden, that's why we are here. Swedish law applies everywhere. Swedish law on discrimination, Swedish law on hate crimes, Swedish law on homophobia applies everywhere, even here. That's why we are here, and that's why we will continue to come here until this, what we have understood to be an intolerant part of Sweden has understood that they are in Sweden.'

Sjunnesson manages to say Sweden/Swedish more than ten times within the first two minutes of the speech and directly introduces its central conflict: the LGBTQ-friendly culture that defines Sweden and Swedishness (it is even enshrined in law) against a diffuse intolerant and homophobic 'they' disrespecting both Swedish culture and Swedish law. It should be pointed out here, however, that while Sweden has legislation on discrimination and hate crimes (among others discrimination based on sexual orientation and gender expression), there is no 'Swedish law on homophobia'. As discussed elsewhere, Sjunnesson's description of Swedishness and its gender exceptionalism is not unique or original. It is a well-established narrative both within and outside of Sweden, making it easy to recognize and easy to identify with, even for people who would not consider themselves supporters of the political right. The kissing reference reminds of 'kiss-ins' staged in front of mosques in Germany, where the gay kiss is portrayed as a revolutionary act of emancipation and protest (while, as Haritaworn writes, always staying within the safe, recognizable boundaries of monogamous long-term relationships [Haritaworn, 2010]). Sjunnesson is, however, also in line with the SD's view of (homo)sexuality as something happening in the privacy of your own bedroom. The word *pussa* in Swedish refers to a chaste kiss on the cheek, at most a peck on the lips – a way of showing a parent's affection for their child rather than between lovers.

Sjunnesson specifies the characteristics of the intolerant Other he is referring to by explaining that most people in Rinkeby, Tensta and around Järva do not have their roots in Sweden. They come instead from "the Middle East, Africa and South Asia" where, he claims, homosexuality is illegal and punishable by death according to Islamic Sharia law. According to him, the inhabitants of Rinkeby/Tensta are thus more intolerant than people living in other parts of Sweden, since they bring their values with them from their countries of origin:

'[N]aturally, if you dislike homosexuals, and you come from Mogadishu or Baghdad, and move here, then you continue to do so. And if somebody moves from Stockholm, and is a native [*infödd*] Swede and moves to Riad, or Addis Ababa, then you continue to be tolerant of homosexuals. … People who have decided to live in Sweden need to understand that we do not tolerate intolerance here!'

Sjunnesson's intolerant Other becomes increasingly more visible as the speech goes on: immigrants (and their descendants), born and raised in homophobic cultures, coming to Sweden with cultural baggage that makes them inevitably intolerant of homosexuality. On the other hand, somebody who is a 'native' or ethnic Swede unquestionably is, and always will be, tolerant of homosexuals. Values such as respect and tolerance are presented as static and unchangeable, determined by the society in which you have your roots. They thus take on almost biological, innate qualities, mirroring historical narratives of race biology where racialized, sexualized Others were ascribed certain innate drives and intellectual capacities (see for example Laskar, 2015a). At the same time, this still resonates with the more widely accepted contemporary constructions of Sweden as a country of tolerance and gender equality.

The problematic language of tolerance

Sjunnesson's repeated use of tolerance as central to the relationship between LGBTQ people and the rest of society indicates clearly how he conceptualizes LGBTQ identities, echoing SD's view on (homo)sexuality as non-political. The concept of tolerance does not equal acceptance or affirmation. Rather, it is about a majority conditionally allowing what actually is considered deviant or even unwanted. It 'iterates the normalcy of the powerful and the deviance of the marginal' (Brown, 2006, p 6). Tolerance is therefore both productive and regulative, it requires and produces a subject who tolerates, and somebody else to be tolerated, reinforcing the distinction as well as the power relation between the two. When Sjunnesson speaks of the need for immigrants to tolerate homosexuality, he employs 'a civilizational discourse that identifies both tolerance and the tolerable with the West' (Brown, 2006, p 6). This is not at all the same as considering LGBTQ identities as equal to (and equally valid as) the heterosexual, cis-binary norm. Later on, he describes LGBTQ identities as anything not heterosexual, "everything else, whichever labels we can put on them", reinforcing the notion that homosexuality, bisexuality, transsexuality (without even considering identities beyond these categories) are a deviation from the norm. Clearly, there exists a heterosexual, cisgender 'we' putting labels on a non-heterosexual, non-cisgender 'them'. The continuous internal Othering of LGBTQ people (racialized or not) within Sweden is barely concealed in this statement. The central problem in the meeting between Swedish culture and the intolerant Other, according to Sjunnesson, is Islam, a religion inherently hostile towards homosexuality. It forces homosexual Muslims in Islamic countries to hide from family and friends:

> 'They live a double life. We did this in Sweden for a long time, I would argue up until the 70s, and we do not want back that time. We do not want back a time where homosexuals, lesbians, and everything else, whichever labels we can put on them, or us, for that matter ... live a double life. That's why we have Stockholm Pride in the city centre, that's why we are here. At some point, you should be able to come out as homosexual or bisexual, or transsexual.'

Sjunnesson supports his claim of Islam being a homophobic religion by arguing that yes, Sweden did have homophobia once, and 'we' do not want to have it back. He creates a temporal segregation between progressive Swedish society and countries with Islamic traditions. Homophobia is thus externalized from Sweden – it is a ghost from the past, re-invigorated only by Muslim communities' traditionalism. This also means that Swedish culture seems to be able to change over time (for the better), while Islam and the morals and values related to it are resistant to or incapable of change. Sjunnesson plays to and repeats classical colonialist-orientalist descriptions of the Middle East and Northern Africa as lagging behind Europe, as having stalled in their development (Said, 1978; Spivak, 2004; Butler, 2008). Sjunnesson's mentioning of the coming-out reinforces this narrative of progress, as it presupposes an LGBTQ subject liberating itself from the violently oppressive structures of collective, non-Swedish identities. He completely ignores the fact that homophobia, transphobia, hate crimes and violence against LGBTQ are not a thing of the past in Sweden. LGBTQ people living a double life did not stop 'in the 70s'. Additionally, much of the legislation Sjunnesson praises was introduced fairly recently, against the vehement resistance of SD, the party he is a member of.

The suburb as a homophobic space

Going on, Sjunnesson claims that "there is an import of people who are homophobic [from Islamic countries]". Again, homophobia is something that is externalized, coming to Sweden from the outside. Swedishness is thus distanced from homophobia, both in time and in space. Dagerlind's comment on Stockholm Pride avoiding the barricades in the suburbs in favour of the safety of the inner city (Dagerlind, 2015) shows how much homophobia is portrayed as something spatially and culturally situated (and thus limited), rather than a social structure that continues to be pervasive in Swedish society. When Sjunnesson identifies homophobic spaces in Sweden, these are not Swedish spaces: the homophobia that has come (back) to Sweden with migrant communities coexists with spheres controlled by religiously motivated honour-based violence. According to him, this applies particularly strongly to homosexuals in the suburbs: "It is haram if the son chooses to fall in love with another boy, it is haram if a girlfriend falls in love with another girlfriend [*sic*]. It is haram to at all show that you have that kind of openness, that [sexual] orientation here in Rinkeby/Tensta." He takes up the example of Nalin Pekgul, Kurdish-Swedish social-democrat and former minister for integration, who publicly said she was worried about radical Islamist ideologies gaining influence in Swedish suburbs (Eriksson, 2014):

'It is even so bad that there are parts of Tensta ... she [Nalin Pekgul] can't go to, and she is Kurdish. She can't go into certain shops here in Tensta and do her shopping, without a headscarf. Can you imagine being gay here, and maybe Swedish? Imagine being blond, Swedish and gay. Gives the word "faggot Swede" [*svennebög*], a whole new meaning, doesn't it? We're all faggot Swedes now.'

Based on his claims about Islam's inherent homophobia, Sjunnesson creates a picture of the suburbs as an unsafe space. More specifically, unsafe along lines of gender, sexuality and race. While being an immigrant woman without a headscarf can make you unsafe, being gay will make you unsafe. Being gay, blond and (White, ethnically) Swedish, Sjunnesson implies, is the most unsafe position that exists in this area of Stockholm. To back up his claim, he mentions that "a transsexual called Jack" was attacked in Rinkeby about six months before Pride Järva 2016. No further information on Jack, the attack itself or the attacker(s) is provided. Listeners are left to make their own connections between the incident and Sjunnesson's description of homophobic migrants. His construction of homophobic violence perpetrated by hateful Others is completely in line with other analysis of hate crime discourses (Haritaworn, 2015; Klatran, 2021; Hagerlid, 2023), while not a word is uttered about the violence and threats that LGBTQ people in Sweden are exposed to by the very groups on the political far right he is a part of. By saying "We're all faggot Swedes now", he even extends the threatened community to encompass all White, blond Swedes, no matter their gender or sexual orientation. Swedishness in general is what is at stake in Rinkeby and Tensta. He thus combines old and new narratives of what it means to be Swedish – the acceptable, recognizable Swede is still blond and White but apparently can now also be gay or transsexual. Finally, Sjunnesson argues that the problems created by Islam's inherent hostility towards homosexuality are not something which established LGTBQ organizations want to talk about:

'They don't dare to come here. And then they have the stomach to stand over there and shout "not in our name!", that we have taken this demonstration and pretend to be Pride-people ... but that's not what this is about. Some of us have a sexual orientation that isn't heterosexual, others maybe are heterosexual, I myself am somewhere in between. But we simply want Swedish law to apply in Sweden, and we think [the people organizing] Stockholm Pride are too much of a coward to tackle this, so we did it ourselves.'

This is where Sjunnesson's narrative of threat and protection comes to its climax, and its conclusion. After constructing a threatening external Other (Islam's homophobia and intolerance, personified in the figure of the homophobic Muslim) and a threatened internal Other (White LGBTQ people, by extension White Swedishness), he turns towards those whose responsibility he thinks it is to defend LGBTQ rights in Sweden. RFSL and Stockholm Pride, he says, fail their mission as state-funded protectors of LGBTQ rights because of their "political correctness". Instead of coming to the suburbs themselves (what about the queer protesters outside the square, one wonders?), they criticize Pride Järva, calling them "Islamophobes and fascists and racists" while actually, they are "just normal people who have decided to get involved in this". This alleged failure to protect and care provides Sjunnesson and his political associates with the opportunity to cast themselves in the role of the concerned speakers of truth, the true protectors of LGBTQ people, despite their track record of anti-LGBTQ policy making. They return once more to established notions of Swedish gender exceptionalism, writing themselves into that narrative as its alleged protector. This is thus the final component in their attempt to enlist LGBTQ rights and activists in Sweden in nationalist projects of racialized Othering and boundary making by using them to construct, reproduce and reinforce exclusionary us–them dichotomies along lines of race, gender and sexuality.

Conclusions

While earlier literature on homonationalism in European contexts shows that LGBTQ organizations have been guilty of using racialized othering to gain support in the political mainstream, this chapter has looked at how right-wing political actors in turn exploit LGBTQ rights for nationalist projects of boundary making that exclude racialized and Muslim Others. Discussing Pride Järva, a march organized by right-wing publicist Jan Sjunnesson in the northern suburbs of Stockholm, I argue that this event is not an instance of LGBTQ emancipation, but an attempt to construct and reproduce certain exclusionary notions of Swedishness. Looking at how LGBTQ identities are conceptualized in both the SD's and Sjunnesson's rhetoric around Pride Järva shows that these identities on the one hand present an attractive tool for the populist right when trying to construct a threatening, externalized Other along lines of race, sexuality and gender. This is, among other things, because they resonate well with existing narratives around Swedish gender exceptionalism, as well as established homonationalist notions of tolerance and progress. They revolve around narrow grids of intelligibility regarding who is recognizable as the right kind of (depoliticized, domesticated) queer, and as such worthy of recognition and protection.

In his speech, Sjunnesson weaves together older colonialist-orientalist discourses about the backwardness of the 'East' with these more contemporary notions of Swedish gender exceptionalism and homonationalist rhetoric. Using a language of threat and protection, he constructs and reproduces notions of enlightened, tolerant and progressive Swedishness opposed to a patriarchal, traditional and oppressive Islamic other. White LGBTQ people play a central role in this narrative as the foremost markers of Swedishness – as the right kind of Other, they are a minority included with the purpose of excluding racialized Others. This inclusion into the nationalist fold, however, requires a defenceless, depoliticized and docile LGBTQ community, aiming for a private life tolerated by a cis-binary, heterosexist majoritarian society rather than challenging and opposing the violent exclusion of all minorities. The alleged failure of established LGBTQ organizations to tackle homophobia among migrants creates an opportunity for the populist right in Sweden to construct themselves as protectors of LGBTQ issues, and thus Swedish values. This narrative is maintained even though these actors have themselves consistently opposed LGBTQ rights and continue with the internal othering of LGBTQ people in Sweden. Recent political developments in Sweden also show that the relevance of LGBTQ rights for right-wing boundary making around exclusionary notions of Swedishness has further declined since the SD gained more political influence on a national level. Instead, grids of intelligibility for acceptable queerness on the right have become even more narrow through anti-LGBTQ rhetoric and pushback on legislation (Lagerman, 2023a).

Crucially, while Sjunnesson's binary Self/Other distinction rests on the White Swedish LGBTQ victim and the dangerous homophobic racialized Other, LGBTQ activists (both White and racialized as non-White) challenge their being-made-intelligible as victims in need of protection by protesting against Pride Järva. Following Butler's conceptualization of the performativity of assembly (Butler, 2015), their physical presence in the very space Sjunnesson determines as the most dangerous for LGBTQ people in Sweden expresses a political challenge to his way of turning the suburbs into an LGBTQ-phobic and thus non-Swedish space. It also upsets the various ways in which his rhetoric makes them intelligible as victims by opening up alternative expressions of being (racialized) LGBTQ people in particular parts of Stockholm. While Pride Järva is an attempt from the populist right to enlist LGBTQ rights in nationalist, xenophobic and racist projects of exclusive boundary making, made possible to a large extent by the established nature of narratives of Swedish gender exceptionalism and homonationalist rhetoric, it is also an occasion of how the apparent stability of these narratives is challenged through activist intervention.

7

A Flag Worth Defending? Rainbows, Pride and the Swedish Armed Forces

The increased mobilization of LGBTQ rights in the creation and maintenance of national(ist) identities takes place both in domestic and foreign policy discourses. State actors have variously used their stances on LGBTQ rights in order to position themselves as 'good' states that support these rights (Weber, 2016b; Rao, 2020) or as defenders of 'traditional family values', challenging LGBTQ rights (Edenborg, 2023). One arena in which this has happened is military recruiting and information campaigns. Military institutions across a number of countries have attempted to mobilize issues around gender and sexuality in efforts to broaden recruiting, to re-define their societal relevance as security organizations, to justify geopolitical interventions and to re-arm and re-territorialize their national defence (Strand and Kehl, 2019; Spade and Belkin, 2021; Baker, 2022; Dolan and Danilova, 2023). Sweden has, as discussed, in various ways been cast as exceptionally progressive with regard to gender equality and LGBTQ rights. It has often been cited as a forerunner for this kind of gender-related recruiting, with the Swedish Armed Forces (SAF) launching a variety of campaigns touching on gender and sexuality having been released in the last ten years (see Gray, 2022 for overview). This process is on the one hand closely related to the shift from conscription to voluntary service in 2012–18 (Strand, 2019). On the other hand, it has been connected to a trend to re-territorialize Swedish defence, not least in the context of growing anti-gender mobilization in parts of Europe, the full-scale Russian invasion of Ukraine in early 2022 and the consequent move by the Swedish government to apply for membership of NATO.

Since the early 2010s, the rainbow flag has re-appeared in campaign and information material published by the SAF in different ways, gaining more prominence as time went by. Two recent campaigns, *En flagga värd att försvara* (A flag worth defending) and *Viktigare än någonsin* (More important than ever), put the flag centre-stage in promoting the defence and protection of LGBTQ rights as part of a set of progressive Swedish values. Drawing on a combined analysis of visual and textual campaign material, this chapter looks at the ways in which LGBTQ rights are employed to ascribe meaning to the SAF as an organization as well as to justify the increasing rearmament and re-territorialization of Swedish defence in the face of anti-gender mobilization across Europe, the Russian invasion of Ukraine and the increasing militarization of European defence discourses. It analyses the various ways in which the pride campaigns perform a certain kind of 'Swedishness' (that is, a normative understanding of who belongs and who does not belong to an imagined Swedish nation) through conveying a specific image of the SAF. Finally, it reflects upon how LGBTQ people are made intelligible within the context of these campaigns, and the possible implications this may have for LGBTQ movements and their fights for LGBTQ rights.

It's complicated: sexuality, gender and/in the military

As discussed across this book, normative notions of gender and sexuality are central to the creation and delimitation of nation states and the communities of belonging that underlie them. Within these boundary-making processes, military institutions occupy a very particular and, in many ways, crucial position as the dedicated defenders of nations/states and, thus, the guarantors of their continued existence (see for example Strand and Kehl, 2019). There is also a well-established link between service in the armed forces and normative – if potentially contradictory – notions of masculinity and (hetero)sexuality (Belkin, 2012; Bulmer, 2013; Welland, 2013; Henry, 2017). However, as discussed by previous research including my own, various notions of 'equal opportunities' military are increasingly called upon in Western European defence discourses, partially due to countries moving from conscription armies to professionalized armed forces with a focus on military service as a career. Within the context of armed forces as career-building social institutions, rather than draft-based organizations, the need to attract individuals interested in pursuing military careers has meant a broadening of recruiting campaigns beyond specific cohorts of young White men (Kronsell, 2012; Stengel and Shim, 2021; Baker, 2022; Strand, 2022).

Attempts to attract non-traditional recruits include not only female soldiers in all branches of military service but increasingly also positions LGBTQ soldiers as serving openly and proudly as defenders of their respective countries (Bulmer, 2013; Montegary, 2015; Mandelbaum, 2018; Baker, 2022). While this could easily be dismissed as a straightforwardly (homo)nationalist political project, the increased visibility of the LGBTQ soldier as a subject position cannot simply be approached through the binary understandings of co-optation versus subversion. In her analysis of the decision to allow LGBTQ troops to participate in their official uniforms in London Pride in 2008, Bulmer analyses how this seems to have made LGBTQ soldiers visible as subjects subverting patriarchy and heteronormativity hegemony within the British military (Bulmer, 2013). However, Bulmer argues that the intense debate prior to this decision and the heteronormative reactions it provoked among military personnel uncovered the military institution and identity as 'always already heterosexual', constituted and haunted by the ghostly homosexual Other (2013, p 145; see also Welland, 2013). In a more recent analysis of UK Armed Forces recruiting campaigns, Baker argues that while 'the British Army now offers some queers a home in the military, that is not the same as a queer military home' (Baker, 2022, p 16). Instead, Baker identifies a specific kind of queerness that is considered acceptable within a military context, closely connected to normative forms of domesticity and family formation as well as Whiteness as a major signifier of belonging (Baker, 2022).

Similarly, Strand and I have argued that the recent employment of LGBTQ subjectivities in various broader SAF marketing campaigns superficially challenges, but at the same time externalizes and hides, existing norms and hierarchies regarding gender and sexuality in Sweden (Strand and Kehl, 2019). Thus, even when rendered visible and available, representations of the LGBTQ soldier can contribute to reproduce military institutions as patriarchal and heteronormative. Along with Bulmer, we might therefore approach the mobilization of LGBTQ identities in defence discourses as potential sites of both 'resistance and co-optation' (Bulmer 2013, p 150). In the Swedish case, this means the SAF might emerge as the very defender of continued Swedish progressiveness through the mobilization of LGBTQ identities, rights and symbols like the rainbow flag while simultaneously justifying military rearmament and a re-territorialization of the Swedish defence along the geographical boundaries of the country (Strand and Kehl, 2019).

So while feminist and queer scholars consider it important to study what gender and sexuality 'do' (see Ahmed, 2006) when called upon in discourses around nationalist bordering and the defence of those borders, they do also warn against employing binary analytical frameworks of either subversion or (homo)normalization (Weber, 2016b; Kehl, 2020). Certain symbols and identities appear in these discourses as *both* perverse *and* normal, in multiple and contradictory ways. This illustrates the importance of contextual analyses of what certain homonationalist practices render (im)possible and (in)visible (Rossdale, 2015), including an openness for going beyond simplistic analysis of either/or, as I discuss in Chapter 2.

The rainbow flag itself is of course a cultural symbol with its own contested history – designed in the 1970s in San Francisco, it spread beyond the United States in the wake of an increasingly professionalized and transnational activism for LGBTQ rights in the 1990s (Picq and Thiel, 2015). The commercialization of pride as an event means that the 2020s now see the flag hoisted no longer only by activists but outside government buildings, banks and multinational businesses. The way in which it has been embraced by companies as well as conservative politicians trying to demonstrate their commitment to notions of 'diversity' and 'tolerance' (including populists like Sjunnesson) means it has reached a status as globalized cultural commodity.

However, as ethnographic research indicates, beyond its market values, the rainbow flag also maintains its meaning as a crucial symbol of resistance, activism and belonging for queer communities across various global contexts (Alm and Martinsson, 2016; Klapeer and Laskar, 2018). On a global geopolitical stage, the rainbow flag has additionally been used to mark deviant, dangerous Others by states such as Russia, Turkey and Hungary, who position themselves as defenders of 'traditional values' by ostracizing and persecuting LGBTQ people in the name of the defence of country, state and heterosexual nuclear families (Edenborg, 2020b; Altay, 2022; Çağatay et al, 2022). This fluidity and diversity of what the rainbow flag 'means' to people globally therefore provides an important backdrop to my analysis of what it 'does' when it appears in SAF marketing campaigns.

In the light of these theoretical calls for nuance, this chapter engages with a limited and specific part of the SAF marketing campaigns in relation to sexuality and gender. It explores the employment of the rainbow flag in campaigns relating to pride month and specifically Sweden's largest pride event, Stockholm Pride, which usually takes place in July. I analyse all six campaign posters that were released in the years 2015 and 2017–22 to coincide with Stockholm Pride, looking at the visual representation of LGBTQ in/as part of the military as well as the messages that accompany the picture. While these yearly campaigns could be seen as merely part of the SAF's overall communication strategy, they tend to create a recurring public debate about LGBTQ rights and the role of the 'political' in relation to the military and other state institutions. I therefore treat the yearly campaigns as separate discursive events, to better understand the role of LGBTQ rights in ascribing meaning to national(ist) boundary-making processes, the SAF as an institution as well as the rearmament and re-territorialization of Swedish defence. Methodologically, the analysis is driven by Ahmed's 'ethnography of text' (Ahmed, 2006) as well as an understanding of how images and words create intertextual meaning (Hansen, 2011b; Adler-Nissen et al, 2020), discussed in more detail in Chapter 5.

The right to serve openly: LGBTQ and SAF until 2017

The history of LGBTQ personnel serving in the SAF is closely connected to the classification of homosexuality and transgender identities as mental illness. While exemption from military duties based on military medical policies around homosexuality was the rule up to the late 1960s, this was contested by the Swedish Federation for Lesbian, Gay, Bisexual, Transgender, Queer and Intersex Rights in the 1970s, and the regulations for homosexual and transexual service members were revised (Sundevall and Persson, 2016). However, homosexuality remained a formal diagnosis within the SAF which could be used to exclude gay men from service until 1989, ten years after the classification was removed from the Swedish Classification of Diseases (Sundevall, 2014; Sundevall and Persson, 2016). The 1990s saw the arrival of Swedish anti-discrimination legislation based on sexual orientation in the workplace, and in 2001 the organization HoF (Homo-, bisexuella och transpersoner inom Försvarsmakten) was founded by active service members to organize LGBTQ personnel in the SAF. In 2005, the SAF as an organization participated in Stockholm Pride for the first time, and since 2008 individual service members have been allowed to march in pride parades dressed in full uniform. Since 2013, the commander-in-chief has attended Stockholm Pride every year, as part of the SAF's work towards diversity and anti-discrimination.

In 2015, the rainbow flag became explicitly visible in the SAF's public image beyond the limited physical space of the actual pride parade in central Stockholm. This happened in two specific ways: on the social media platform Facebook, the SAF replaced their profile picture (usually showing a shield of armour against a white background) with the same shield of armour against a rainbow-coloured background. Several hours after its publication, the picture was removed and replaced by the original shield of armour again. Communication officer Jesper stated that this was because "the shield of armour should not stand for anything else ... and should look the same way at all times". According to him, this did not mean that the SAF did not stand behind pride but that the shield of armour as a symbol already included the values symbolized by the rainbow flag (Carlsson, 2015).

Around the same time, HoF also released a poster campaign with the slogan 'Some things you should not need to camouflage.' The poster was positioned prominently across Stockholm and distributed across various SAF social media channels. It shows a person in camouflage jacket and hat, with their face covered in camouflage paint, standing against a camouflage-patterned background. Two things stick out from the green-and-beige pattern: the person's blue eyes, and the rainbow flag positioned on the right arm, the place where the uniform insignia would sit otherwise. The text underneath reads as follows: 'Equality is an important part of a democracy. In the Swedish Armed Forces, we treat each other with respect and see each others' differences as a strength. We are an inclusive organization where everybody who belongs and contributes to our operation should feel welcome and respected.' This advertisement creates the image of an equal opportunities employer who demands and promises respect for LGBTQ soldiers. The message is communicated through a prominent placement of the rainbow flag in a visual setting that is otherwise clearly readable as military. However, by implying that LGBTQ people might camouflage their identity outside of the SAF, it also strongly reproduces the idea of LGBTQ people as inherently closeted and in need of 'coming out' (see also Baker, 2022). Much of the early debates on LGBTQ people in relation to the SAF can therefore be seen as concerning questions of discrimination in the workplace, which positions the SAF in line with other public employers – the early campaigning mirrors this focus on LGBTQ people within the SAF and their right to serve openly and safely.

While no pride-related campaign was released in 2016, my analysis indicates a clear shift in the message that accompanies the campaigns released in the years since 2017. This shift coincided with the several larger information and marketing campaigns disseminated by the SAF between 2016 and 2018 which drew on sexuality and gender as ways to ascribe meaning to the SAF, and by extension to the rearmament and re-territorialization of Swedish defence. Campaigns like 'Thou New, Thou Free' (in reference to the national anthem 'Thou old, thou free'), 'How many reasons do you need', 'Come as you are' and 'We let Sweden be at peace' featured, to an unprecedented degree, non-normative representations of gender and sexuality, including same-sex kisses and gender-non-conforming expressions (Strand and Kehl, 2019). They were also decidedly 'demilitarized', showing few classical components of military marketing (such as tanks, uniforms or soldiers in the field). Instead, they centred on everyday life, civilian clothing and domestic scenery from Sweden 'at peace'. They also took up questions of religion and non-normative body types and included a spectrum of bodies racialized as non-White in an attempt to 'create relevance' and relatability, to demystify and dehomogenize a military institution that was in need of re-branding itself as much as it was in need of recruits (Strand and Berndtsson, 2015). As will become clear from the analysis in this chapter, even with the rainbow flag present in all of them, the explicitly pride-related campaigns stay much closer to classical military iconography than the larger campaigns, while also drawing on a very limited register of diversity. In the following sections, I will analyse the six SAF pride campaigns published between 2017 and 2022 chronologically in the order of their publication.

Protect and defend: pride campaigns 2017–20

The 2017 pride campaign centres on a photo of a pair of army boots, laced up with rainbow shoelaces. The photo is accompanied by the message 'We are ready to go as far as it takes. Your right to live as you want to, as the one you want to be and with whom you want to, is our task to defend.' While the picture maintains the approach of combining military field equipment with a rainbow detail (as in the HoF campaign from 2015), the shift in the communicated message is quite striking. Now the campaign addresses an individual 'you' and their rights to be who and with whom they want to be, from the position of a collective 'we' promising to defend these rights. The campaign thus moves away from the language of anti-discrimination and equality at the workplace which portrayed the SAF as being an inclusive and safe organization for its LGBTQ employees according to democratic values and Swedish anti-discrimination legislation. Instead, the narrative shifts towards a discourse around the defence of LGBTQ rights as part of the duty of the SAF. LGBTQ people are now called upon as 'rights holders' (Weber, 2016b), normalized as citizens and thus explicitly included in the nation that should be secured and protected by the SAF.

Not least the reference to marching 'as far as it takes' indicates that this protection is not only aimed at internal challenges within the organization (or even the country) but instead directed towards an external enemy and threat. As discussed elsewhere, the notion that there are certain progressive Swedish values, ideas and freedoms which are considered 'extreme in the eyes of others' is an integral part of how boundaries around Swedishness are constructed discursively (Aggestam and Bergman-Rosamond, 2016; Agius and Edenborg, 2019; Strand and Kehl, 2019). Following established patterns of threat and protection, Sweden is ascribed meaning in relation to (sometimes not so) distant, but always dangerous Others (Campbell, 1998; Stern, 2006). The message of this campaign thus aligns with other statements that perform Sweden as an exceptionally progressive, tolerant and inclusive nation/state. LGBTQ rights and, by extension, LGBTQ individuals, are not only included in the nation (to be protected by the SAF); they even serve as the 'markers' of its value-based boundaries. Arguably, this also means that the rainbow flag as a symbol acquires meaning beyond the earlier message of anti-discrimination and becomes entangled in notions of protection and defence connected to national(ist) understandings of Sweden and its borders.

The campaign posters from the following year reinforce right-based discourses while at the same time continuously expanding the notion that LGBTQ rights and LGBTQ people need to be defended at and beyond Swedish borders. In 2018, the SAF campaign was published exclusively in English. Since Stockholm Pride was also the venue for the 2018 EuroPride Festival (a pan-European international event, hosted by a different European city each year), campaigners perhaps anticipated a more international audience. The main campaign visual consists of two individual photos of soldiers in uniform, one with long hair in a braid across the shoulder, the other with short hair. Both of them are White, blue-eyed and blond-haired, thus living up to a very specific embodiment of 'Swedishness' (Mulinari and Neergaard, 2017). They are photographed in the process of covering their faces in paint, but instead of the camouflage paint present in the 2015 campaign, they are painting their faces with rainbow colours. Both of them look at the camera defiantly as they are smearing out the colours across their faces. The campaign slogan for these images reads 'We don't always march straight', accompanied by the following caption: 'But no matter where or when we march, we always stand up for your right to live the way you want with whoever you want. Read more about how we work to protect freedom and the right to choose the way we live at forsvarsmakten.se.'

Several of the messages from the previous year are repeated in this campaign. The notion of the 'right to live the way you want and with whoever you want' re-appears, as does the SAF as the protector of that right and the freedoms associated with it. The idea of marching is even more central to this campaign, not least because of the slogan's play on words with the term 'straight', referring both to the straight marching line of soldiers, and heterosexuality as straightness. SAF soldiers, the campaign indicates, are open and proud LGBTQ people, but they are also dedicated defenders of LGBTQ rights in their professional role as soldiers. This clearly troubles more traditional binary understandings of who is the one in need of protection (the LGTBQ person) and who is the protector (the masculinized soldier) (Bulmer, 2013; Duncanson, 2015). At the same time, the two soldiers' camouflage outfits, complete with combat vest and ammunition, reproduce established militarized iconography to the same extent that their blue-eyed blond exterior reproduces established notions of White Swedishness. Defending LGBTQ rights might be a task conducted by LGBTQ people in uniform, but in the context of these campaigns it is definitely also one done exclusively by White people. This resembles widespread notions about White people having to protect racialized LGBTQ people from their own racialized communities and families, as analysed across a number of contexts (Haritaworn, 2015; Jungar and Peltonen, 2015; Hiller, 2022). These ideas appear both in Sjunnesson's speech at Pride Järva and in the experiences of racialized LGBTQ people discussed in Chapter 8. The soldiers' White Swedishness can also be seen as a first indicator that the diversity portrayed in these campaigns might apply to 'one minority position only'. The soldiers portrayed do not challenge or disturb any social norms beyond their being LGBTQ in the context of a traditionally heteronormative institution. This approach to diversity becomes clearer as more campaigns are launched, and I will therefore return to it in the following paragraphs.

The 2019 campaign was the first one to appear as a full-page ad in major Swedish daily newspapers. Among others, it was published on the front page of *Svenska Dagbladet*, one of Sweden's more conservative news media. This publication strategy has since been maintained, with one pride-themed advert being released every year. The 2019 campaign features a picture of a table with a multi-storey wedding cake on top, decorated with roses, hearts and camouflage icing in a grey colour scale that strongly resembles the camouflage pattern of Swedish naval vessels. A piece has been cut out at the top to show a layered rainbow sponge cake inside. There is, no pun intended, a colourful rainbow underneath the camouflaged exterior. The slogan says 'To the defence of love', and the caption reads as follows: 'Your right to be who you are, live how you want to with whom you yourself chose – is our task to defend' (Axbom, 2021). The message is starting to become familiar and reiterates the individual 'you' and their right to be who they want to be, to live with whom they choose as a part of the mission and duty of national defence.

Of course, the same-sex wedding hinted at with the elaborate wedding cake is one of the achievements Sweden has prided itself on with regard to its progressive legislation, being among the earlier countries to allow civil partnership between same-sex couples in 1995 and moving towards a fully gender-neutral marriage law in 2009 – exactly ten years prior to the release of this campaign. Swedish marriage law also features prominently on the SAF website, as part of a timeline of 'Swedish progressiveness' in relation to gender equality and LGBTQ rights, where 2009 is referred to as 'a decisive year for your right to live how you like, with whom you like'. And when asked about specific aspects of what makes Sweden 'extreme' or 'exceptional' in international comparison, one SAF market strategist put same-sex marriage on the top of their list (Strand and Kehl, 2019).

At the same time, the right to marry is frequently called upon as a hallmark symbol of homonormativity, critiqued as a crucial building block for queer assimilation into the social institutions of heteronormativity and achieved at the cost of more encompassing social reforms (Duggan, 2002; Wilkinson, 2017). The focus on 'love' in the campaign slogan also indicates a depoliticized understanding of queer movements' fight against gender and sexuality norms. Here, this fight is merely portrayed to be about love and acceptance, rather than the discrimination and stigmatization of non-normative gender and sexual identities in various legal, social and institutional arenas – including incarceration and militarized violence. As LGBTQ activists in various national contexts point out – including the activists whose experiences are discussed in Chapter 8 – this depoliticized love is accessible primarily to those parts of LGBTQ communities who otherwise occupy privileged positions in society based on their ethnicity, citizenship status and economic situation. Interestingly, the promise of protecting LGBTQ people's 'right to be who they are', which reappears as a discursive pillar throughout all the campaigns, can be seen as contributing to this depoliticized message in its own way. The focus on protecting rights implies that these rights are already well established in Sweden, which in turn suggests there is no need for a continued political struggle.

In 2020, the SAF pride campaign shows a group of soldiers pictured from behind, standing at ease in uniforms in a sunlit nature surrounding. As the person closest to the camera has their hands folded behind their back, we can see that the nails of all ten fingers are painted in different colours, forming the colour palette of the rainbow flag. 'Our strength consists of our differences' reads the slogan, and the caption declares that 'We are proud to stand up for all people's equal worth. Together we defend Sweden, our freedom and the right to live as we ourselves chose' (Axbom, 2021). This picture connects some of the earlier messages: it alludes to the strengths of the equal opportunities organization, where everybody contributes their part to the overall mission. It also connects the defence of Sweden as a nation to the defence of a certain set of values and the freedom to choose a particular way of life. Interestingly, the language has once more shifted in this campaign: instead of addressing an individual 'you' whose rights are defended by a collective SAF 'we', the 'we' has now become more all-encompassing. 'We' are defending 'our' freedom and 'our' rights, which again relates back to LGBTQ soldiers being part of the forces defending these rights. However, even in this group the four soldiers who are visible are White, and most of them are, yet again, blond. The 'differences' (or diversity) that the campaign alludes to seem to stretch only so far.

Rainbow under arms: pride campaigns 2021–22

While the campaigns in 2017–20 all featured camouflage patterns and uniforms, the 2021 campaign introduced an additional aspect of classical military iconography: for the first time, it showed fully armed soldiers. While this might simply be mirroring what Swedish defence agencies argue to be a deteriorating security situation in Europe at large, it can also be interpreted as part of a slow normalization of placing the rainbow flag next to military equipment that more explicitly refers to the use of weaponized force. In the campaign image released in July 2021, four soldiers in field uniforms, helmets and combat vests, with camouflage-painted faces and carrying rifles, are pictured walking across a landscape with brush and small trees. While the three soldiers in the background hold their rifles in a way that indicates they are on patrol, the one closest to the camera carries a large rainbow flag twice the soldier's height. The flag-bearing soldier in the front looks at the camera with a determined expression. The slogan across the picture reads 'A flag worth defending', and the caption claims that 'We defend human rights, everybody's equal worth and our right to live as we ourselves chose to' (Axbom, 2021).

While the depiction of weapons is one departure from previous images, the picture of the flag bearer also marks the most prominent placement of the rainbow flag throughout all the campaigns so far. The way in which it is positioned in the centre of the picture, as well as the fact that the campaign slogan explicitly refers to it, elevates the flag's role as an important symbol, representing a variety of things. The caption equates it with human rights, the equal worth of all people and the right to live as they choose to. Read in relation to the previous campaigns, it is also equated with the defence of Swedish values and, eventually, Swedish borders. Defending the rainbow flag, and all it stands for, means defending Sweden. While, as this book shows, the equation between Sweden and LGBTQ rights has been present in various discourses across the political spectrum, the statement that this flag is worth defending through the use of weapons and (implicitly) by the loss of Swedish soldiers' lives, elevates the message to a new level. Read in the context of existing research on, for example, the promotion of Sweden's feminist foreign policy and the increasing escalation of geopolitical conflicts framed as being (among other things) about 'traditional values', this statement positions Swedish military force in open opposition to countries such as Russia and Hungary. The imagery connected to this statement makes it clear that, for the SAF, the defence of LGBTQ rights is connected to a territorial defence, and one that is increasingly orienting itself towards an outward threat coming from the East.

As Strand and I discuss elsewhere, campaigns relating LGBTQ identities to organizations such as armed forces might superficially challenge gender binaries and heteronormativity. However, they also make discrimination based on these norms more difficult to address by repeating, reinforcing and stabilizing the notion of a gender-exceptional Sweden (Strand and Kehl, 2019). These campaigns portray 'the right to be who you are' as something that needs to be protected, rather than achieved through political action, as if it was already self-evident for each and every member of LGBTQ communities across Sweden. Discrimination on the basis of gender identity and sexual orientation is discursively externalized from Swedish borders in these campaigns, while the continued LGBTQ-phobia, discrimination and harassment within Swedish society (and within institutions like the SAF) remain concealed. As Lagerman puts it: 'Swedish sexual exceptionalism is so common-sensical, that it is reproduced even when describing domestic events contradicting its validity' (Lagerman, 2023a, p 15).

Despite this, the reception of the SAF ad campaigns which make use of LGBTQ people, LGBTQ rights and symbols also illustrates the continued existence of anti-LGBTQ sentiments and attitudes. The pride campaign from 2021 is no exception. While the message in the caption in and by itself might not be seen as controversial for a state institution in the Swedish context, the prominent placement of the flag as well as the claim that it is 'worth defending' sparked a heated debate across social media. Voices were raised in favour of and against the use of the rainbow flag as a symbol, one of the main critical arguments being that it was a 'political' symbol and that the Swedish national flag should be the only one featuring in SAF campaigns. Contrary to 2015, when criticism led to the rainbow flag being removed from a Facebook post after criticism, in 2021 the SAF did not back down on the campaign. Instead, the commander in chief referred to a statement he made in 2020: 'Our participation at Pride means we are actively taking the position of all human beings' equal values, which is also a natural part of our responsibility as employer. … The SAF are simply confident with regard to their values' (Försvarsmakten, 2020).

This statement was republished on social media in connection to the most recent pride-related SAF campaign, which was published in August 2022. In the context of the Russian invasion of Ukraine and the subsequent move by the Swedish government to apply for NATO membership, the campaign's slogan is 'More important now than ever.' Its by-line reads: 'Unsafe times do not mean we stop defending human rights, everybody's equal value and your right to live as you are. That is why we are participating in Pride – even this year' (Axbom, 2021). Its release was accompanied by press statements from the PR company that created the campaign, claiming that

> Russia's invasion of Ukraine in February made it painfully clear that we cannot take our rights for granted. It therefore feels particularly important this year to emphasize why the SAF are participating in Pride. We should be proud to have armed forces that defend all inhabitant, no matter who you are. (Price, 2022)

The campaign image itself shows six soldiers standing in a field in a V-formation, each of them holding a different-coloured smoke grenade in one raised hand. Together, the colourful smoke clouds create a rainbow plume over the group of fully armed and camouflaged soldiers. The angle of the photograph, shot from below, and the dark and seemingly stormy sky against which they are positioned creates a powerful, almost threatening atmosphere. The picture is one of a military unit ready to engage in combat, while the high-visibility smoke grenades allude to them having no reason to hide. Instead, they are openly signalling their support of LGBTQ people, to be seen across a long distance.

On their website, the SAF anticipate some of the by-now expected critique against this campaign by stating that

> [w]hen the world is in an unsafe state, it is easy to pitch rights against each other. There are those who claim that the SAF have more important things to do right now than waving pride-flags. Rights are pitched against rights, and you ask yourself what is more important: a strong defence or everybody's equal value? For us, these are no opposites. SAF duty is to defend Sweden, everybody who lives here, our democracy and our rights. For in the end, it's the person without rights who stands without protection.

However, as discussed elsewhere, research shows that there are LGBTQ people in Sweden who are quite clearly not being included in the 'duty to defend'. This includes LGBTQ asylum seekers, who frequently experience that Sweden is indeed *not* a country protecting the rights of all LGBTQ people within its borders, as they are being subjected to invasive migration interviews, questioning of their sexual identities and, eventually, may face deportation (Peltonen and Jungar, 2018; Akin, 2019; Hedlund and Wimark, 2019). To them, this final reference to 'the person without rights who stands without protection' might sound almost cynical.

Conclusions

The SAF's yearly pride campaigns could merely be seen as part of a wider attempt by the organization to create relevance for themselves in Swedish society and to aid recruitment. However, in their close connection to pride and the specificities of their messages, these campaigns are distinct discursive events, creating a recurring debate about LGBTQ rights, anti-discrimination and the role of the 'political' in relation to the military and other state institutions. Throughout, the messages conveyed in the slogans and the captions circulate around a number of key signifiers: the right (eventually described as a human right) to be who and with whom you want to be, the defence and protection of those rights by the SAF, as well as the marching and standing up for the defence of those rights wherever it is needed. Starting from the initial image of the SAF as an equal opportunities employer, who demands and promises respect for LGBTQ soldiers, the military organization has now become the face of the guarantor of LGBTQ rights in Sweden (and potentially beyond). Simultaneously, LGBTQ soldiers are portrayed as an important, capable and self-evident part of the forces defending those rights. In the context of pride, the SAF appear as both participants and potential employer, but even overall guarantor of the event taking place at all in the face of growing anti-gender mobilization in eastern parts of Europe and Russian aggression against Ukraine (Petö and Kováts, 2017; Paternotte and Kuhar, 2018; Korolczuk, 2020a; Edenborg, 2023).

It becomes apparent that even with the rainbow flag present in all of them, the explicitly pride-related campaigns stay very close to classical military iconography, much closer than other campaigns drawing on sexuality and gender identity during the same time span (Strand and Kehl, 2019). While the rainbow flag is used as the re-appearing visual marker of LGBTQ rights and identities, elements like camouflage patterns, military uniforms and increasingly also combat equipment are present to 'ground' the rainbow representation. They connect it visually to the military organization that is the SAF. Nor is there anything non-normative about the soldiers pictured in the campaigns, as they present seemingly conventional notions of masculinity and femininity in the context of military employment. Beyond that, they are exclusively White, predominantly blond and blue-eyed, representing a military institution that rests on (and in this case actively reproduces) racialized conventions about 'Swedishness' as Whiteness. As Baker points out in her analysis of similar campaigns by the British Armed Forces, such representations can 'evidently only cope with one axis of diversity at a time' (Baker, 2022, p 8). Crucially, the representation of LGBTQ love through the symbol of the wedding cake places that love firmly within the conventions of institutionally approved monogamy (even potentially alluding to the benefits extended to married couples as part of being employed by the SAF). Grids of intelligibility for who is the right kind of queer in these campaigns follow established normative ideals of sexuality, gender and race.

In the context of the SAF's pride campaigns, it appears as if the presence of the rainbow is considered sufficiently controversial, and sufficiently symbolically powerful, to raise attention and convey the message of the SAF being the defenders of LGBTQ rights within and outside of Swedish borders. While creating some kind of LGBTQ representation, they thus fail to effectively challenge normative assumptions about gender and sexuality beyond specific kinds of acceptable 'queerness' resting on normalizing intersections of race, binary gender and socially sanctioned forms of monogamy. This can be seen as counterpointing some of the alleged self-evidence in which 'pro-LGBTQ' attitudes are brought forward – if it was so self-evident, why would they have to tone it down?

As the narrative in the campaigns shifts towards a discourse around the defence of LGBTQ rights as part of the duty of the SAF, the rainbow flag as a symbol acquires meaning beyond earlier messages of anti-discrimination and becomes entangled in notions of protection and defence connected to national(ist) understandings of Sweden and its borders. Sweden is portrayed as an equal, tolerant and progressive nation/state, currently under threat from various Others (most prominently Russia). As part of these defence discourses, discrimination against and dangers for LGBTQ people are externalized from Swedish territory, being instead (dis)placed to distant locations and external threats. Despite this externalization of discrimination, the openly homo- and transphobic opinions voiced by right-wing commentators in reaction to the SAF's pride campaigns every year reflects Sweden's contradictory environment towards LGBTQ rights. The SAF's promise of defending and protecting LGBTQ people's rights implies that these rights are already well established within Sweden, foreclosing the need for a continued political struggle towards the recognition and protection of all members of LGBTQ communities.

At the same time, these recurring campaigns normalize the visual proximity of the rainbow flag and camouflaged, uniform-wearing, gun-bearing military professionals. Following the campaigns chronologically makes this increasingly clear, as the rainbow flag, accompanied by the 'the right to be who you are', becomes one of the established visual-discursive pillars that justify the continued existence, financing and staffing of a military organization. If LGBTQ rights are equated with Swedish progressiveness and these campaigns position the SAF as the defender of this continued progressiveness, LGBTQ symbolism contributes to the military preparedness and renewed focus on securing Sweden's geographical borders by providing legitimacy. Previous research demonstrates clearly how the mobilization of normalized LGBTQ subjectivities in discourses on national defence makes possible homo-colonialist and homo-imperialist projects (Puar, 2007; Rahman, 2014; Weber, 2016b). My analysis suggests that the use of these symbols in current SAF campaigns also justifies a military defence of Swedish territory, casting Sweden's ongoing rearmament and re-territorialization policy as progress in the face of potential external aggression. When called upon in these campaigns, the figure of the 'LGBTQ rights holder' (and the LGBTQ soldier) therefore becomes part of a 'reinvigorated militarism … that is arguably more palatable to the Swedish public than previous appeals' (Stern and Strand, 2021). Flying the rainbow flag, in other words, enables the SAF to appear equal parts progressive and reassuringly militaristic while doing rather little to challenge the limitations that normative grids of intelligibility for gender and sexuality put on the liveability of queer lives in Sweden.

8

Racialized Grids of Intelligibility in Swedish LGBTQ Contexts

In November 2015, three young Swedish activists started an Instagram account, a 'platform by and for LGBTQ people who are racialized', in order to 'give visibility to racialized people and their personal experiences of growing up and living outside heteronormativity and/or cisnormativity as "blatte" in Sweden/the West'. Their initiative points to a wider social phenomenon: the various ways in which LGBTQ people racialized as non-White and/or Muslim are perceived and made intelligible in relation to LGBTQ rights featuring ever more prominently in discourses on immigration across Western European contexts (Haritaworn, 2015; Tschalaer, 2020; Altay, 2023).

As discussed previously, LGBTQ rights have increasingly become political markers of 'Western values': tolerance, gender equality, sexual liberation and general social progressiveness. A variety of actors in a number of countries construct them as being under threat from the LGBTQ-phobic backwardness ascribed to communities racialized as non-White and/or Muslim (Haritaworn, 2015; Hiller, 2022; Tschalaer, 2021). This rhetoric puts people who are racialized as non-White and/or Muslim as well as LGBTQ in precarious positions: they become 'exceptions to the rule' (Bracke, 2012), facing assumptions that being both LGBTQ and racialized as non-White and/or Muslim are mutually exclusive. They also feature in ongoing processes of racist and Islamophobic othering – Pride Järva is one instance where this has happened in a Swedish context. As they are embraced into Western European societies as the 'good [racialized] other' (Sabsay, 2012, p 611), various dangerous bad Others are (re)produced – communities racialized as non-White and/or Muslim are constructed as being not queer-friendly enough, while those challenging assumptions about what it can mean to be queer and Muslim are too queer. The power that rests with these normalizations of certain bodies and experiences (Puwar, 2004) means especially young people might be unable to make sense of their own experiences or feel the need to adjust the ways in which they perform their sexuality and gender identity in order to become intelligible as a 'proper sexual subject' in White, Western European contexts.

By taking a closer look at the experiences of young LGBTQ people racialized as non-White and/or Muslim within predominantly White Swedish LGBTQ contexts, this chapter investigates some grids of intelligibility that make up the 'field of the recognisable' (Butler, 2015, p 34) in these contexts. How are LGBTQ bodies racialized as non-White and/or Muslim and their experiences made intelligible? Which assumptions around their sexuality, race and gender identity do they encounter, and which positionalities are thus suggested as 'liveable' for them? It does so through an analysis of experiences shared on an activist Instagram account, identifying predominant grids of intelligibility for LGBTQ people racialized as non-White and/or Muslim within White Swedish LGBTQ contexts.

This chapter identifies four major ways in which LGBTQ people racialized as non-White and/or Muslim are made intelligible in predominantly White Swedish LGBTQ contexts: as the victims of a hateful Other, through coming-out narratives, via exotification and tokenism and via experiences of lacking representation. All of these revolve around notions of LGBTQ people racialized as non-White and/or Muslim as never quite belonging, never quite recognizable. They are instead frequently situated between White, gender-equal and LGBTQ-friendly 'Swedishness' and threatening, LGBTQ-phobic racialized 'Others', made intelligible only in relation to these.

Intelligibility, racialization and Swedish gender exceptionalism

As discussed in Chapter 3 on boundaries and intelligibility, this book investigates ways in which we have to perform and produce ourselves as particular, seemingly coherent subjects in order to be recognizable and therefore deserving of rights (Foucault, 1978; Butler, 1993). Being intelligible to individuals, groups and institutions as well as to ourselves is a condition for at all being able to bring oneself into (social) existence. While Butler's earlier work stresses moments of resistance and instability in these acts of subjection (Butler, 1993, 1999), more recent writings point out the importance of 'norms of recognition' (Butler, 2015, p 34) that make up the boundaries of the 'field of the recognisable' (Butler, 2015, p 34), creating and (re)producing violent hierarchies between those who are more and those who are less intelligible in certain social contexts. Looking at these norms as grids of intelligibility helps us understand how certain experiences and identities are assigned legitimacy and relevance, while others remain unacknowledged, delegitimized or even vilified.

An intersectional perspective draws our attention to the ways in which these grids are (among other things) shaped by issues of race, gender and sexual orientation. In the Swedish context, processes of racialization clearly sharpen the ways in which grids of intelligibility around gender and sexuality create the right kind of queers. As discussed in more detail in Chapter 4 on racialization, the social construction and ascription of race to certain bodies includes hierarchies and domination (Grosfoguel et al, 2015), the creation of constitutive outsides (Laskar, 2007) and the objectification of those racialized as non-White as the oppositional (potentially dangerous) Other of Whiteness and its privileges (Ahmed, 2007b, p 161). Acknowledging that racialization processes apply to everybody – that is, Whiteness does not exist in a position of neutrality or 'non-race' (Ahmed, 2007a) – this chapter uses the term 'racialized' in two different ways. In the quotes, it is directly translated from the Swedish word *rasifierat*, a self-identifier used by Swedish activists of colour. The analytical term 'racialized as non-White and/or Muslim' allows for the nuanced engagement with how the ascription of race (in the sense of having a body that is racialized as non-White) and the ascription of religion (as ethno-cultural signifier of 'foreignness' [El-Tayeb, 2008]) make LGBTQ people (un-)intelligible in different ways.

As the other empirical chapters indicate, Sweden is a particularly interesting context for exploring grids of intelligibility around sexuality, gender and race because of longstanding narratives describing it as exceptionally progressive with regard to gender equality and sexual rights (Alm et al, 2021). They predate, overlap with and reinforce more recent homonationalist and homonormative narratives and are frequently accompanied by ideas of 'bad patriarchies' located in distant places and racialized bodies (Keskinen et al, 2009, p 5). Constructing gender equality and LGBTQ inclusiveness as Swedish 'national traits' (as discussed in relation to the other empirical sites) is thus closely linked to racialization processes. These inscribe only certain people as White, Swedish, feminist and LGBTQ-friendly, whereas others are marked as non-White and/or Muslim, non-Swedish, non-gender-equal and LGBTQ-phobic. Trans-, bi- and homophobia are located outside normative White Swedishness and are instead projected on to communities racialized as non-White and/or Muslim. The way in which these communities are talked about as second-, third-, even fourth-generation immigrants shows that racialization in Western European contexts often includes the ascription of migration to certain bodies racialized as non-White – they are constructed as 'never at home' in these societies (Tudor, 2018). As touched upon previously, the Swedish term *blatte*, which is used throughout the material analysed here, describes the experience of being assigned this position as an 'eternal migrant' (El-Tayeb, 2011, p xxv), even if you are a Swedish citizen, born and raised in Sweden. *Blatte* is originally a racist slur, reclaimed as a self-identifier by some people racialized as non-White and/or Muslim in Sweden. I have therefore decided not to translate it.

Contextualizing the account

This chapter analyses experiences shared on a Swedish-based Instagram account created as a virtual space by and for LGBTQ people racialized as non-White and/or Muslim with around 4,600 followers at the time of writing. While it is used for information sharing, organizing and emotional support, its main function is that of a so-called 'relay account' (*stafettkonto* in Swedish), a way of sharing a social media account between different people (Christensen, 2013). By having a different person write about their experiences of being LGBTQ and racialized as non-White and/or Muslim every week, the account aims to provide particularly young people with a variety of stories to identify with. Existing research stresses the community- and identity-building potential of social media platforms, especially for members of minority groups (Gray, 2009; Marino, 2015; Lucero, 2017). Positive representation of marginalized identities and the ability to claim identification with multiple social groups allows them to positively affirm their unique intersectional positioning within society (Tynes et al, 2016, p 33), thus to a certain extent countering the negative social effects of occupying a stigmatized identity (Howarth, 2006).

The account is particularly interesting because of its continuity, its relevance within the activist community and the issue of access. Between 2015 and 2019, it was continuously updated with content, providing a richness of experiences and a somewhat stable reference in notoriously volatile social media settings (see Kozinets, 2015). The administrators organized or participated in various events on being both LGBTQ and racialized as non-White and/or Muslim, becoming a recurring voice with regard to how these experiences are described within the wider Swedish LGBTQ community. Additionally, the account's privacy setting is 'open', which means anybody can read it without the administrators' admission. It also enables reading without actively having to 'follow' the account, an important option for anybody who for various reasons might not want to be visibly associated with LGBTQ issues (Marwick and Boyd, 2018). As White people are not allowed to post or comment, the account still provides a virtual space that is predominantly for LGBTQ people who are racialized without being completely closed off (see for example Collins, 2009 on empowerment through shared minority spaces). At a public event in 2018, the administrators encouraged the audience to widely share the account, stating that one of the reasons for its existence was to raise awareness about the experiences of racialized LGBTQ people beyond the limited group who already followed the account and recognized themselves in the stories shared. As somebody with White privileges myself, this openness and the administrators' encouragement was crucial for me when conducting this research, something which I also discuss in Chapter 5 on research methodology.

Research on social media, especially on sensitive topics like sexuality, requires particular attention to privacy and data protection (Markham and Buchanan, 2012). Privacy in virtual spaces is experienced and negotiated contextually, mainly through 'the ability to strategically control a social situation by influencing what information is available to others' (Marwick and Boyd, 2018, p 1158). Most writers post with an identifiable name, including links to personal accounts on other platforms. Those writing anonymously usually state that they are not 'out' and fear being discovered. While feminist researchers have argued against anonymizing research material in order to enable authors to maintain full ownership of their stories (Luka and Millette, 2018), this research follows the (re-)appearance of grids of intelligibility throughout all the posts rather than individual narratives, looking at the account as a collective entity. Additionally, there have been cases where social media accounts were used in asylum cases, exposing asylum seekers to involuntary outing and danger of persecution in their countries of origin (Andreassen, 2020). I therefore decided to anonymize all material by removing user names and publication dates, a decision that was sanctioned by the account's administrators.

The analysis is based on around 700 entries published by 86 different writers between November 2015 and December 2017. The writers are in their late teens up to early 30s, predominantly living in urban parts of Sweden. They are refugees, children of immigrants or racialized Swedes or adopted into White Swedish families. Their entries show various specific ways in which race, religion, sexuality and gender intersect, while also containing re-appearing common themes. Based on the assumptions that intelligibility functions according to norms creating hierarchies between those who are more and those who are less intelligible within certain contexts (Butler, 1993, 2008) and that these norms are both racialized, (cis-)gendered and sexualized, I identified instances where the writers shared experiences of being made intelligible (by others or themselves) through norms and expectations based on sexuality–gender–race in relation to a White majority society. I organized these experiences into broader themes, which generated a number of recurring narratives and figures. Four of them were so recurring that the majority of writers referred to at least one of them: the oppositional narrative of the LGBTQ victim and the racialized hateful other, coming out as an LGBTQ identity milestone, experiences of exotification and tokenism in White LGBTQ communities, and a general feeling of there being a lack of representation of LGBTQ people racialized as non-White and/or Muslim. By maintaining long quotes, I try to give as much space as possible to the writers' own voices.

Being the victim of the 'hateful Other'

> I know that not all *blattekids* have had the luck I've had, but I still get so tired of all White people who are always worried about how my family reacts to finding out that I am queer. (W 12)

> For a lot of us, white LGBTQ spaces are incredibly unsafe because our existence is constantly being questioned. ... How can you be both Muslim and gay??? What do your parents say about you being gay??? (W 11)

> I am so bothered by having to 'come out' etc. I constantly get the question about whether I am open and what my parents think. (W 65)

Throughout, it becomes clear that one underlying assumption is that communities racialized as non-White and/or Muslims are inherently negatively predisposed against LGBTQ identities and LGBTQ rights, frequently expressed by questions about 'what your parents think' with regard to writers being LGBTQ. Two major themes make up the frame of intelligibility with regard to this assumption: the 'rescue narrative' (Bracke, 2012) and the 'hateful Other' (Haritaworn, 2015). As its re-occurrence across empirical arenas shows, the rescue narrative is a well-established practice of Othering with regard to LGBTQ people racialized as non-White and/or Muslim. It describes them as in need of liberation and protection from their own communities and these communities' oppressive societal structures. Various LGBTQ organizations have been criticized for perpetuating these themes and for rendering LGBTQ people racialized as non-White and/or Muslim into exceptional, but voiceless figures, always only portrayed as in need of help (El-Tayeb, 2012; Haritaworn, 2015; Jungar and Peltonen, 2015):

> You would think that those who've had the hardest time accepting me and my sexual orientation are my dad and my relatives in Morocco, but I'll tell u. It's fkn wrong. Let us criticize the queer world once and for all. In those chalk white queer spaces where everything that matters is to look sufficiently lesbian and to 'free the nipple'. (W 30)

> If there is one place where I've been treated badly because of my faith, gender and sexuality, it is among WHITE LGBTQIA+ people. They almost love to question my faith as soon as they get the chance. 'Has your dad forced you?' 'Have you been brainwashed?' 'Will you be beaten at home otherwise?' ... Like nooo this is something I believe. White LGBTQIA+ people can easily exclude a LGBTQIA+ person of faith, especially if they are poc. Because of course, of course we don't

belong in your world? … Of course it is so much easier to be able to think that all POC of faith are narrow-minded homophobes? (W 48)

[My mum] thinks it's great fun and important to support the LGBTQ-fight, but she also marches in the parade to destroy racist ideas about migrant parents not backing their queer children. Tired of unnuanced debates and reports about migrants and everyone in the *förort*, poc working class, being LGBTQ-phobes. That openness quietly equals 'Western values', whiteness and well educated. As if being white, doctor, psychologist and journalist automatically turns people into some kind of unicorn tearing up from joy when seeing a rainbow flag. While the combination migrant, dishwasher, cleaner, dinner lady leads to you boo as soon as a dyke turns up. But mami says that no 'viejas pitucas' [old hags] who 'worry about LGBTQ-immigrants' while at the same time being blatant racists are allowed to lecture her or ascribe homophobic views to her. And she doesn't let anybody do it either. (W 75)

The rescue narrative is to a large extent maintained via the notion of 'the hateful Other', that is, the racialized and/or Muslim migrant perpetrating violence against LGBTQ people (Haritaworn, 2015). In various European countries, specific education campaigns about tolerance have been directed towards communities racialized as non-White and/or Muslim (Haritaworn, 2015; Jungar and Peltonen, 2015). One specific Swedish example of these attempts to 'teach the hateful other a lesson' is of course Pride Järva, discussed in Chapter 6 of this book. Taking place in the northern outskirts of Stockholm, the marches were used to portray certain parts of Swedish cities as unsafe for LGBTQ people because of the 'hateful Others' who live there. These areas (*förorten* or *orten*) were built in the 1960s and 1970s, with their inhabitants often being both immigrants and racialized Swedes. The abbreviation *orten*, much like the term *blatte*, has been reclaimed by those who live there in order to tackle the stigmatization accompanying it. Suffering from high unemployment rates and crammed living conditions, these areas (and their inhabitants) are regularly portrayed as chaotic, lawless and dangerous, while also marked as 'un-Swedish'. Grids of intelligibility with regard to Swedishness as Whiteness and Swedishness as LGBTQ-friendliness converge here, externalizing and othering communities racialized as non-White and/or Muslim as well as complicating the intelligibility of being both LGBTQ and racialized as non-White and/or Muslim in the Swedish context.

Expectations to come out

One much discussed issue throughout the posts is coming out. Coming out to oneself, but particularly coming out to others. While some speak of it as liberating, coming out is also described as a strong norm regarding what makes one intelligible as a 'proper LGBTQ person', to the extent that people feel pressured to do so:

> People have gotten this idea that the best you can do is to come out to everybody you know and to be open with your sexuality at all times to show your pride. However, for many of us that would mean strained relations, to be thrown out from your community etc. So that's why many decide not to come out. I myself have no plans whatsoever to ever come out to my family/community because it would be awkward and uncomfortable and no i rather not. (W 11)

> I decided to post anonymously on this account partially because I come from a country where it is illegal to be anything else than straight. I still travel there sometimes to be able to meet my relatives who are not allowed to come here (because of Sweden's disgusting immigration politics) and I want to continue travelling there without risking the death penalty. I might also expose my relatives there for risks if I was to come out publicly, they can be connected to me. It's sometimes been a problem in the white queer world I have moved around, and there's been expectations that I should speak publicly about being queer/pan/bi/lesbian (whatever I might be defined as), and some people I've dated haven't always been understanding. …
>
> The whole thing about how one absolutely has to come out to precisely everybody was putting a real strain on me a few years back. I was constantly worried and anxious about it and my mental health declined. How should I come out to my parents who follow a fairly strict interpretation of religion where LGBTQ people are not part of the picture. I knew then and I know now that if I was to come out to them it would end with me not having a home or a family left. I'm at peace with that thought today, and I am just waiting until I have economic stability first. … But once again, what's the deal with the whole coming-out culture that drives young people who are in unsafe environments to come out, that everything will be better if only they do it. I was in such bad shape when I was 16 years old because I wanted so very much to come out because I believed I was forced to do so. … Today my parents know nothing and I have no problems with that, because I know that they and I are not ready yet. (W 50)

These entries stress the way in which coming out is a norm in White Swedish LGBTQ circles that disregards different social aspects, making it hard to comply with, such as destroying family relations or impacting upon one's ability to travel. Another aspect of coming out – showing your relationship openly (for example, by holding hands or kissing) is described as being potentially unsafe in relation to a White majority society, especially when you are racialized as non-White and/or Muslim: 'It's simply not always safe to be open and out, but it gives me a feeling of safety and serenity to know that my partner understands' (W 31). This entry describes the potential danger of hate crimes that are motivated by both racism and homophobia, and the benefit of having a partner who instinctively understands this based on their own experience, making them less inclined to see somebody who strategically decides not to be open as a coward or oppressed. A sentiment that is echoed in another entry: 'The few gay friends I had during that time pretty quickly no longer gave a shit about me since they couldn't be bothered to hang out with a closet-boy who could not stand up for himself' (W 67). White LGBTQ people, the entries indicate, expect you to be out, otherwise they will consider you a coward or refuse to date you. Mirrored in these posts are of course the writers' own assumptions that White LGBTQ people can come out whenever and to whomever without experiencing any repercussions or anxiety – an assumption that to some extent re-inscribes the strict discursive binary between the 'open' White LGBTQ person and the 'closeted' person racialized as non-White and/or Muslim (Horton, 2018). A further testament to people experiencing strong pressure to come out are the appeals to their readers that it is ok to not come out and that nobody should rush this step if they are not 'ready':

> I am still working on becoming comfortable with my sexuality. Something which has been increeeeeeedibly helpful has been the mindset that I do not need to come out. I hate that expression, btw. It feels like its definite that all LGBTQI+ people at some point in their lives have to start writing on their foreheads that they are queer. I don't feel the need to tell my parents, I don't feel the need to tell the whole world that I am queer. What does it matter? Why can't I just be without having to make such a big deal out of it? (W 41)

> Sometimes I throw the closet door wide open and roll out all glittery. Sometimes I just have a toe outside the closet. And that's ok. There should be space for being able to be as open or closed as oneself is comfortable with. You don't have to be an encyclopaedia. You are 100% valid even if you are not 'out'. (W 54)

> Remember that none of you has to come out if you don't want to or can't. Sometimes it is safer not to do it. (W 9)

> To all of you who haven't come out and feel that you can't cope or don't need to, go ahead as usual, as long as you feel good. (W 57)

All of the entries point to coming out as a crucial aspect when it comes to becoming intelligible as LGBTQ in White, Western contexts. Coming out has historically been used as a political strategy by activists in Europe and North America, creating the foundation for struggles for rights and recognition by making the existence of LGBTQ people publicly visible (Horton, 2018). This emphasis on 'visibility via verbal disclosure' (Horton, 2018, p 2) requires and reproduces a subject that is 'out and proud'. Dhawan describes this as a deeply developmental narrative, from closeted, 'prepolitical' same-sex acts to liberated, politicized, modern, gay identities (Dhawan, 2013, p 201). This mirrors linear temporalities characterizing the 'West' as more developed than 'the Rest' with regard to LGBTQ rights within which LGBTQ people racialized as non-White and/or Muslim play a central role (Butler, 2008). The process of coming out also plays to narratives around threat and protection – in order to be included into the safety of gay-friendly liberal-secular Western communities, LGBTQ people racialized as non-White and/or Muslim have to liberate themselves from the oppressive structures of collective identities. Jivraj and de Jong show how the focus on 'speakability' and dialogue 'reinforces the perception of queer Muslims being "positioned in between"' (Jivraj and de Jong, 2011, p 145), thus once more strengthening the dichotomy between the LGBTQ-friendly West and homophobic Muslims. Additionally, coming out is seen as an 'important means by which to achieve not only individual emancipation, but also broader social acceptance' (Jivraj and de Jong, 2011, p 149), raising the expectation that every LGBTQ person should want to come out.

Non-public ways of living and inhabiting LGBTQ identities are read as morally inferior or out of place. Queerness that 'both operationalizes and persists through [strategic] silence might be seen as constricting, oppressive, and backwards' (Horton, 2018, p 2) instead of acknowledging the need to manage different social contexts. El-Tayeb calls coming out a 'decontextualized fetish' according to which 'queers of color are expected to catch up, to overcome their inherent cultural disadvantage' (El-Tayeb, 2012, p 89). The Instagram entries show that coming out is a major frame of intelligibility in these young LGBTQ people's lives but also indicate that they relate to it by 'working around it', opening up alternative ways to the open/closeted and out-and-proud/silent dichotomies (see also Barglowski et al, 2018).

Exotification, (de-)sexualization and tokenism

Beyond being the victim of a hateful Other, bodies racialized as non-White and/or Muslim are made intelligible in White LGBTQ contexts in Sweden through frames of exotified othering, both sexualized and non-sexualized.

One recurring aspect is the way in which they feel they are read as tokens by White LGBTQ people:

I didn't want white queers to look at me like some kind of sidekick, like 'oh, she's Arab AND lesbian, that's a catch'. (W 33)

I've been working with LGBTQ issues since mid-2014. Megafonen [a grassroot organization working for social justice in disadvantaged areas of Stockholm] was still hot. *Orten* became hotter. I have never been hit on by women as much as I was then. One friend put it like this 'You are a trophy wife. You are *blatte*, activist, and from the *förort*. You are one of the best ways for all white anti-racists to get more anti-racist points by showing that they hang out with you in front of their white friends.' (W 26)

Afterwards I heard that one person I had hung out with had talked about me as 'orten-tjejen' [the girl from the *förort*]. Yes, I think I know that you are reading this. I have a name. I am *orten*, but I am not 'orten-tjejen' from your bucket list whom you can brag about in front of your other white anti-racists. (W 26)

When I came out as non-binary I realized that I got invited to white spaces which I earlier on not had been invited to, I was seen in a new light. ... Before I was just this angry, bitchy racialized girl who would constantly point out POC's existence, rights and the damn shit we're forced to go through in this society built on and by normative whiteness for white people. Now suddenly you include me in a whole new way. Why? Yes; identification with my sexuality. So I thought it was a little weird when these people contacted me and invited me to their space. And it got even more weird when I opened the door and saw that the space was constituted of only white people. I was the only *blatte*-queer person in the room. My first thought was: What the fuck is this? Am I some kind of damn trophy they think they've won and need to show like 'LOOK!!! MY CIRCLES AREN'T SOOOO WHIIIIITE!!' Neither me nor any other of my racialized LGBTQ-siblings are some damn addition to your circles supposed to make you look like something 'better'. (W 52)

Research shows that particularly LGBTQ people racialized as Muslims have been made intelligible through the frame of the 'token victim' (Erdem et al, 2008, p 78). 'Tokenized' LGBTQ people racialized as non-White and/or Muslim are in in this context again seen as 'exceptions' who have emancipated themselves from oppressive cultural context, thus re-inscribing the narrative of 'the West' as safe and progressive (Jungar and Peltonen, 2015), constituting itself against threat of the 'hateful other'. While it could be argued that the token inclusion described in the quotes opens up spaces and opportunities to activists racialized as non-White and/or Muslim, the writers frame this distinctly as a particular version of exotification, where they are turned into an accessory in spaces otherwise dominated by White people (who might even gain extra credibility through their association with LGBTQ people racialized as non-White).

Beyond the issue of tokenism, sexualized exotification or fetishization is a common grid of intelligibility. The writers are exposed to strongly racialized notions of masculinity or femininity, which are accorded value in very different ways:

> Another thing you are often exposed to as *blatte* is exotification. I definitely feel very clearly how I am seen as exotic, as foreign, as the 'masculine' and 'dominant' *blatte* who should take control. I have several times gotten comments like that I 'look dangerous'. (W 4)

> Sometimes the person I meet manages to get through the first date completely without exotifying me or saying something femmephobic; they save it till during or after [sexual] contact. 'I think it's unsexy with feminine guys, you *blattar* are more masculine with your beards.' Girl please. 'You Arabs are so …' When did I become 'you [Arabs]'. When did I become representative for all Arab men? I'm here to get laid, not to talk about the Gulf War. (W 78)

> I'm not your damn Persian prince you can 'ride the flying carpet' with. … Exotification. We *blattar* have all experienced it, right? (W 27)

> Honestly, I don't go clubbing much. One of the last times I was out it was at a queer club here in Stockholm. Almost everybody apart from me and my friends were white. White Swedes spoke English to me, complimented me in English, made me feel bad and quickly leave them because I couldn't handle it. (W 63)

> Exotification, when people treat you like a mango or a papaya because of the way you look, your ethnicity etc. Might seem like a small thing, but you who experience it do know that it is tough in the long term to be called things like 'mocha caramel queen', getting to hear 'lets mix that coco with the cream' etcetc. (W 58)

The way in which racialization and exotification intersect in these examples shows that the writers' sexual orientation or gender identity is made intelligible based on highly stereotypical notions of racialized identities:

> As a racialized person, especially as a Japanese person in the West I constantly get exotified and fetishized. East Asian girls are always seen as straight and to be existing for (white) men … As East Asian girl (as whom I get misgendered) I more frequently have my queer identity put into doubt than white girls. I am denied my own sexuality and my queerness. (W 63)

> To constantly be sexualized [as an East Asian woman]. To see East Asian men be desexualized, denied a sexuality and representation because of that. (Or when mostly white people fetishize us as objects, as decorations and parts of their 'aesthetic'.) I am so tired of this bullshit. I'm not exotic, I'm exhausted. (W 63)

> Because I am East-Asian and are sometimes taken for a girl and sometimes for a guy I get very different reactions in public. When I one day get taken for East-Asian girl I get over-sexualized, while when I get taken as East-Asian guy I get totally de-sexualised. Being taken for an East-Asian guy has led to a lot of gender dysphoria for me. Because East-Asian guys are so de-sexualised by society I have felt ugly and disgusting and inadequate when people take me for a guy. … No matter what I look like or what I get taken for, it's seldomly on my terms because I am trans and East-Asian. (W 36)

Desexualization combined with openly expressed racism on the dating market adds to these experiences:

> I've seen on different dating sides that some write that they are not looking for dates with a certain type of racialized. Some bodies are desexualised. (W 27)

> I can still see people on the apps grindr or scurff (mostly cis-gay-bi men there) who write 'no blacks/not hot for blacks'. Sick!! (W 34)

Both hyper-sexualization and desexualization are central and longstanding narratives in the exotification and externalization of bodies racialized as non-White in Western societies (Han, 2007; Laskar, 2007; Massad, 2007). Notions of the Other as both sexually exciting and dangerous are closely connected to European colonial history, and, yet again, position 'civilized' White societies in opposition to communities and individuals racialized as non-White (Laskar, 2015a). Laskar demonstrates how images of racialized others were used to 'steadily produc[e] counter-images and deterrents to the [Swedish] majority society's ideals of gender, sexuality, class and race' (Laskar, 2015b, p 138). The hyper-sexuality accorded to Black bodies and

Asian women, the dangerous masculinity ascribed to bodies orientalized as 'Arab' and the emasculation of Asian men as described in the Instagram entries all function as a 'constitutive outside' (Haritaworn, 2015, p 85) to a normalized sexuality ascribed to White bodies.

These grids of intelligibility portray the subject position of LGBTQ people racialized as non-White and/or Muslim as objects of desire, pity or fascination by White LGBTQ people. Tokenism and sexualized exotification further re-inscribe LGBTQ people racialized as non-White and/or Muslim as externalized others, made intelligible in an oppositional relation to White LGBTQ people, who are therefore once more established as the main frame of reference for how sexuality and gender identity become intelligible in the Swedish context.

(Lack of) representation

For most of the writers, entering LGBTQ spaces in Sweden entails the instant realization that these spaces are predominantly White. Some refer to themselves being read as threatening in White LGBTQ spaces, they are themselves read as threatening, based on their being racialized as non-White and/or Muslim. The ascription of LGBTQ-phobia to racialized communities and racialized bodies follows them into these spaces, requiring a careful adjustment in order to make themselves less 'threatening'. They describe this as turning themselves into a 'nice *blatte*' or 'conscious *blatte*', which marks them out as the 'liberal exception' from the homo-/transphobic racialized norm, and thus as legitimate and 'safe' in White LGBTQ contexts. This entails one more conditional intelligibility on the terms of a White majority LGBTQ community, with entry being granted to those being queer in 'the right way':

> Somewhere in between I came out and started hanging out with queers I realized that that it would not go smoothly. In these [LGBTQ] spaces I was clearly the black sheep. I could not identify as lesbian. In these spaces I was Arab. (W 33)

> At the same time I tried to join the public spaces for LGBTQI+ people, but I found mostly white spaces and people who did not at all share my experiences of the world. We had completely different perspectives and it was clear to me that they often lacked a wider perspective. But I thought there was something wrong with me and that's why I tried to fit into their template. (W 77)

> Because queer safe spaces in Sweden often have been dominated by and built by white LGBTQ people they are also built according to that

group's needs and notions of where the danger is. WHO the danger is. Which body potentially is homo-, bi- or transphobic. Beyond POC-LGBTQs often not being read as LGBTQ because queerness in Sweden = openness/enlightenment and thus = whiteness, POCs are also seen as bearers of homo-, bi- or transphobia in a racist world view. To be allowed belonging to a 'safe queer space' in Sweden can therefore require different forms of adjustment from a POC. Through making oneself unthreatening though language, not taking up for much space, not being too many *blattar* at the same time, to be a 'fin blatte', assume the current queer norm, style, opinion, taste etc that whiteness has created. (W 75)

It's hard to find a community for queer POC. There are spaces for LGBTQI people. And there are spaces for POC. But there are no communities for LGBTI PO. It's hard to find a safe space. When you are exposed to both racism and homophobia. In POC spaces there is not a lot of talk about homophobia. And in queer spaces you don't talk about racism. There is no combination. For people who are subjected to both racism and homophobia you need a space which gets all of your identity. (W32)

Sometimes it feels like queer-style is a guard. The focus is more on my crazy style than me being *blattetrans*. But it only works in the white queer world and sometimes in the white cis-heteronormative world. Because then you are seen as a conscious *blatte* and get cred for that. (W 25)

I stopped talking like I had grown up talking, avoided my friends from home because I knew that they never would understand. Did everything to fit in with queer white contexts but it always felt forced and wrong, I was never as comfortable as I was with other kids from the *förort*. (W 50)

'The right kind of queer' seems to always already be racialized as White, with norms around style and beauty being based on bodies racialized as White. Experiences and bodies of LGBTQ people racialized as non-White and/or Muslim are exotified in these contexts through the various frames of intelligibility discussed earlier. Many writers point out the general lack of representation as one of the reasons why they were insecure about whether they can actually *be* LGBTQ while also being racialized as non-White and/or Muslim:

There are so many norms in the trans community that I know that I am not the only one who sometimes feels that they are not 'sufficiently trans'. Just like hegemonic whiteness fucked with my brain and told me that I could not be non-binary if I wasn't 175 cm tall and had really pale skin. (W 36)

It was obviously also harder to realize because the few LGBTQ people I saw in the media or read about in school were all white. It would have felt less unthinkable and alien, and I had realised a lot earlier if I just had got to see people who looked like me, who had the same experiences as me, were lesbian and happy. But I didn't get that, so I interpreted it simply as something that other people were, but never I myself. (W 32)

I was very religious during my early teens, wore niqab for a while, and during that period I avoided even thinking about my queerness. If I didn't think about it, it did not exist. In my head Islam and LGBTQ were completely separated, I would never be accepted + did queer Muslims even exist? (W 50)

To not see your own skin colour (in all its nuances) represented is one thing, and something all non-whites experience during their lives. … However, to not see yourself represented with regard to sexuality is another thing. ARE there even 'people like me'? ARE there at all black women, who love other women? (W 31)

The search results I find when I google 'lesbian Latinas' are links to pornhub, xvideo, xxnx. My sexual orientation and my ethnicity are therefore both individually and in combination with each other only material for men to jerk off to. How can you realize that you are lesbian, that you are allowed to be lesbian, that being lesbian is a real alternative if you never get to see it anywhere apart from distorted, overly sexualised and exploitative contexts? (W 43)

Sometimes it feels like the white culture is the only culture that has somewhat normalized non-straight relationships. Among non-white families this isn't even a question. Or? Is there a lack of representation of non-white families with queer children that makes me feel this way? Is there an overrepresentation of white families with white queer children that makes me feel that the only families who accept and understand and love their child not matter what partner they chose is the majority of white families? (W 57)

So: representation is important! Here in Sweden, with white trans people and non-binary people as the constant public face for all of us etc it is damn hard for us trans poc to make space for ourselves when we can't see our existence mirrored in the queer or non-white spaces. (W 63)

These entries speak of a complete lack of representation with regard to being both racialized as non-White and/or Muslim and LGBTQ, and the ways in which this made the writers question their own identities. While the other narratives (the victim, the coming out, the exotified other) make their experiences intelligible in certain specific ways in White LGBTQ contexts, these entries show that lack of representation in itself constitutes an important framework of (non-)intelligibility. It renders the positionality of being LGBTQ people racialized as non-White and/or Muslim impossible, to others, but also to themselves (see also Held, 2023). This mirrors existing research on the importance of (positive) representation for identity formation (Phoenix et al, 2015). Without exception, all writers expressed immense gratitude and relief that the Instagram account existed, as a place in which to find one's identity represented and thus strengthened by the existence of other LGBTQ people racialized as non-White and/or Muslim.

Conclusions

The overall experience verbalized in the Instagram entries is one of being made intelligible as an 'externalized other', mapped out along various grids of intelligibility around race, religion, sexuality and gender. When entering predominantly White Swedish LGBTQ contexts, the young people posting on the account are made intelligible as non-Swedish, with Swedishness being closely connected to Whiteness, in contrast to their being racialized as non-White and/or Muslim. Based on the close discursive relationship between Swedishness and gender/LGBTQ equality (so-called Swedish gender exceptionalism) and its constitutive other, the LGBTQ-phobic immigrant community, they thus also become intelligible as potential victims of LGBTQ-phobia ascribed to their own communities – the hateful Other(s) (Haritaworn, 2015). Related to this is the noticeable importance accorded to the notion of 'coming out' as the quintessential act of asserting one's own sexuality and gender identity, in relation to oneself and to others. With the coming out as one of the most central frames of intelligibility for being LGBTQ in a Western European context (Horton, 2018), their way of navigating their sexuality/gender identity is frequently interpreted (to a certain degree even by themselves) as a failure to liberate themselves, rather than a conscious strategy for handling various ways of 'being LGBTQ'. They (and their racialized bodies) are also othered and exotified in both sexualized and non-sexualized ways that echo earlier historical renderings of the 'exotic other' (Laskar, 2015a). They are made intelligible as the token racialized friend or hook-up, the fetishized exotic object of desire or the desexualized body. Additionally, the experience of LGBTQ contexts being predominantly (even exclusively) White means that 'the right kind of queer' inhabiting these spaces comfortably is always already racialized as White, further exotifying rather than normalizing racialized LGBTQ experiences. This lack of representation in itself constitutes an important grid of non-intelligibility to the extent that the writers question whether they can actually *be* LGBTQ if they are racialized as non-White and/or Muslim. The way in which they become an 'impossible other' even to themselves points towards the importance of analysing grids of intelligibility – they have severe consequences for individuals' identities, personal well-being and sense of self (Jaspal and Cinnirella, 2012).

The prevailing grids of intelligibility can therefore be seen to objectify LGBTQ people racialized as non-White and/or Muslim, making them intelligible either in relation to White, LGBTQ-friendly 'Swedishness' or threatening, LGBTQ-phobic racialized 'others'. In the light of these findings, separatism (in the way this particular Instagram account practises it) can be considered an important political strategy used to deal with the lack of representation and to expand the grids of intelligibility available to LGBTQ people racialized as non-White and/or Muslim.

9

Conclusions and Ways Ahead

Prologue: an unexpected encounter

In August 2018, I was invited to participate in a panel on homonationalism at Sweden's second-largest pride festival, West Pride in Gothenburg. There were familiar faces among both panellists and audience, some of them researchers, some of them activists. Greetings and introductions were exchanged while we were waiting for the actual event to begin, which no doubt would pass in an atmosphere of mutual recognition and encouragement. As we were taking our seats, the door opened once more, and four members of the Swedish Armed Forces (SAF) entered the room. Two were wearing navy blue, the other two were dressed in camouflage fatigues. All of them had replaced the detachable badge with the Swedish flag worn on the right arm with a rainbow flag. As they sat down in the back of the room, there was a slight apprehensive murmur among the audience. I was flabbergasted. Suddenly, the physical manifestation of the very article I had recently published, and was now preparing to present, marched right into this space I occupied so comfortably. It took me a minute or so to find my way back into the panel discussion.

There is much to unpack here: Do the SAF encourage their soldiers to swap out the national flag for the rainbow flag when it is pride week? Do soldiers get to attend these events on duty? How do we make sense of the predominantly LGBTQ-identified audience's reaction? But it was my own reaction that intrigued me the most. As a researcher, no matter my commitment to my activist identity, I had apparently lost track of the fact that my research dealt with the lives of 'real' people, and that it would sooner or later encounter these lives. That in fact, it had always been my expressed aim that this project *should* encounter people and lives beyond academic circles. Instead, the performance aspect required of us for the sake of academic career building had gotten the better of me. As I write the concluding chapter, this project has come to a point where it is more than ready to live its own life beyond academia. I sincerely hope it provides insights that provoke the interest not only of those already invested in the issues I discuss but also of those I did not anticipate. In this final chapter, I will take a concluding look at what this book set out to do, summarize the findings and provide some suggestions on what future avenues have opened up during the course of the project, both with regard to research interventions and activist action.

Boundary making, race and intelligibility

The placement of flags, blue-and-yellow in combination with rainbow-striped ones, has of course played a central role in the way this project came about, symbolizing one of the various ways in which LGBTQ rights appear in contemporary projects of nationalist boundary making. Inspired by research on homonationalism, homonormativity and Swedish gender exceptionalism, this book set out to provide new insights into the role played by race, sexuality and gender in constructions of nationhood and (non-)belonging. It does so by asking, first, *how LGBTQ rights are mobilized in these constructions*. Secondly, this book investigates *which subject positions are suggested and experienced as intelligible* within these processes of nationalist boundary making around normative notions of sexuality, race and gender. Since neither boundary-making processes nor normative grids of intelligibility can conclusively determine the ways in which we make sense of ourselves and others around us, it also looks at *how these are negotiated, particularly by LGBTQ people racialized as non-White and/or Muslim*. Finally, acknowledging the ways in which both boundary-making processes and the grids of intelligibility enabled by them are built on racialized notions of Otherness, it pays particular attention to the *role played by racialization in these constructions*. By doing so, it covers central aspects that characterize contemporary (homo)nationalist attempts at boundary making around sexuality, race and gender while also accounting for the important implication these attempts have for the lives of LGBTQ people through the creation of 'right' and 'wrong' kinds of queers in different contexts.

Constructing Swedishness through LGBTQ rights

The book shows that notions of Swedishness are constructed with explicit reference to values and rights related to the acceptance, recognition and, crucially, protection of LGBTQ people. This is done in two main ways. First, constructions of Swedishness rely on Swedishness being equated with positive signifiers regarding LGBTQ rights and pro-LGBTQ attitudes, including references to tolerance, openness and the ability to 'be who you want to be'. This notion of Swedish progressiveness is formulated in the SAF campaign slogans about protecting 'everybody's right to live our lives the way we want to', and it positions and constructs Swedishness within wider contexts of tolerant and progressive 'Europeanness'. Secondly, and much more pronouncedly so, constructions of Swedishness through LGBTQ rights rely on the comparison with – and thus differentiation from – LGBTQ-phobic Others. These Others are constructed as either existing outside of Sweden, or, if found within, as not 'originally' from Sweden (and should therefore be considered non-Swedish). This externalization of LGBTQ-phobia occurs across all three empirical cases discussed in the book: Sjunnesson locates homophobia within immigrant communities based on their 'cultural heritage'; the SAF refer to distant Others that threaten Swedish progressiveness (thus justifying a re-territorialization of the Swedish defence along its national borders) and the Instagram writers describe how their families and communities are made intelligible as LGBTQ-phobic Others based on real or ascribed experiences of migration into Sweden. The externalization of anti-LGBTQ sentiments happens both territorially (in relation to Sweden as a place where LGBTQ rights are upheld) and temporally (in relation to these rights being an expression of Swedish modernity and progressiveness).

Both of the main narratives underlying constructions of Swedishness in relation to LGBTQ rights (the 'positive' one about Swedishness, and the 'negative' one about dangerous Otherness) crucially rely on a language of threat and protection. LGBTQ people in Sweden are, throughout the material I analysed, performed as being in need of protection from LGBTQ-phobic and thus threatening Others, and it is first and foremost the actors engaged in the boundary-making constructions of Swedishness that claim to be able to provide that protection. Sjunnesson draws on established notions of Swedish gender exceptionalism at Pride Järva, writing himself into that narrative as its protector. The SAF's portrayal of Sweden as an 'exceptionally' good country to be queer in establishes, as well as relies on, the continued existence of an LGBTQ-phobic threat somewhere else, and thus the continued need for protection. Interestingly, the SAF campaigns make LGBTQ people intelligible as both the ones in need of protection and the potential protectors (in the form of LGBTQ-identified armed personnel), an aspect I will discuss in more detail later. Even in the material on the Instagram account, the dangerous Other is present in White LGBTQ people's assumptions about the writers' families and communities as LGBTQ-phobic.

I found that the binary ways in which Swedishness/the Swedish Self is constructed by way of separation and distancing from dangerous Others do a number of things beyond attempts at boundary making around communities of belonging. By externalizing anti-LGBTQ attitudes from Swedishness (both in space and time), homo-, bi- and transphobia are portrayed as spatially and culturally situated (and thus limited), rather than as social structures which continue to exist also in Swedish society. Constructions of Swedishness as LGBTQ-friendly, particularly those constructions that rely on a dangerous (and externalized) Other, thus conceal discrimination and violence on the basis of gender identity and sexual orientation within Sweden. The lived experiences of LGBTQ people in Sweden are replaced with depersonalized markers (like the rainbow flag) in these constructions of Swedishness, which can make it difficult to address the continued existence of LGBTQ-phobia within Swedish society. While LGBTQ rights might be mobilized in various attempts at boundary making around notions of Swedishness, these mobilizations also externalize and hide, and thus at best superficially challenge, existing norms regarding gender and sexuality.

Dangerous Others, racialized Others

My analysis of boundary-making processes around notions of Swedishness through positive attitudes towards and protection of LGBTQ rights also shows how these processes are profoundly racialized in their construction of the Self and the Other, relying crucially on the differentiation of Others by way of racialization. This applies to racialization as a social process for ascribing different varieties of non-Whiteness, but also for ascription of religion, more specifically Islam, as a signifier of Otherness. The LGBTQ-phobic Other is marked by these processes of racialization while simultaneously serving as the constitutive outside to notions of Swedishness as being accepting but also protective of LGBTQ rights and LGBTQ people. Throughout, the racialized Other is constructed, and thus made intelligible, as a threat to LGBTQ people (both White and racialized). The racialization of the threatening Other is least explicit in Chapter 7, with the SAF instead relying on an externalization of anti-LGBTQ sentiments into unnamed distant Others. Here, Swedish values (symbolized by, among other things, the rainbow flag) are described as 'extreme in the eyes of others', without actually defining these Others. However, once we read these differentiating moves alongside other externalizations of LGBTQ-phobia on to distant Others inhabiting racialized bodies, it becomes clear that, at the very least, even the boundary-making moves employed by the SAF tap into established notions of racialized Othering. As the security situation in Central Europe deteriorates following the Russian invasion of Ukraine, a homophobic threat from a non-European Russian Other increasingly becomes the centre of these campaigns.

Throughout, the analysis shows that Otherness is frequently reinforced by notions of communities racialized as non-White and/or Muslims having their own 'culture' of LGBTQ-phobia. Again, religion (and particularly Islam) as an ethno-cultural signifier of difference plays an important role in these narratives. The 'cultural' aspect alluded to by references to Islam also includes an understanding of temporality that positions Othered communities into a civilizational discourse of development, within which they are considered to be stuck in an LGBTQ-phobic past. LGBTQ-friendly Swedishness, on the other hand, is a marker of progress, the present, even the future. Crucially, the ascription of certain anti-LGBTQ attitudes to bodies racialized as Other happens not only in the more depersonalized constructions of Swedishness analysed in Chapters 6 and 7 but appears in similar ways in Chapter 8, where LGBTQ people racialized as non-White and/or Muslim express recurring experiences of having been made intelligible in relation to these attitudes. This happens with regard to their racialized families and communities being made intelligible as potentially dangerous but also with regard to they themselves feeling they have to adjust to expectations from White LGBTQ people because of their being-racialized when entering White LGBTQ contexts. In the contemporary constructions of Swedishness analysed, in particular, in Chapters 6 and 8, I would, therefore, argue that racialization, not sexuality or gender, is the central marker of the particular boundary-making processes that separate the included from the excluded in relation to LGBTQ rights. However, as we see in the case of the Instagram Account, this is modulated by sexuality and gender, when people racialized as non-White and/or Muslim are made intelligible as 'the right kind of queer'.

Manoeuvring (non-)intelligibility

As discussed throughout the book, collective constructions of (non-)belonging through boundary making both draw upon and enable normative grids of intelligibility, thus producing certain subjectivities as more easily recognizable, whereas the intelligibility of others is less self-evident. Analysing the ways in which Swedishness is constructed through racialized boundary making in relation to LGBTQ rights is therefore important in order to understand which LGBTQ positionalities are recognized as intelligible within the context of these constructions. As the book shows, this is particularly true for those who are both LGBTQ and racialized as non-White and/or Muslim. While the discursive boundary-making moves analysed here only make up a limited part of how Swedishness is constructed through LGBTQ rights, they still produce certain lives as 'liveable' through contemporary attempts at boundary making around notions of Swedishness. Looking at this aspect thus gives us important indications of what constructions of nationhood and national belonging through LGBTQ rights 'do' with regard to the lives of LGBTQ people that unfold in the context of these constructions.

The boundary-making moves that construct Swedishness in relation to LGBTQ rights rely on a number of narratives. Particularly crucial to these constructions is the demarcation of a pro-LGBTQ Swedishness under threat from a dangerous LGBTQ-phobic (and racialized) Other, and thus in need of protection; a protection that is offered by the very actors involved in the boundary making. These attempts at boundary making make LGBTQ people at large intelligible first and foremost as potential victims of discrimination and violence based on gender identity and sexuality. While boundary-making moves enable this victim positionality, they also crucially rely on it – if LGBTQ people were not (potential) victims, there would be no need for anybody to offer protection from dangerous Others; without the dangerous Others at the boundaries of belonging, these constructions of Swedishness would lack their constitutive outside. At the same time, this being-made-intelligible through victimhood is crucially challenged or complicated across all three sites. While Sjunnesson's rhetoric most clearly rests on binary Self/Other distinctions with regard to the White Swedish LGBTQ victim and the dangerous homophobic racialized Other, the LGBTQ activists who protest Pride Järva challenge their being-made-intelligible as victims in need of protection. Their physical presence and political expression in the very space Sjunnesson determines as the most dangerous for LGBTQ people in Sweden – due to its alleged existence 'outside' of Swedish legal and value systems – upsets the ways in which they are made intelligible as victims but also how the suburbs become an LGBTQ-phobic and thus non-Swedish space. There is, in Butler's words, a performative aspect to their assembling to protest Pride Järva that crucially challenges Sjunnesson's attempts at making them intelligible by opening up alternative expressions of being racialized LGBTQ people in particular parts of Stockholm (Butler, 2015).

This book also shows how, in a slightly more complicated move, the SAF campaigns mobilize LGBTQ people as both the ones in need of protection and the potential protector (in the role of the LGBTQ soldier). While LGBTQ people are still made intelligible as potential victims here, in this narrative they also become capable protectors as part of a newly inclusive military force. However, their positionalities as both victims and/or protectors remain within constructions of tolerant and modern Swedishness that crucially rely on notions of distant LGBTQ-phobic Others. Here, the complexity lies more in looking beyond the ways in which LGBTQ people are made intelligible as victims and/or protectors, and towards the wider contexts of boundary making in relation to national defence and re-armament that maintain the binary distinction between the Swedish Self as a defender of LGBTQ rights and the LGBTQ-phobic externalized Other. LGBTQ people are thus made intelligible as victims and/or defenders only in relation to threats from the outside. With anti-LGBTQ attitudes firmly located elsewhere, these constructions of Swedishness in relation to LGBTQ rights make domestic discrimination on the basis of gender identity and sexual orientation more difficult to address. Intriguingly, this is both despite and because of the rainbow flag being proudly displayed on Swedish military uniforms.

While Chapters 6 and 7 indicate that the racialized Other is described not only as being externalized but also as being threatening to LGBTQ people, the personal testimonies in Chapter 8 provide a more in-depth insight into which narratives LGBTQ people racialized as non-White and/or Muslim experience as making them intelligible, as well as how they manoeuvre these grids of intelligibility. Major grids of intelligibility, as described in their stories, include LGBTQ people racialized as non-White and/or Muslim being victims of 'hateful Others', strong expectations to come out, exotification and tokenism (both sexualized and otherwise) and a general lack of representation. Throughout, these include the recurring experience of being made intelligible in relation to either constructions of tolerant pro-LGBTQ Swedishness (built simultaneously on notions of Swedishness-as-Whiteness) or to constructions of externalized, non-White (and therefore non-Swedish) Otherness. Being LGBTQ and racialized as non-White and/or Muslim seems to rarely have been feasible as a subjectivity in itself without people going back to assumptions about these two identities being mutually exclusive, or at least in conflict with each other.

However, this book shows that these grids of intelligibility are also contested, navigated and manoeuvred in various ways by the writers on the Instagram account. One important aspect is the actual community building around sharing these experiences, where being LGBTQ and racialized as non-White and/or Muslim becomes an intelligible positionality in itself by relating to others who occupy the same or similar social position. Throughout the entries, the writers point out the importance of being able to relate to others who share experiences of being LGBTQ and racialized as non-White and/or Muslim as a way of negotiating existing, and creating alternative, grids of intelligibility. There is also recurring encouragement to 'do what works for you', rather than to follow any assumed expectations with regard to LGBTQ positionalities in Swedish contexts. This kind of encouragement is particularly present when people talk about questions of coming out. The existence of the account itself but also the ways in which it is used are clear indications that despite their experiences of being made intelligible through normative grids that diminish or erase aspects of their identity, those who write on the account carve out 'liveable lives' for themselves. They do so by negotiating, rather than just trying to comply with these normative notions of intelligibility.

Contributions and interventions

Studying Pride Järva, the SAF pride campaigns and the activist Instagram account shows that similar narratives of Swedishness as LGBTQ-friendly as well as of dangerous racialized Otherness are re-occurring across different contexts. This indicates that they are well established and readily available for mobilization in particular boundary-making processes as well as in the enablement of normative grids of intelligibility. While this book certainly cannot tell us everything about all the ways in which this happens, it enables us to learn something about how contemporary notions of nationhood and belonging are constructed through mobilization of sexuality, gender and race; how these mobilizations draw upon and enable normative grids of intelligibility; and how LGBTQ people manoeuvre, negotiate and contest them. By providing these insights, the book goes beyond the context of Sweden and Swedish gender exceptionalism and speaks to wider issues on racialized Othering, (homo)nationalist mobilizations of LGBTQ rights and questions of who gets to have access to 'liveable lives' in the context of these mobilizations.

Empirically, the analysis of contemporary constructions of Swedishness through LGBTQ rights contributes new knowledge to existing research on Swedish gender exceptionalism. It expands what has previously been a discussion focused predominantly on notions of feminism and gender equality towards including boundary-making mobilizations of non-normative sexualities and gender identities. As this book shows, not only is Sweden performed as a *gender*-exceptional country both at home and abroad; this exceptionalism increasingly extends also to the promotion and defence of LGBTQ rights. In relation to various Others who are mobilized in attempts at nationalist boundary making, LGBTQ rights are portrayed as so exceptional(ly Swedish) that they are under constant threat and in need of protection both from official state institutions like the SAF and, at a specific point in time, actors on the populist right (otherwise not known for any particular interest in the promotion of LGBTQ rights). By looking at the coexistence of these two sites as well as by analysing the recurrence of narratives of threat and protection in their attempts at boundary making, this book shows that similar narratives have been employed by actors with diverging political standpoints. This also indicates that they are well established, or at least close to already existing narratives (such as notions of Swedish exceptionality performed through gender equality). While the political landscape in Sweden is changing, with the political right increasingly turning away from homonationalist statements, the question of whether there is a need to defend LGBTQ rights weapon in hand against an intolerant Other has only become more present in the public awareness after the full-scale Russian invasion of Ukraine in 2022.

Importantly, this book also increases our understanding of how racialization plays into attempts at boundary making around notions of Swedishness. It contributes thus to interrogations of race within the context of a number of fields, including queer migration studies, queer international relations and postcolonial studies with a focus on the Nordic context. It shows some of the crucial ways in which the Others mobilized in these boundary-making moves appear as racialized, and how this racialization spills over into grids of intelligibility for LGBTQ people, continually re-inscribing Whiteness as an essential part of Swedishness. The contemporary constructions of Swedishness analysed in this book locate threats to LGBTQ rights within racialized communities and bodies and place these outside of Swedishness both with regard to space and time. This externalization not only separates the lives of people racialized as non-White and/or Muslim from notions of Swedishness; it also forecloses the possibility of threats to LGBTQ rights and LGBTQ people being located 'within' White Swedishness. The insights gained from the stories shared on the activist Instagram account show what this means with regard to being both LGBTQ and racialized as non-White and/or Muslim, when being made intelligible as both LGBTQ (included) and racialized (excluded) means becoming non-intelligible in contemporary constructions of Swedishness.

Finally, the book contributes important insights into how attempts at boundary making both draw upon and enable particular normative grids of intelligibility for what it means to be the 'right kind of queer'. It thus moves from discussions of what homonormativity and homonationalism *is* to what it *does*, particularly with regard to the LGBTQ people living their lives in various contexts marked by nationalist boundary making through LGBTQ rights. Two important contributions can be drawn from the analysis. First, constructions of nationhood and belonging through LGBTQ rights draw on binary notions of tolerant Self/LGBTQ-phobic Other, which can effectively silence violence and discrimination based on gender identity and sexuality 'at home', making it harder to address these issues. In other words, if the danger is clearly delimited as coming from 'outside', there is no need to engage with the problems LGBTQ people are experiencing 'within' normative Swedishness. Secondly, boundary-making moves rely upon making people intelligible in particular ways, thus delimiting the horizon of what can be considered 'liveable lives' within specific contexts (Butler, 2005, 2015). This is most acutely felt with regard to the negation and silencing of experiences of LGBTQ people racialized as non-White and/or Muslim, but it relates also to the silencing of discrimination within, making it even harder for those racialized as White to challenge notions of LGBTQ-friendly Swedishness. In both cases, the empirical material analysed within the context of this project can support activist claims towards a continued need for the protection and support of LGBTQ rights and LGBTQ people even within (national) contexts that are built around notions of tolerance, progress and LGBTQ-friendliness.

However, by also providing insights into how normative grids of intelligibility are challenged, negotiated and manoeuvred, *particularly* by LGBTQ people racialized as non-White and/or Muslim, this book opens up space for a broader discussion of the instability of attempts at boundary making. Herein lies the main theoretical contributions of this project. When reading the theoretical framework and empirical material together, it becomes clear that boundary-making moves and grids of intelligibility are always co-constitutive of each other. As scholars, but also as activists, this can draw our attention away from the normative power of these moves (which many previous studies have focused on) towards the various ways in which they are challenged and contested. By combining theoretical literature on politics of belonging and boundary making with queer theorists' conceptualizations of subjectivity through performative grids of intelligibility and a plural logic of and/or, this book thus makes a crucial contribution to our understanding of how attempts at boundary making never completely manage to distinguish inside from outside, Self from Other. Approaching (homo)nationalist boundary-making moves through queer understandings of the Self as enabled by grids of intelligibility thus stresses their inevitable instability.

Boundary-making moves and the grids of intelligibility they enable and draw upon may be normalizing, but they are also never *not* contested. Seeing this constant coexistence of both normative violence and the irresolvable instability of normative grids of intelligibility does not only improve our academic analyses by making them more complex. It also enhances our capacity for political and activist interventions, as it puts at the centre of the analysis those people and positionalities that have the potential to show up the norm simply by way of existing at all. It thus can guide our activist interventions to spaces where engagement is not only most needed but also most likely to be efficient in questioning normative grids of intelligibility. Within the context of this book, this has become particularly clear in relation to how LGBTQ people racialized as non-White and/or Muslim negotiate and manoeuvre the ways in which they are made intelligible as victims or non-existent (when their LGBTQ-ness is fore-fronted), and/or a threat to White LGBTQ people (when they become intelligible as the dangerous Other). I have also identified the instability of LGBTQ positionalities in processes of boundary making in the ways in which the SAF campaigns make LGBTQ people intelligible as the soldier-protectors (of Swedishness-qua-LGBTQ rights) and/or the ones in need of protection (from a distant LGBTQ-phobic Other).

Throughout, this book aims to further develop a theoretical approach that encourages and presupposes looking closely at these kinds of complexities and contradictions, in order to be able to conduct a nuanced analysis of boundary-making moves and the grids of intelligibility they enable and draw upon. I have striven to maintain and further the relevance of critical concepts such as homonationalism, homonormativity and, by extension, Swedish gender exceptionalism by creating a theoretical framework that allows us to employ them as nuanced analytical tools. Only then can they help us account for the ambiguities, contradictions and complexities that occur as some LGBTQ people become boundary markers for national(ist) projects of belonging, while others find themselves continually othered, exoticized and excluded. Only then can we find a way to turn academic analysis into activist intervention. As I discuss in Chapters 2, 3 and 4, this requires both theoretical expansions and a renewed focus on some central aspects of the original concepts, most pressingly issues of racialization. Racialization variously positions people with regard to, for example, the access to civil rights that comes about when LGBTQ rights become part of national – and even international – boundary making. This means simple binary narratives of homonationalism (and, in this particular context, Swedish gender exceptionalism) as 'bad politics' which are to be rejected miss the mark. Instead of creating accounts of 'bad' and 'good' LGBTQ activism, we need to continue to deconstruct complex power relations and pay attention to the complex ways in which the individual and collective ability to want or 'not want' access to rights and recognition varies widely. It includes acknowledging how certain individuals and groups are more susceptible to the risks associated with not being included in the 'gay-rights-as-human-rights' discourses. This has implications not only for individual 'liveable lives'; it also impacts the potential for different kinds of collective LGBTQ activism and mobilization in any given context. New backlashes against LGBTQ rights as well as sexual and reproductive rights across the globe (including in countries previously considered 'LGBTQ-friendly') question the possibility for 'liveable lives' even for the most privileged among us. Fights for legal rights and protections will therefore have to continue to go hand in hand with our most nuanced critiques of these kinds of systems of recognition in all their homonationalist forms. At the same time, queer and feminist calls to arm Ukraine in the fight against Russian invasion and neo-imperialism point towards situations in which military protection as promised by SAF advertising is a precondition not only for specific kinds of 'liveable lives' but for any life at all. In light of the contributions made by this book, this complexity of positionalities and contexts remains one of the main challenges with regard to researching nationalist boundary making in relation to LGBTQ rights.

Continuing the conversation: ways ahead

Notwithstanding the changing political landscapes for LGBTQ people in Europe and beyond, there remains a need to engage critically with constructions of (non-)belonging in relation to notions of LGBTQ-friendliness and how they affect the lives of those who challenge normative notions of Whiteness, heterosexuality and binary cis-gender. Three main avenues of further research seem particularly relevant and urgent at this point.

First, my critique of boundary-making processes, and the inclusions/exclusions accompanying them, needs to be developed by looking more closely at the lived experiences of LGBTQ people. This includes those racialized as non-White and/or Muslim, but also those who might be excluded from constructions of belonging for other reasons. This book reads boundary making around LGBTQ rights through a particular lens focusing on *racialized* Othering, thus neglecting additional ways in which Othering might occur in relation to LGBTQ rights. What kinds of normative grids of intelligibility do people experience with regard to notions of being 'too queer'? Where do, for example, the boundaries of LGBTQ-friendliness go with regard to normative notions of romantic relationships and parenting? How do normative notions of (dis)ability play into who becomes intelligible as the 'right kind of queer'? While some work on these issues has been done (Rydström, 2012; Mery Karlsson, 2020; Dahl and Andreassen, 2021), there remains great need and potential for a continued critical engagement with various notions of nationhood and belonging as defined through LGBTQ rights and how these notions are experienced and manoeuvred by LGBTQ people. In the Swedish contexts, this is particularly true with regard to the experience of LGBTQ people within indigenous Sámi communities, whose lives play out in a specific (post)colonial context in relation to historical and contemporary constructions of nationhood and belonging. Additionally, the arrival of Ukrainian refugees since 2022 has further complicated processes of externalization via racialization, as this group's Whiteness is contingent in similar ways to those coming from the Balkans during the 1990s (Odynets, 2022; Palmgren et al, 2023).

An additional area in which more research around notions of Swedish gender/LGBTQ exceptionalism seems both feasible and necessary concerns the international geopolitical implications of these constructions, not least because the political landscape in Sweden has become more conservative one since 2022. While this book has turned its focus almost exclusively towards the domestic arena (apart from some cursory references), there remains a need to examine how constructions of Swedishness as 'a good place to be queer' play out on an international stage. To what extent are these notions employed by other countries or international actors, both as a counter-example and as a model to strive for? What role do countries like Sweden play in the eyes of other international actors with regard to LGBTQ rights? And how does the Swedish bid to abandon notions of neutrality and join NATO change that role? Edenborg et al have started down this research path (Hedling et al, 2022; Rosamond and Hedling, 2022; Edenborg, 2023; Eduards and Jansson, 2023), and as countries like Russia, Brazil and the United States have steered variously towards anti-LGBTQ politics, Sweden's and other countries' international image as defenders of LGBTQ rights provides continued potential for important analysis.

Finally, and potentially closest to my heart as a researcher who is also an LGBTQ activist, there is an urgent need for an analysis of what I call 'the homophobic Other within'. Even here, the overall shift in political direction, in Sweden and beyond, has only increased this need. As indicated in Chapter 5 on research methods, contestations of and reactions to homonationalist statements by both the SAF and around Pride Järva were not part of my analysis for various reasons. This book has therefore focused mostly on attempts at (homo)nationalist boundary making, neglecting the aspect of contestation and debate. However, it remains crucially important to investigate the ways in which symbols like the rainbow flag or public statements in defence of LGBTQ rights evoke virulent LGBTQ-phobia 'in the comment sections', be it in right-wing online forums or in a response to SAF campaign material. Additionally, the arrival of the Sweden Democrats on the political main stage in 2022 means that anti-LGBTQ statements are no longer confined to the comment sections, as emerging research shows (Lagerman, 2023a, 2023b).

The ways in which notions of Sweden as a safe place for LGBTQ people to live in neglect to engage with the existence of these voices, instead projecting homo- and transphobia on to distant Others and racialized bodies, is not only racist; it is also dangerous. It erases the hatred towards and continued discrimination of LGBTQ people expressed in these statements. This is particularly important because recent years have seen a (renewed) presence of anti-gender movements within the country, mobilizing around questions such as the status of gender studies as a field of research, the right to abortion and transgender youths' access to gender-reaffirming medical care (Martinsson, 2020; Selberg, 2020; Norocel et al, 2022), as well as a political mainstream moving towards more conservative values. Further research which engages with these 'native' challengers to notions of Swedish gender/LGBTQ exceptionalism would therefore be of great value for both the academic and political debate.

Across the globe, normative notions of sexuality and gender continue to feature prominently in national narratives about (non-)belonging, with processes of racialization playing a crucial role in making LGBTQ people variously intelligible as 'right' or 'wrong' kinds of queers. Carving out liveable queer lives for ourselves in this situation might require, if nothing else, an acute awareness of the many ambiguities and contingencies that undermine *any* absolute claim to coherence of such attempts at delineating belonging.

References

Ackerly, B., Stern, M. and True, J. (eds) (2006) *Feminist Methodologies for International Relations*, Cambridge: Cambridge University Press.

Adelson, L.A. (2005) *The Turkish Turn in Contemporary German Literature: Toward a New Critical Grammar of Migration*, New York: Palgrave Macmillan.

Adler-Nissen, R., Andersen, K.E. and Hansen, L. (2020) 'Images, emotions, and international politics: the death of Alan Kurdi', *Review of International Studies*, 46(1): 75–95. DOI: 10.1017/S0260210519000317

Aggestam, K. and Bergman-Rosamond, A. (2016) 'Swedish feminist foreign policy in the making: Ethics, politics, and gender', *Ethics and International Affairs*, 30(3): 323–34. DOI: 10.1017/S0892679416000241

Aggestam, K., Bergman Rosamond, A. and Kronsell, A. (2019) 'Theorising feminist foreign policy', *International Relations*, 33(1): 23–39. DOI: 10.1177/0047117818811892

Agius, C. (2013) *The Social Construction of Swedish Neutrality*, Manchester: Manchester University Press. DOI: 10.7765/9781847791993.

Agius, C. and Edenborg, E. (2019) 'Gendered bordering practices in Swedish and Russian foreign and security policy', *Political Geography*, 71: 56–66. DOI: 10.1016/j.polgeo.2019.02.012

Ahlstedt, S. (2016) 'The feeling of migration: narratives of queer intimacies and partner migration', PhD Thesis. Institute for Research on Migration, Ethnicity and Society (REMESO) at the Department of Social and Welfare Studies, Linköping University.

Ahmed, S. (2004a) 'Affective economies', *Social Text*, 22(2): 117–39.

Ahmed, S. (2004b) 'Declarations of Whiteness: the non-performativity of anti-racism', *Borderlands*, 3(2): 1–14.

Ahmed, S. (2004c) *The Cultural Politics of Emotion*, New York: Routledge.

Ahmed, S. (2006) 'The nonperformativity of antiracism', *Meridians: Feminism, Race, Transnationalism*, 7(1): 104–26. DOI: 10.2979/MER.2006.7.1.104

Ahmed, S. (2007a) 'A phenomenology of Whiteness', *Feminist Theory*, 8(2): 149–68. DOI: 10.1177/1464700107078139

Ahmed, S. (2007b) 'The language of diversity', *Ethnic and Racial Studies*, 30(2): 235–56. DOI: 10.1080/01419870601143927

REFERENCES

Ahmed, S. (2009) 'Embodying diversity: problems and paradoxes for Black feminists', *Race Ethnicity and Education*, 12(1): 41–52. DOI: 10.1080/13613320802650931

Ahmed, S. (2014) 'Mixed orientations', *Subjectivity*, 7(1): 92–109. DOI: 10.1057/sub.2013.22

Åkesson, J. and Herrstedt, C. (2010) SD – ett parti för hbt-personer. Aftonbladet, 30 March. Available from: http://www.aftonbladet.se/debatt/debattamnen/jamstalldhet/article12256370.ab [Accessed 16 October 2016].

Akin, D. (2019) 'Discursive construction of genuine LGBT refugees', *Lambda Nordica*, 23(3–4): 21–46. DOI: 10.34041/ln.v23.549

Alinia, M. (2020) 'White ignorance, race, and feminist politics in Sweden', *Ethnic and Racial Studies*, 43(16): 249–67. DOI: 10.1080/01419870.2020.1775861

Alm, E. and Martinsson, L. (2016) 'The rainbow flag as friction: transnational, imagined communities of belonging among Pakistani LGBTQ activists', *Culture Unbound*, 8(3): 218–39. DOI: 10.3384/cu.2000.1525.1683218

Alm, E., Berg, L., Hero, M.L., Johansson, A., Laskar, P., Martinsson, L. et al (eds) (2021) *Pluralistic Struggles in Gender, Sexuality and Coloniality*, Cham: Springer International. DOI: 10.1007/978-3-030-47432-4

Altay, T. (2022) 'The pink line across digital publics: political homophobia and the queer strategies of everyday life during COVID-19 in Turkey', *European Journal of Women's Studies*, 29(1_suppl): 60S–74S. DOI: 10.1177/13505068221076329

Altay, T. (2023) 'Translating difference: Whiteness, racialisation and queer migration in Berlin', *European Journal of Politics and Gender*, 7(1): 27–44. DOI: 10.1332/25151088Y2023D000000012

Altermark, N. and Edenborg, E. (2018) 'Visualizing the included subject: photography, progress narratives and intellectual disability', *Subjectivity*, 11(4): 287–302. DOI: 10.1057/s41286-018-0057-y

Andersen, A., Hvenegård-Lassen, K. and Knobblock, I. (2015) 'Feminism in postcolonial Nordic spaces', *NORA: Nordic Journal of Feminist and Gender Research*, 23(4): 239–45. DOI: 10.1080/08038740.2015.1104596

Anderson, B. (1991) *Imagined Communities: Reflections on the Origin and Spread of Nationalism*, New York: Verso.

Andreassen, R. (2020) 'Social media surveillance, LGBTQ refugees and asylum', *First Monday*, 26(1). DOI: 10.5210/fm.v26i1.10653

Andreassen, R. and Vitus, K. (eds) (2015) *Affectivity and Race: Studies from Nordic Contexts*, Burlington, VT: Ashgate.

Anthias, F. and Yuval-Davis, N. (1992) *Racialized Boundaries: Race, Nation, Gender, Colour and Class and the Antiracist Struggle*, London: Routledge.

Avpixlat (2016) 'Jan Sjunnesson talar på Järva PRIDE 2016', Avpixlat (YouTube channel), Available from: https://www.youtube.com/watch?v=nbuyeOXNI7w&t=176s [Accessed 1 August 2016].

Axbom, P. (2021) 'Försvarsmakten och flaggan', Available from: https://axbom.se/forsvarsmakten-och-flaggan/ [Accessed 12 October 2021].

Bacchetta, P. (2010) 'Decolonial praxis: enabling intranational and queer coalition building', *Qui Parle: Critical Humanities and Social Sciences*, 18(2): 147–92. DOI: 10.1353/qui.0.0021

Bacchetta, P. (2017) 'Murderous conditions and LTQ + POC decolonial, anti-capitalist and anti-misogyny life imaginings in France', *lambda nordica*, 22(2–3): 153–73.

Baker, C. (2017) 'The "gay Olympics"? The Eurovision Song Contest and the politics of LGBT/European belonging', *European Journal of International Relations*, 23(1): 97–121. DOI: 10.1177/1354066116633278.

Baker, C. (2019) '"If love was a crime, we would be criminals": the Eurovision Song Contest and the queer international politics of flags', in J. Kalman, B. Wellings and K. Jacotine (eds) *Eurovisions: Identity and the International Politics of the Eurovision Song Contest since 1956*, Singapore: Palgrave Macmillan, pp 175–200. DOI: 10.1007/978-981-13-9427-0_9

Baker, C. (2021) 'The contingencies of Whiteness: gendered/racialized global dynamics of security narratives', *Security Dialogue*, 52(1): 124–32. DOI: 10.1177/09670106211024408

Baker, C. (2022) '"Can I be gay in the army?": British army recruitment advertising to LGBTQ youth in 2017–18 and belonging in the queer military home', *Critical Military Studies*, 9(3): 442–61. DOI: 10.1080/23337486.2022.2113960

Balibar, E. and Wallerstein, I.M. (1991) *Race, Nation, Class: Ambiguous Identities*, London: Verso. DOI: 10.3892/mmr.2011.655

Barglowski, K., Amelina, A. and Bilecen, B. (2018) 'Coming out within transnational families: intimate confessions under Western eyes', *Social Identities*, 24(6): 836–51. DOI: 10.1080/13504630.2017.1310041

Barthes, R. (1973) *Mythologies*, London: Paladin.

Barthes, R. (1974) *S/Z*, Paris: Blackwell.

Basham, V.M. and Vaughan-Williams, N. (2013) 'Gender, race and border security practices: a profane reading of "muscular liberalism"', *British Journal of Politics and International Relations*, 15(4): 509–27. DOI: 10.1111/j.1467-856X.2012.00517.x

Bazeley, P. (2013) *Qualitative Data Analysis: Practical Strategies*, London: Sage.

Belkin, A. (2012) *Bring Me Men: Military Masculinity and the Benign Facade of American Empire, 1898–2001*, London: Hurst.

Bergman Rosamond, A. (2020) 'Swedish feminist foreign policy and "gender cosmopolitanism"', *Foreign Policy Analysis*, 16(2): 217–35. DOI: 10.1093/fpa/orz025

Bhaba, H. (1994) *The Location of Culture*, New York: Routledge.

Bjerknes, C. (2023) 'Queer narratives in Nordic Sami literature: coming-out narratives and final exposures in Savior of the Lost Children (2008) and Himlabrand (2021)', *NORA: Nordic Journal of Feminist and Gender Research*, 31(2): 195–205. DOI: 10.1080/08038740.2023.2207040

Bleiker, R. (2015) 'Pluralist methods for visual global politics', *Millennium: Journal of International Studies*, 43(3): 872–90. DOI: 10.1177/0305829815583084

Bleiker, R. (2018a) 'Mapping visual global politics', in R. Bleiker (ed) *Visual Global Politics*, Abingdon: Routledge, pp 1–29. DOI: 10.4324/9781315856506

Bleiker, R. (ed) (2018b) *Visual Global Politics*, Abingdon: Routledge, 2018. DOI: 10.4324/9781315856506

Bleiker, R. (2019) 'Writing visual global politics: in defence of a pluralist approach; a response to Gabi Schlag, "Thinking and writing visual global politics"', *International Journal of Politics, Culture and Society*, 32(1): 115–23. DOI: 10.1007/s10767-018-9299-5

Bosia, M.J. (2020) 'Global sexual diversity politics and the trouble with LGBT rights', in M.J. Bosia, S.M. McEvoy and M. Rahman (eds) *The Oxford Handbook of Global LGBT and Sexual Diversity Politics*, Oxford: Oxford University Press, pp 432–49. DOI: 10.1093/oxfordhb/9780190673741.013.22.

Boulila, S.C. and Browne, K. (2023) 'Heteroactivism, homonationalism and national projects', *ACME: An International Journal for Critical Geographies*, 22(3): 1015–24.

Bracke, S. (2012) 'From "saving women" to "saving gays": rescue narratives and their dis/continuities', *European Journal of Women's Studies*, 19(2): 237–52. DOI: 10.1177/1350506811435032

Braidotti, R. (2002) 'Identity, subjectivity and difference: a critical genealogy', in G. Griffin and R. Braidotti (eds) *Thinking Differently: A Reader in European Women's Studies*, London: Zed Books, pp 158–81.

Breitbart News (2016a) 'Breitbart's Milo to lead gay pride march through Swedish Muslim ghetto', 26 June, Available from: http://www.breitbart.com/milo/2016/06/26/milo-to-lead-gay-pride-march-through-muslim-ghetto-sweden/ [Accessed 1 August 2016].

Breitbart News (2016b) 'Breitbart News cancels Milo Yiannopoulos appearance at Swedish gay pride march', 25 July. Available from: http://www.breitbart.com/milo/2016/07/25/milos-gay-pride-march-in-sweden-cancelled-after-threat-revealed/ [Accessed 1 August 2016].

Brock, M. (2023) 'The necropolitics of Russia's traditional family values', *Lambda Nordica*, 27(3–4): 173–8. DOI: 10.34041/ln.v27.840

Brock, M. and Edenborg, E. (2020) '"You cannot oppress those who do not exist"', *GLQ: A Journal of Lesbian and Gay Studies*, 26(4): 673–700. DOI: 10.1215/10642684-8618730

Brovold, M. (2023) 'Sámi feminism and activism in Ann-Helén Laestadius' novel Stöld', *NORA: Nordic Journal of Feminist and Gender Research*, 31(2): 184–94. DOI: 10.1080/08038740.2023.2214376

Brown, L. and Strega, S. (eds) (2005) *Research as Resistance: Critical, Indigenous, & Anti-oppressive Approaches*, Toronto: Canadian Scholars' Press/Women's Press.

Brown, W. (2006) *Regulating Aversion: Tolerance in an Age of Identity and Empire*, Princeton: Princeton University Press.

Browne, K. and Nash, C. (eds) (2016) *Queer Methods and Methodologies: Intersecting Queer Theories and Social Science Research*, New York: Routledge. DOI: 10.1002/9781118663219.wbegss229

Bulmer, S. (2013) 'Patriarchal confusion?', *International Feminist Journal of Politics*, 15(2): 137–56. DOI: 10.1080/14616742.2012.746565

Buruma, I. (2009) 'Parade's end: Dutch liberals get tough', *New Yorker*, 29 December, Available from: www.newyorker.com/magazine/2009/12/07/parades-end-2

Butler, J. (1988) 'Performative acts and gender constitution: an essay in phenomenology and feminist theory', *Theatre Journal*, 40(4): 519–531. DOI: 10.2307/3207893

Butler, J. (1990) *Gender Trouble: Feminism and the Subversion of Identity*, New York: Routledge.

Butler, J. (1993) 'Gender is burning: questions of appropriation and subversion', in *Bodies That Matter: On the Discursive Limits of Sex*, New York: Routledge, pp 121–41.

Butler, J. (1997) *Excitable Speech: A Politics of the Performative*, New York: Routledge.

Butler, J. (1999) *Gender Trouble: Feminism and the Subversion of Identity*, New York: Routledge.

Butler, J. (2004) *Undoing Gender*, New York: Routledge.

Butler, J. (2005) 'On being beside oneself: on the limits of sexual autonomy', in N. Bamforth (ed) *Sex Rights: The Oxford Amnesty Lectures 2002*, Oxford: Oxford University Press, pp 48–78.

Butler, J. (2008) 'Sexual politics, torture, and secular time', *The British Journal of Sociology*, 59(1): 1–23. DOI: 10.1111/j.1468-4446.2007.00176.x

Butler, J. (2009) 'Performativity, precarity and sexual politics', *AIBR Revista de Antropologia Iberoamericana*, 4(3): 1–23. DOI: 10.1111/j.1468-4446.2007.00176.x

Butler, J. (2010) *Frames of War: When Is Life Grievable?*, New York: Verso.

Butler, J. (2011) *Bodies That Matter: On the Discursive Limits of 'Sex'*, Abingdon: Routledge.

Butler, J. (2015) *Notes towards a Performative Theory of Assembly*, Cambridge, MA: Harvard University Press.

REFERENCES

Butler, J. and Athanasiou, A. (2013) *Dispossession: The Performative in the Political*, Malden, MA: Polity.

Butler, J. and Spivak, G.C. (2010) *Who Sings the Nation State? Language, Politics, Belonging*, London: Seagull Books.

Çağatay, S., Liinason, M. and Sasunkevich, O. (eds) (2022) *Feminist and LGBTI+ Activism across Russia, Scandinavia and Turkey: Transnationalizing Spaces of Resistance*, Cham: Palgrave Macmillan.

Campbell, D. (1998) *Writing Security* (2nd edn), Minneapolis: Minnesota University Press.

Carlsson, J. (2015) 'Försvarsmakten hade prideflagga som profilbild på Facebook – tog sedan bort den', Nyheter24, Available from: https://nyheter24.se/nyheter/internet/804816-forsvarsmakten-hade-prideflagga-som-profilbild-pa-facebook-tog-sedan-bort-den [Accessed 27 September 2020].

Christensen, C. (2013) '@Sweden: curating a nation on Twitter', *Popular Communication*, 11(1): 30–46. DOI: 10.1080/15405702.2013.751855

Cohen, C.J. (1997) 'Punks, bulldaggers, and welfare queens: the radical potential of queer politics?', *GLQ: A Journal of Lesbian and Gay Studies*, 3(4): 437–65.

Collins, P.H. (2009) *Black Feminist Thought: Knowledge, Consciousness, and the Politics of Empowerment* (2nd edn), New York: Routledge.

Collins, P.H. (2015) 'Intersectionality's definitional dilemmas', *Annual Review of Sociology*, 41(1): 1–20. DOI: 10.1146/annurev-soc-073014-112142

Colyar, J. (2009) 'Becoming writing, becoming writers', *Qualitative Inquiry*, 15(2): 421–36. DOI: 10.1177/1077800408318280

Conrad, R. (ed) (2014) *Against Equality: Queer Revolution, Not Mere Inclusion*, Oakland: AK Press.

Cuesta, M. and Mulinari, D. (2018) 'The bodies of others in Swedish feminism', *Gender, Place & Culture*, 25(7): 978–93. DOI: 10.1080/0966369X.2018.1435510

Dagerlind M (2015) Fega HBTQ-hycklare borde la° ta den rosa PRIDE-champagnen tysta munnen. Avpixlat.se, 27 June. Available from: http://avpixlat.info/2015/07/27/fega-hbtq- hycklare-borde-lata-den-rosa-pride-champagnen-tysta-munnen/ [accessed 16 September 2016].

Dahl, U. (2011) 'Queer in the Nordic region: telling queer (feminist) stories', in L. Downing and R. Gillett (eds) *Queer in Europe: Contemporary Case Studies*, London: Ashgate, pp 143–57.

Dahl, U. (2017) 'Becoming fertile in the land of organic milk: lesbian and queer reproductions of femininity and motherhood in Sweden', *Sexualities*, 21(7): 1021–38. DOI: 10.1177/1363460717718509

Dahl, U. (2018) '(The promise of) monstrous kinship? Queer reproduction and the somatechnics of sexual and racial difference', *Somatechnics*, 8(2): 195–211. DOI: 10.3366/soma.2018.0250.

Dahl, U. (2021) 'Nordic academic feminism and Whiteness as epistemic habit', in S. Keskinen, P. Stoltz and D. Mulinari (eds) *Feminisms in the Nordic Region*, Cham: Springer International, pp 87–100. DOI: 10.1007/978-3-030-53464-6_13

Dahl, U. and Andreassen, R. (2021) 'Donors we choose: race, nation and the biopolitics of (queer) assisted reproduction in Scandinavia', *BioSocieties*, 18(1): 79–101, Available from: https://doi.org/10.1057/s41292-021-00256-2

Dahl, U. and Gabb, J. (2019) 'Trends in contemporary queer kinship and family', *Lambda Nordica*, 24(2–3): 209–37.

Dankertsen, A. (2019) 'I felt so White: Sámi racialization, indigeneity, and shades of Whiteness', *Native American and Indigenous Studies*, 6(2): 110–37, Available from: DOI: 10.5749/natiindistudj.6.2.0110

Dankertsen, A. (2021) 'Indigenising Nordic feminism: a Sámi decolonial critique', in S. Keskinen, P. Stoltz and D. Mulinari (eds) *Feminisms in the Nordic Region*, Cham: Springer International, pp 135–54.

DasGupta, D. and Dasgupta, R.K. (2018) 'Being out of place: non-belonging and queer racialization in the U.K.', *Emotion, Space and Society*, 27(September): 31–8. DOI: 10.1016/j.emospa.2018.02.008

De los Reyes, P. and Mulinari, D. (2020) 'Hegemonic feminism revisited: on the promises of intersectionality in times of the precarisation of life', *NORA: Nordic Journal of Feminist and Gender Research*, 28(3): 183–96. DOI: 10.1080/08038740.2019.1705905

De los Reyes, P., Molina, I. and Mulinari, D. (eds) (2002) *Maktens (olika) förklädnader: kön, klass & etnicitet i det postkoloniala Sverige*, Stockholm: Atlas.

De Saussure, F. (1974) *A Course in General Linguistics*, London: Fontana.

Derrida, J. (1978) *Writing and Difference*, London: Routledge & Kegan Paul.

Dhawan, N. (2013) 'The empire prays back: religion, secularity, and queer critique', *Boundary 2*, 40(1): 191–222. DOI: 10.1215/01903659-2072918

Dhawan, N. (2016) 'Homonationalism and state-phobia: the postcolonial predicament of queering modernities', in M.A. Viteri and M. Lavinas Picq (eds) *Queering Paradigms V: Queering Narratives of Modernity*, Oxford: Peter Lang, pp 51–68.

Dolan, E. and Danilova, N. (2023) '"To those who choose to follow in our footsteps": making women/LGBT+ soldiers (in)visible through feminist "her-story" theater', *International Feminist Journal of Politics*, 25(3): 434–60. DOI: 10.1080/14616742.2022.2097936

Duggan, L. (2002) 'The new homonormativity: the sexual politics of neoliberalism', in D. Nelson and R. Castronova (eds) *Materializing Democracy: Toward a Revitalized Cultural Politics*, Durham: Duke University Press, pp 175–94.

Duncanson, C. (2015) 'Hegemonic masculinity and the possibility of change in gender relations', *Men and Masculinities*, 18(2): 231–48. DOI: 10.1177/1097184X15584912

Dyer, R. (2005) 'The matter of Whiteness', in P. Rothenberg (ed) *White Privilege: Essential Readings on the Other Side of Racism*, New York: Worth Publishers, pp 9–14.

Edenborg, E. (2016) 'Nothing more to see: contestations of belonging and visibility in Russian media', PhD thesis, Lund University, Malmö University, Available fromn: http://lup.lub.lu.se/record/8840122

Edenborg, E. (2020a) 'Endangered Swedish values: immigration, gender equality, and "migrants' sexual violence"', in O.C. Norocel, A. Hellström and M.B. Jørgensen (eds) *Nostalgia and Hope: Intersections between Politics of Culture, Welfare, and Migration in Europe*, Cham: Springer, pp 101–17. DOI: 10.1007/978-3-030-41694-2

Edenborg, E. (2020b) 'Russia's spectacle of "traditional values": rethinking the politics of visibility', *International Feminist Journal of Politics*, 22(1): 106–26. DOI: 10.1080/14616742.2018.1560227

Edenborg, E. (2020c) 'Saving women and bordering Europe: narratives of "migrants' sexual violence" and geopolitical imaginaries in Russia and Sweden', *Geopolitics*, 25(3): 780–801. DOI: 10.1080/14650045.2018.1465045

Edenborg, E. (2020d) 'Visibility in global queer politics', in M.J. Bosia, S.M. McEvoy and M. Rahman (eds) *The Oxford Handbook of Global LGBT and Sexual Diversity Politics*, Oxford: Oxford University Press, pp 348–63. DOI: 10.1093/oxfordhb/9780190673741.001.0001

Edenborg, E. (2023) '"Traditional values" and the narrative of gay rights as modernity: sexual politics beyond polarization', *Sexualities*, 26(1–2): 37–53. DOI: 10.1177/13634607211008067

Edkins, J. and Pin-Fat, V. (1999) 'Introduction: the subject of the political', in J. Edkins, N. Persram and V. Pin-Fat (eds) *Sovereignty and Subjectivity*, London: Lynne Rienner, pp 1–18.

Eduards, M. and Jansson, M. (2023) 'KÖN, HETEROSEXUALITET OCH (O) TRYGGHET En feministisk analys av svenska säkerhetsdebatter i skuggan av kriget i Ukraina', *Tidskrift för genusvetenskap*, 43(2–3): 37–60. DOI: 10.55870/tgv.v43i2-3.8446

El-Tayeb, F. (2008) '"The birth of a European public": migration, postnationality, and race in the uniting of Europe', *American Quarterly*, 60(3): 649–70. DOI: 10.1353/aq.0.0024

El-Tayeb, F. (2011) *European Others: Queering Ethnicity in Postnational Europe*, Minneapolis: University of Minnesota Press.

El-Tayeb, F. (2012) '"Gays who cannot properly be gay": queer Muslims in the neoliberal European city', *European Journal of Women's Studies*, 19(1): 79–95. DOI: 10.1177/1350506811426388

El-Tayeb, F., Haritaworn, J. and Bacchetta, P. (2015) 'Queer of colour formations and translocal spaces in Europe', *Environment and Planning D: Society and Space*, 33(5): 769–78. DOI: 10.1177/0263775815608712

Elsner, R. (2019) 'New wave of persecutions against LGBTI★ people in Chechnya', ZOiS Spotlight, Available from: https://www.zois-berlin.de/en/publications/zois-spotlight/archiv-2019/new-wave-of-persecutions-against-lgbti-people-in-chechnya [Accessed 14 September 2020].

Erdem, E., Haritaworn, J. and Tauqir, T. (2008) 'Gay imperialism: the role of gender and sexuality discourses in the "War on Terror"', in A. Kuntsman and E. Miyake (eds) *Out of Place: Interrogating Silences in Queerness/Raciality*, York: Raw Nerve Books, pp 71–95.

Eriksson, T. (2014) 'Jag utmanar starka krafter', *Dagens Samhälle*, 30 October, Available from: http://www.dagenssamhalle.se/nyhet/jag-utmanar-starka-krafter-11659

Essed, P. (1996) *Diversity: Gender, Color, and Culture*, Amherst: University of Massachusetts Press.

Fabian, J. (1983) *Time and the Other: How Anthropology Makes Its Object*, New York: Columbia University Press.

Fanon, F. (1967) *Black Skin, White Masks*, New York: Grove Press.

Försvarsmakten (2020) 'Varför deltar försvarsmakten i Pride?', Available from: https://www.facebook.com/forsvarsmakten/photos/a.287926437898544/3467355946622228/?type=3 [Accessed 3 March 2021].

Foucault, M. (1977) *Discipline and Punish: The Birth of the Prison*, edited and translated by A. Sheridan, New York: Pantheon.

Foucault, M. (1978) *The History of Sexuality: Volume 1; An Introduction*, New York: Pantheon.

Gerbaudo, P. (2018) 'Social media and populism: an elective affinity?', *Media, Culture and Society*, 40(5): 745–53. DOI: 10.1177/0163443718772192

Gilroy, P. (1993) *The Black Atlantic: Modernity and Double Consciousness*, Cambridge, MA: Harvard University Press.

Gilroy, P. (2006) 'Colonial crimes and convivial cultures', Rethinking Nordic Colonialism, pp 1–9. DOI: 10.1080/17448689.2015.1045698

Girma, S. and Atto, J. (2017) 'Black queers Sweden', *lambda nordica*, 22(2–3): 174–5.

Goldberg, D.T. (2006) 'Racial Europeanization', *Ethnic and Racial Studies*, 29(2): 331–64. DOI: 10.1080/01419870500465611

Göteborgs Posten (2016) 'Pride Järva: Sverigevänner får också fira Pride', 27 July.

Graff, A. (2022) 'Solidarity with Ukraine, or: why East–West still matters to feminism', *Gender Studies*, 26(1): 57–61.

Graff, A. and Korolczuk, E. (2021) *Anti-gender Politics in the Populist Moment*, London: Routledge. DOI: 10.4324/9781003133520

Gray, H. (2022) 'Disparities and diversification: feminists in Europe study war and/or militaries', in M. Stern and A. Towns (eds) *Feminist IR in Europe*, Palgrave Macmillan, pp 9–32.

Gray, M.L. (2009) 'Negotiating identities/queering desires: coming out online and the remediation of the coming-out story', *Journal of Computer-Mediated Communication*, 14(4): 1162–89. DOI: 10.1111/j.1083-6101.2009.01485.x

Grosfoguel, R., Oso, L. and Christou, A. (2015) '"Racism", intersectionality and migration studies: framing some theoretical reflections', *Identities*, 22(6): 635–52. DOI: 10.1080/1070289X.2014.950974

Habel, Y. (2012) 'Challenging Swedish exceptionalism? Teaching while Black', in K. Freeman and E. Johnson (eds) *Education in the Black Diaspora: Perspectives, Challenges, and Prospects*, London: Routledge, pp 99–122. DOI: 10.4324/9780203152973

Hagerlid, M. (2023) 'Discursive constructions of race and gender in racial hate crime targeting women in Sweden', *NORA: Nordic Journal of Feminist and Gender Research*, 31(1): 49–61. DOI: 10.1080/08038740.2022.2076738

Halberstam, J. (1998) *Female Masculinity*, Durham: Duke University Press.

Halberstam, J. (2011) *The Queer Art of Failure*, Durham: Duke University Press. DOI: 10.1215/9780822394358

Hall, S. (1990) 'Cultural identity and diaspora', in J. Rutherford (ed) *Identity: Community, Culture, Difference*, London: Lawrence & Wishart, pp 222–37.

Hall, S. (1992) 'The West and the rest: discourse and power', in S. Hall and B. Gieben (eds) *Formations of Modernity*, Cambridge, MA: Polity Press, pp 275–32.

Hall, S. (1996) 'Introduction: who needs identity?', in S. Hall and P. Du Gay (eds) *Questions of Cultural Identity*, London: Sage, pp 1–17.

Hall, S. (1997a) *Representation: Cultural Representations and Signifying Practices*, London: Sage.

Hall, S. (1997b) 'The spectacle of the other', in S. Hall (ed) *Representation: Cultural Representation and Signifying Practices*, London: Sage, pp 225–79. DOI: 10.1017/S0964028299310168

Hall, S. (2021) 'Race, the floating signifier', in P. Gilroy and R.W. Gilmore (eds) *Selected Writings on Race and Difference*, Durham: Duke University Press, pp 359–73. DOI: 10.2307/j.ctv1hhj1b9.23

Hall, S. and Gieben, B. (1992) *Formations of Modernity*, Cambridge: Polity Press.

Halpin, Z.T. (1989) 'Scientific objectivity and the concept of "the other"', *Women's Studies International Forum*, 12(3): 285–94. DOI: 10.1016/S0277-5395(89)80006-8

Han, C.S. (2007) 'They don't want to cruise your type: gay men of color and the racial politics of exclusion', *Social Identities*, 13(1): 51–67. DOI: 10.1080/13504630601163379

Hansen, L. (2011a) 'The politics of securitization and the Muhammad cartoon crisis: a post-structuralist perspective', *Security Dialogue*, 42(4–5): 357–69. DOI: 10.1177/0967010611418999

Hansen, L. (2011b) 'Theorizing the image for security studies: visual securitization and the Muhammad cartoon crisis', *European Journal of International Relations*, 17(1): 51–74. DOI: 10.1177/1354066110388593

Hansen, L. (2015) 'How images make world politics: international icons and the case of Abu Ghraib', *Review of International Studies*, 41(2): 263–88. DOI: 10.1017/S0260210514000199

Hansen, L. (2018) 'Images and international security', in A. Gheciu and W.C. Wohlforth (eds) *The Oxford Handbook of International Security*, Oxford: Oxford University Press, pp 592–606. DOI: 10.1093/oxfordhb/9780198777854.013.39

Hansen, L., Adler-Nissen, R. and Andersen, K.E. (2021) 'The visual international politics of the European refugee crisis: tragedy, humanitarianism, borders', *Cooperation and Conflict*, 56(4): 367–93. DOI: 10.1177/0010836721989363.

Haraway, D.J. (1988) 'Situated knowledges: the science question in feminism and the privilege of partial perspective', *Feminist Studies*, 14(3): 575–99. DOI: 10.2307/3178066

Haraway, D.J. (1994) 'A game of cat's cradle: science studies, feminist theory, cultural studies', *Configurations*, 2(1): 59–71. DOI: 10.1353/con.1994.0009

Haritaworn, J. (2010) 'Queer injuries: the racial politics of "homophobic hate crime" in Germany', *Social Justice*, 37(1): 69–89. DOI: 10.2307/41336936

Haritaworn, J. (2012) 'Women's rights, gay rights and anti-Muslim racism in Europe: introduction', *European Journal of Women's Studies*, 19(1): 73–8. DOI: 10.1177/1350506811426384

Haritaworn, J. (2015) *Queer Lovers and Hateful Others: Regenerating Violent Times and Places*, London: Pluto Press.

Haritaworn, J., Kuntsman, A. and Posocco, S. (2013) 'Murderous inclusions', *International Feminist Journal of Politics*, 15(4): 445–52. DOI: 10.1080/14616742.2013.841568

Haritaworn, J., Kuntsman, A. and Posocco, S. (eds) (2014) *Queer Necropolitics*, London: Routledge.

Hedling, E., Edenborg, E. and Strand, S. (2022) 'Embodying military muscles and a remasculinized West: influencer marketing, fantasy, and "the face of NATO"', *Global Studies Quarterly*, 2(1): 1–12. DOI: 10.1093/isagsq/ksac010

Hedlund, D. and Wimark, T. (2019) 'Unaccompanied children claiming asylum on the basis of sexual orientation and gender identity', *Journal of Refugee Studies*, 32(2): 257–77. DOI: 10.1093/jrs/fey026

Held, N. (2023) '"As queer refugees, we are out of category, we do not belong to one, or the other": LGBTIQ+ refugees' experiences in "ambivalent" queer spaces', *Ethnic and Racial Studies*, 46(9): 1898–918. DOI: 10.1080/01419870.2022.2032246

Hendl, T. (2022) 'Towards accounting for Russian imperialism and building meaningful transnational feminist solidarity with Ukraine', *Харьковский Национальный Университет Им.В.Н. Каразина*, 26: 62–90. Available from: http://kcgs.net.ua/gurnal/26/06-hendl-gs26.pdf/

Henry, M. (2017) 'Problematizing military masculinity, intersectionality and male vulnerability in feminist critical military studies', *Critical Military Studies*, 3(2): 182–99. DOI: 10.1080/23337486.2017.1325140

herising, F. (2005) 'Interrupting positions: critical thresholds and queer pro/positions', in L. Brown and S. Strega (eds) *Research as Resistance: Critical, Indigenous, and Anti-oppressive Approaches*, Toronto: Canadian Scholars' Press/Women's Press, pp 127–52.

Hesse, B. (2004) 'Im/plausible deniability: racism's conceptual double bind', *Social Identities: Journal of the Study of Race, Nation and Culture*, 10(1): 9–29.

Hiller, L.J. (2022) 'Queer asylum politics of separation in Germany: homonationalist narratives of safety', *Gender, Place and Culture*, 29(6): 858–79. DOI: 10.1080/0966369X.2021.1931048

hooks, b. (1989) 'Choosing the margin as a space of radical openness', *Framework: The Journal of Cinema and Media*, 36: 15–23, Available from: http://www.jstor.org/stable/44111660

Horton, B.A. (2018) 'What's so "queer" about coming out? Silent queers and theorizing kinship agonistically in Mumbai', *Sexualities*, 21(7): 1059–74. DOI: 10.1177/1363460717718506

Howarth, C. (2006) 'Race as stigma: positioning the stigmatized as agents, not objects', *Journal of Community & Applied Social Psychology*, 16(6): 442–51. DOI: 10.1002/casp.898

Hübinette, T. and Lundström, C. (2011) 'Sweden after the recent election: the double-binding power of Swedish Whiteness through the mourning of the loss of "old Sweden" and the passing of "good Sweden"', *NORA: Nordic Journal of Feminist and Gender Research*, 19(1): 42–52. DOI: 10.1080/08038740.2010.547835

Hübinette, T. and Lundström, C. (2023) 'White melancholia: a historicised analysis of hegemonic Whiteness in Sweden', in R. Andreassen, C. Lundström, S. Keskinen and S.A. Tate (eds) *The Routledge International Handbook of New Critical Race and Whiteness Studies*, London: Routledge, pp 308–20. DOI: 10.4324/9781003120612-31

Hübinette, T., Lundström, C. and Wikström, P. (2023) *Race in Sweden: Racism and Antiracism in the World's First 'Colourblind' Nation*, London: Routledge. DOI: 10.4324/9781003345763

Huuki, T. and Kyrölä, K. (2023) '"Show yourself": indigenous ethics, Sámi cosmologies and decolonial queer pedagogies of Frozen 2', *Gender and Education*, 35(2): 171–185. DOI: 10.1080/09540253.2021.2023112

Infowars (2016) 'Milo Yiannopoulos to hold gay pride march in "Swedish Muslim ghetto"', 27 June, 2016, Available from: http://www.infowars.com/milo-yiannopoulos-to-hold-gay-pride-march-in-swedish-muslim-ghetto [Accessed 15 November 2016].

Irani, S. (2015) '"Pride är vårt inte rasisternas"', *Feministiskt Perspektiv*, 21 July, Available from: https://feministisktperspektiv.se/2015/07/21/pride-ar-vart-inte-rasisternas/

Janoff, D. (2022) 'International relations, human rights diplomacy and LGBT rights, in *Queer Diplomacy: Homophobia, International Relations and LGBT Human Rights*, Cham: Palgrave Macmillan, pp 41–69.

Jaspal, R. and Cinnirella, M. (2012) 'Identity processes, threat, and interpersonal relations: accounts from British Muslim gay men', *Journal of Homosexuality*, 59(2): 215–40. DOI: 10.1080/00918369.2012.638551

Jezierska, K. and Towns, A. (2018) 'Taming feminism? The place of gender equality in the "progressive Sweden" brand', *Place Branding and Public Diplomacy*, 14(1): 55–63. DOI: 10.1057/s41254-017-0091-5

Jivraj, S. and de Jong, A. (2011) 'The Dutch homo-emancipation policy and its silencing effects on queer Muslims', *Feminist Legal Studies*, 19(2): 143–58. DOI: 10.1007/s10691-011-9182-5

Johansson, H. (2015) 'IRM avslöjar: Pride Järva ett evenemang skapat av homofober bakom Avpixlat', Inte rasist men, Available from: https://www.interasistmen.se/granskning/irm-avslojar-pride-jarva-ett-evenemang-skapat-av-homofober-bakom-avpixlat/ [Accessed 1 August 2016].

Jørgensen, M. and Phillips, L. (2002) *Discourse Analysis as Theory and Method*, London: Sage.

Jungar, K. and Peltonen, S. (2015) '"Saving Muslim queer women from Muslim hetero- patriarchy": savior narratives in LGBTI youth work', *NORMA: International Journal for Masculinity Studies*, 10(2): 136–49. DOI: 10.1080/18902138.2015.1050862

Jungar, K. and Peltonen, S. (2016) 'Acts of homonationalism: mapping Africa in the Swedish media', *Sexualities*, 20(5–6): 715–37. DOI: 10.1177/1363460716645806

Kahlina, K. (2015) 'Local histories, European LGBT designs: sexual citizenship, nationalism, and "Europeanisation" in post-Yugoslav Croatia and Serbia', *Women's Studies International Forum*, 49: 73–83. DOI: 10.1016/j.wsif.2014.07.006

Kapur, R. (2005) *Erotic Justice: Law and the New Politics of Postcolonialism*, London: Routledge. DOI: 10.4324/9781843146193

Kehl, K. (2020) 'Homonationalism revisited: race, rights, and queer complexities', *Lambda Nordica*, 25(2): 17–38. DOI: 10.34041/ln.v25.673

Keller, R. (2017) 'Michel Foucault', in R. Wodak and B. Forchtner (eds) *The Routledge Handbook of Language and Politics*, Abingdon: Routledge, pp 65–80. DOI: 10.4324/9781315183718

Keskinen, S., Tuori, S., Irni, S. and Mulinari, D. (eds) (2009) *Complying with Colonialism: Gender, Race and Ethnicity in the Nordic Region*, Abingdon: Routledge.

Keskinen, S., Stoltz, P. and Mulinari, D. (eds) (2021) *Feminisms in the Nordic Region*, Cham: Springer International, DOI: 10.1007/978-3-030-53464-6

Klapeer, C.M. and Laskar, P. (2018) 'Transnational ways of belonging and queer ways of being: exploring transnationalism through the trajectories of the rainbow flag', *Identities*, 25(5): 524–41. DOI: 10.1080/1070289X.2018.1507958

Klatran, H.K. (2021) 'Queer citizens and the perils of the neoliberal city: racialized narratives of homophobic hate crime in Oslo, Norway', *Sexualities*, 26(3): 261–76. DOI: 10.1177/13634607211019365

Knobblock, I. (2021) 'Att skriva från gränslandet: dekoloniala berättelser från Sábme', *Kulturella Perspektiv: Svensk Etnologisk Tidskrift*, 30(1): 1–7.

Knobblock, I. and Kuokkanen, R. (2015) 'Decolonizing feminism in the North: a conversation with Rauna Kuokkanen', *NORA: Nordic Journal of Feminist and Gender Research*, 23(4): 275–81. DOI: 10.1080/08038740.2015.1090480

Kokkola, L. and Siltanen, E. (2021) '"My hard-earned (Sámi) identity": the hard work of uncomfortable reading', *Scandinavian Studies*, 93(2): 216–40. DOI: 10.5406/scanstud.93.2.0216

Kølvraa, C. (2017) 'The discourse theory of Ernesto Laclau', in R. Wodak and B. Forchtner (eds) *The Routledge Handbook of Language and Politics*, London: Routledge, pp 49–62. DOI: 10.4324/9781315183718.ch6

Korolczuk, E. (2020a) 'Poland's LGBT-free zones and global anti-gender campaigns', ZOiS Spotlight, Available from: https://www.zois-berlin.de/en/publications/polands-lgbt-free-zones-and-global-anti-gender-campaigns [Accessed 14 September 2020].

Korolczuk, E. (2020b) 'The fight against "gender" and "LGBT ideology": new developments in Poland', *European Journal of Politics and Gender*, 3(1): 165–7. DOI: 10.1332/251510819X15744244471843

Kosnick, K. (2015) 'A clash of subcultures? Questioning queer–Muslim antagonisms in the neoliberal city', *International Journal of Urban and Regional Research*, 39(4): 687–703. DOI: 10.1111/1468-2427.12261

Kozinets, R.V. (2015) *Netnography: Redefined*, London: Sage.

Kratochvíl, P. and O'Sullivan, M. (2023) 'A war like no other: Russia's invasion of Ukraine as a war on gender order', *European Security*, 32(3): 347–66. DOI: 10.1080/09662839.2023.2236951

Krivonos, D. (2020) 'Swedish surnames, British accents: passing among post-Soviet migrants in Helsinki', *Ethnic and Racial Studies*, 43(16): 388–406. DOI: 10.1080/01419870.2020.1813319

Kronsell, A. (2012) *Gender, Sex, and the Postnational Defense: Militarism and Peacekeeping*, Oxford: Oxford University Press. DOI: 10.1093/acprof:oso/9780199846061.001.0001

Kulpa, R. (2014) 'Western leveraged pedagogy of Central and Eastern Europe: discourses of homophobia, tolerance, and nationhood', *Gender, Place & Culture*, 21(4): 431–48. DOI: 10.1080/0966369X.2013.793656

Kyrölä, K. and Huuki, T. (2021) 'Re-imagining a queer indigenous past: affective archives and minor gestures in the Sámi documentary Sparrooabbán', *Journal of Cinema and Media Studies*, 60(5): 75–98. DOI: 10.1353/cj.2021.0020

Laclau, E. and Mouffe, C. (1985) *Hegemony and Socialist Strategy: Towards a Radical Democratic Politics*, London: Verso.

Lagerman, J. (2023a) 'Homonationalism on the defensive: news media responses to nationalist anti-LGBTQ attacks in Sweden', *Antipode*, 56(2): 1–20. DOI: 10.1111/anti.12987.

Lagerman, J. (2023b) 'Neo-Nazi heteroactivism and the Swedish nationalist contradiction', *Acme*, 22(3): 1093–114. DOI: 10.7202/1102114ar

Langlois, A.J. (2012) 'Human rights in crisis? A critical polemic against polemical critics', *Journal of Human Rights*, 11(4): 558–70. DOI: 10.1080/14754835.2012.702473

Langlois, A.J. (2015) 'Human rights, LGBT rights, and international theory', in M.L. Picq and M. Thiel (eds) *Sexualities in World Politics*, London: Routledge, pp 23–37.

Langlois, A.J. (2022) 'Queer temporalities and human rights', in K. McNeilly and B. Warwick (eds) *The Times and Temporalities of International Human Rights Law*, Oxford: Hart Publishing, pp 31–41. DOI: 10.5040/9781509949939.ch-008

Laskar, P. (2007) 'Förnuft och instinkt: föreställningar om ras, klass och sexualitet under 1800-talet', in P. de los Reyes and S. Gröndahl (eds) *Framtidens feminismer: intersektionella interventioner i den feministiska debatten*, Stockholm: Tankekraft förlag, pp 44–65.

Laskar, P. (2014) 'The illiberal turn: aid conditionalis and the queering of sexual citizenship', *Lambda Nordica*, 1: 87–100.

Laskar, P. (2015a) 'De andras sexualitet som hot-och motbild', in K. Arnberg, P. Laskar and F. Sundevall (eds) *Sexualpolitiska Nyckeltexter*, Stockholm: Leopard, pp 158–66.

Laskar, P. (2015b) 'The construction of "Swedish" gender through the g-other as a counter-image and threat', in J. Selling, M. End, H. Kyuchukov, P. Laskar and B. Templer (eds) *Antiziganism: What's in a Word?*, Newcastle upon Tyne: Cambridge Scholars Publishing, pp 138–53.

Lentin, A. (2011) 'What happens to anti-racism when we are post race?', *Feminist Legal Studies*, 19(2): 159–68. DOI: 10.1007/s10691-011-9174-5

Liinason, M. (2018) 'Borders and belongings in Nordic feminisms and beyond', *Gender, Place & Culture*, 25(7): 1041–56. DOI: 10.1080/0966369X.2018.1461076

Liinason, M. (2023) '"The loved home" and other exclusionary care discourses: a multiscalar and transnational analysis of heteroactivist resistances to gender and sexual rights in Sweden', *Acme*, 22(3): 1047–68.

Liinason, M. and Alm, E. (2018) 'Ungendering Europe: critical engagements with key objects in feminism', *Gender, Place & Culture*, 25(7): 955–62. DOI: 10.1080/0966369X.2018.1471049

Linander, I., Alm, E., Goicolea, I. and Harryson, L. (2019) '"It was like I had to fit into a category": care-seekers' experiences of gender regulation in the Swedish trans-specific healthcare', *Health*, 23(1): 21–38. DOI: 10.1177/1363459317708824

Linander, I., Lauri, J. and Lauri, M. (2023) 'Swedish LGBTQ activists' responses to neo-Nazi threats', *Lambda Nordica*, 27(3–4): 51–75. DOI: 10.34041/ln.v27.830

Loftsdóttir, K. and Jensen, L. (2012) *Whiteness and Postcolonialism in the Nordic Region: Exceptionalism, Migrant Others and National Identities*, Farnham: Ashgate.

Long, R. (2018) 'Sexual subjectivities within neoliberalism: can queer and crip engagements offer an alternative praxis?', *Journal of International Women's Studies*, 19(1): 78–93.

Lorde, A. (1984) *Sister Outsider: Essays and Speeches*, Trumansburg: Crossing Press.

Lucero, L. (2017) 'Safe spaces in online places: social media and LGBTQ youth', *Multicultural Education Review*, 9(2): 117–28. DOI: 10.1080/2005615X.2017.1313482

Luibhéid, E. (2008) 'Sexuality, migration, and the shifting line between legal and illegal status', *GLQ: A Journal of Lesbian and Gay Studies*, 14(2–3): 289–315. DOI: 10.1215/10642684-2007-034

Luka, M.E. and Millette, M. (2018) '(Re)framing big data: activating situated knowledges and a feminist ethics of care in social media research', *Social Media and Society*, 4(2): 1–10. DOI: 10.1177/2056305118768297

Lunau, M. (2019) 'The trouble with "truth": on the politics of life and death in the assessment of queer asylum seekers', *Kvinder, Køn & Forskning*, 102(3–4): 12–23. DOI: 10.7146/kkf.v28i2-3.116305

Mandelbaum, M.M. (2018) '"I'm a proud Israeli": homonationalism, belonging and the insecurity of the Jewish-Israeli body national', *Psychoanalysis, Culture & Society*, 23(2): 160–79. DOI: 10.1057/s41282-018-0093-0

Marino, S. (2015) 'Making space, making place: digital togetherness and the redefinition of migrant identities online', *Social Media and Society*, 1(2): 1–9. DOI: 10.1177/2056305115622479

Markham, A. and Buchanan, E. (2012) 'Ethical decision-making and internet research recommendations from the AoIR Ethics Working Committee', Recommendations from the AoIR Ethics Working Committee (Version 2.0), Available from: https://aoir.org/reports/ethics2.pdf

Martinsson, L. (2020) 'When gender studies becomes a threatening religion', *European Journal of Women's Studies*, 27(3): 293–300. DOI: 10.1177/1350506820931045

Martinsson, L., Griffin, G. and Giritli Nygren, K. (eds) (2016) *Challenging the Myth of Gender Equality in Sweden*, Bristol: Policy Press.

Marwick, A.E. and Boyd, D. (2018) 'Understanding privacy at the margins', *International Journal of Communication*, 12: 1157–65.

Massad, J. (2007) *Desiring Arabs*, Chicago: University of Chicago Press.

McClintock, A. (1995) *Imperial Leather: Race, Gender and Sexuality in the Colonial Context*, London: Routledge.

McQueen, P. (2015) *Subjectivity, Gender and the Struggle for Recognition*, London: Palgrave Macmillan.

McRuer, R. (2006) *Crip Theory: Cultural Signs of Queerness and Disability*, New York: New York University Press.

Meijer, I.C. and Prins, B. (1998) 'How bodies come to matter: an interview with Judith Butler', *Signs*, 23(2): 275–86.

Mery Karlsson, M. (2020) *'Gå eller rulla: alla vill knulla!' Funktionsrättsaktivism nyliberala landskap*, Lund: Arkiv förlag.

Meyer, D. (2020) 'Omar Mateen as US citizen, not foreign threat: homonationalism and LGBTQ online representations of the Pulse nightclub shooting', *Sexualities*, 23(3): 249–68. DOI: 10.1177/1363460719826361

Mills, C. (2007) 'Normative violence, vulnerability, and responsibility', *Differences: A Journal of Feminist Cultural Studies*, 18(2): 133–56. DOI: 10.1215/10407391-2007-005

Moffette, D. and Vadasaria, S. (2016) 'Uninhibited violence: race and the securitization of immigration', *Critical Studies on Security*, 4(3): 291–305. DOI: 10.1080/21624887.2016.1256365

Molina, I. (2005) 'Rasifiering', in P. de los Reyes and M. Kamali (eds) *Bortom Vi och Dom: Teoretiska Reflektioner om Makt, Integration och Strukturell Diskriminering*, Stockholm: Fritzes offentliga publikationer, pp 95–112.

Montegary, L. (2015) 'Militarizing US homonormativities: the making of "ready, willing, and able" gay citizens', *Signs*, 40(4): 891–915. DOI: 10.1086/680333

Mottier, V. and Gerodetti, N. (2007) 'Eugenics and social democracy: or, how the European left tried to eliminate the "weeds" from its national gardens', *New Formations*, 60: 35–49.

Mulinari, D. and Neergaard, A. (2013) 'We are Sweden Democrats because we care for others: exploring racisms in the Swedish extreme right', *European Journal of Women's Studies*, 21(1): 43–56. DOI: 10.1177/1350506813510423

REFERENCES

Mulinari, D. and Neergaard, A. (2017) 'Theorising racism: exploring the Swedish racial regime', *Nordic Journal of Migration Research*, 7(2): 88–96. DOI: 10.1515/njmr-2017-0016

Mulinari, D. and Neergaard, A. (2022) *The Swedish Racial Welfare Regime in Transition, Marx, Engels, and Marxisms*, edited by Perocco. Springer International, pp 91–116. DOI: 10.1007/978-3-031-06071-7_4

Mulinari, D., Keskinen, S., Irni, K. and Tuori, S. (2009) 'Introduction: postcolonialism and the Nordic models of welfare and gender', in S. Keskinen, S. Tuori, S. Irni and D. Mulinari (eds) *Complying with Colonialism: Gender, Race and Ethnicity in the Nordic Region*, Aldershot: Ashgate, pp 16–46.

Naum, M. and Nordin, J.M. (2013) *Scandinavian Colonialism and the Rise of Modernity: Small Time Agents in a Global Arena*, New York: Springer.

Norocel, O.C., Saresma, T., Lähdesmäki, T. and Ruotsalainen, M. (2022) 'Performing "us" and "other": intersectional analyses of right-wing populist media', *European Journal of Cultural Studies*, 25(3): 897–915. DOI: 10.1177/1367549420980002

Nylund, M.L., Håkansson, S. and Bjarnegård, E. (2023) 'The transformative potential of feminist foreign policy: the case of Sweden', *Journal of Women, Politics and Policy*, 44(3): 257–73. DOI: 10.1080/1554477X.2022.2113662

Odynets, S. (2022) 'Ukrainian refugees in Scandinavia, or how to talk about migration without talking about it', *Topos*, 2: 31–7. DOI: 10.24412/1815-0047-2022-2-31-36

Osanami Törngren, S. (2022) 'Understanding race in Sweden', *Nordic Journal of Social Research*, 13(1): 51–66. DOI: 10.18261/njsr.13.1.5

Palmgren, A., Åkerlund, M. and Viklund, L. (2023) 'Refugees versus "refugees": the role of Islamophobia in Swedish alternative media's reporting on Ukrainian asylum seekers', *Media, Culture and Society*, 45(7): 1400–17. DOI: 10.1177/01634437231179363

Parker, N. and Vaughan-Williams, N. (2012) 'Critical border studies: broadening and deepening the "lines in the sand" agenda', *Geopolitics*, 4: 727–33. DOI: 10.1080/14650045.2012.706111

Paternotte, D. and Kuhar, R. (2018) 'Disentangling and locating the "global right": anti-gender campaigns in Europe', *Politics and Governance*, 6(3): 6–19. DOI: 10.17645/pag.v6i3.1557

Peltonen, S. and Jungar, K. (2018) 'The ascendency of Whiteness: on understanding racialized queerness in LGBTQI refugee work', in T. Shefer, J. Hearn, K. Ratele and F. Boonzaier (eds) *Engaging Youth in Activism, Research and Pedagogical Praxis: Transnational and Intersectional Perspectives on Gender, Sex, and Race*, New York: Routledge, pp 57–75.

Petö, A. and Kováts, E. (2017) 'Anti-gender discourse in Hungary: a discourse without a movement?', in R. Kuhar and D. Paternotte (eds) *Anti-gender Campaigns in Europe: Mobilizing against Equality*, London: Rowman & Littlefield, pp 117–31.

Phillips, N. and Hardy, C. (2011) *Discourse Analysis*, Thousand Oaks: Sage, pp 18–39. DOI: 10.4135/9781412983921

Phoenix, A., Howarth, C. and Philogene, G. (2015) 'The everyday politics of identities and social representations: a critical approach', *Representations*, 26(1): 1–15.

Picq, M.L. and Thiel, M. (eds) (2015) *Sexualities in World Politics: How LGBTQ Claims Shape International Relations*, London: Routledge.

Plakhotnik, O. and Mayerchyk, M. (2023) 'Pride contested', *Lambda Nordica*, 28(2–3): 1–28. DOI: 10.34041/ln.v.874

Polkov, K. (2023) 'Homotolerant versus homophobic? Swedish sexual exceptionalism and the Russian Other', *Sexuality & Culture*, 27: 2038–64. DOI: 10.1007/s12119-023-10149-0

Price, A. (2022) 'Försvarsmakten kampanjar för Pride: "vi kan inte ta våra rättigheter för givna"', Resume, Available from: https://www.resume.se/marknadsforing/kampanj/forsvarsmakten-kampanjar-for-pride-vi-kan-inte-ta-vara-rattigheter-for-givna/ [Accessed 10 August 2022].

Stockholm Pride. (2016) 'Statement from RFSL regarding the initiative "Pride Järva"', Stockholmpride.org, Available from: http://www.stockholmpride.org/statement-from-rfsl-regarding-the-initiative-pride-jarva/ [Accessed 1 August 2016].

Puar, J.K. (2006) 'Mapping US homonormativities', *Gender, Place & Culture*, 13(1): 67–88. DOI: 10.1080/09663690500531014

Puar, J.K. (2007) *Terrorist Assemblages: Homonationalism in Queer Times*, Durham: Duke University Press.

Puar, J.K. (2013) 'Rethinking homonationalism', *International Journal of Middle East Studies*, 45(2): 336–9. DOI: 10.1017/S002074381300007X

Puar, J.K. (2022) 'Whither homonationalism?', in A. Sifaki, C.L. Quinan and K. Lončarević (eds) *Homonationalism, Femonationalism and Ablenationalism: Critical Pedagogies Contextualised*, London: Routledge, pp 2–8. DOI: 10.4324/b22813-2

Puwar, N. (2004) *Space Invaders: Race, Gender and Bodies out of Place*, Oxford: Berg Publishers.

Quensel, A.-S. and Vergara, D. (2016) 'Transfobisk medieprofil till antimuslimsk prideparad', Expo, Available from: https://expo.se/nyhet/transfobisk-medieprofil-till-antimuslimsk-prideparad/ [Accessed 1 August 2016].

Rahman, M. (2014) 'Queer rights and the triangulation of Western exceptionalism', *Journal of Human Rights*, 13(3): 274–89. DOI: 10.1080/14754835.2014.919214

Rahman, M. (2015) 'Sexual diffusions and conceptual confusions', in M.L. Picq and M. Thiel (eds) *Sexualities in World Politics*, London: Routledge, pp 92–107.

Rahman, M. (2020) 'Queer Muslim challenges to the internationalization of LGBT rights: decolonizing international relations methodology through intersectionality', in M.J. Bosia, S.M. McEvoy and M. Rahman (eds) *The Oxford Handbook of Global LGBT and Sexual Diversity Politics*, Oxford: Oxford University Press, pp 417–32. DOI: 10.1093/oxfordhb/9780190673741.001.0001

Rao, R. (2010) *Third World Protest*, Oxford: Oxford University Press. DOI: 10.1093/acprof:oso/9780199560370.001.0001

Rao, R. (2014a) 'Queer questions', *International Feminist Journal of Politics*, 16(2): 199–217. DOI: 10.1080/14616742.2014.901817

Rao, R. (2014b) 'The locations of homophobia', *London Review of International Law*, 2(2): 169–99. DOI: 10.1093/lril/lru010

Rao, R. (2018) 'The state of "queer IR"', *GLQ: A Journal of Lesbian and Gay Studies*, 24(1): 139–49. DOI: 10.1215/10642684-4254531

Rao, R. (2020) *Out of Time: The Queer Politics of Postcoloniality*, Oxford: Oxford University Press. DOI: 10.1093/oso/9780190865511.001.0001

The Rebel (2016) 'Video: gay rights march in Muslim areas of Sweden opposed by leftists', The Rebel, Available from: https://twitter.com/RebelNewsOnline/status/758686474015428609 [Accessed 11 November 2016].

Rexhepi, P. (2016) 'From orientalism to homonationalism: queer politics, Islamophobia and Europeanization in Kosovo', *Southeastern Europe*, 40: 32–53. DOI: 10.1163/18763332-03903014

Rexhepi, P. (2018) 'Arab others at European borders: racializing religion and refugees along the Balkan route', *Ethnic and Racial Studies*, 41(12): 2215–34. DOI: 10.1080/01419870.2017.1415455

RFSL (2015) 'Uttalande från Stockholm Pride och RFSL angående initiativet "Pride Järva"', RFSL, Available from: https://www.facebook.com/rfsl.forbundet/posts/10152903725142301 [Accessed 1 August 2016].

RFSU (2020) 'Attacker och tystnad: en rapport om hotet mot hbtq- och srhr-frågor i Sveriges kommuner', Stockholm: RFSU, Available from: https://www.rfsu.se/globalassets/pdf/attacker-och-tystnad-en-rapport-om-hotet-mot-hbtq-och-srhr-fragor-webb.pdf [Accessed 15 January 2021].

Richards, D. (1980) 'European mythology: the ideology of "progress"', in M.K. Asante and A.S. Vandi (eds) *Contemporary Black Thought*, Beverly Hills: Sage, pp 59–79.

Richardson, D. (2017) 'Rethinking sexual citizenship', *Sociology*, 51(2): 208–24. DOI: 10.1177/0038038515609024

Richardson, L. and Adams St. Pierre, E. (2005) 'Writing: a method of inquiry', in N.K. Denzin and Y.S. Lincoln (eds) *The SAGE Handbook of Qualitative Research* (3rd edn), Thousand Oaks: Sage, pp 959–78.

Rivkin-Fish, M. and Hartblay, C. (2014) 'When global LGBTQ advocacy became entangled with new Cold War sentiment: a call for examining Russian queer experience', *The Brown Journal of World Affairs*, 21(1): 95–111.

Rosamond, A.B. and Hedling, E. (2022) 'The digital storytelling of feminist foreign policy: Sweden's state feminism in digital diplomacy', *European Journal of Politics and Gender*, 5(3): 303–21. DOI: 10.1332/251510821X16523466058289

Rossdale, C. (2015) 'Enclosing critique: the limits of ontological security', *International Political Sociology*, 9(4): 369–86. DOI: 10.1111/ips.12103

Rubbestad, M. and Broman, B. (2023) 'Även sverigedemokrater måste få vara HBT+', *Expressen*, Available from: https://www.expressen.se/debatt/aven-sverigedemokrater--maste-fa-vara-hbt-/ [Accessed 8 February 2023].

RuptlyTV (2016) 'Sweden: LGBT parade marches through Muslim areas to "educate"', Ruptly TV (YouTube channel), Available from: https://www.youtube.com/watch?v=GMhi-gPoQzg [Accessed 27 July 2016].

Rydström, J. (2012) 'Introduction: crip theory in Scandinavia', *Lambda Nordica*, 17(1–2): 9–20.

Sabsay, L. (2012) 'The emergence of the other sexual citizen: orientalism and the modernisation of sexuality', *Citizenship Studies*, 16(5–6): 605–23. DOI: 10.1080/13621025.2012.698484

Sager, M. and Mulinari, D. (2018) 'Safety for whom? Exploring femonationalism and care-racism in Sweden', *Women's Studies International Forum*, 68(May–June): 149–56. DOI: 10.1016/j.wsif.2017.12.002

Said, E. (1978) *Orientalism*, New York: Pantheon Books.

Scicchitano, D. (2021) 'The "real" Chechen man: conceptions of religion, nature, and gender and the persecution of sexual minorities in postwar Chechnya', *Journal of Homosexuality*, 68(9): 1545–62. DOI: 10.1080/00918369.2019.1701336

Selberg, R. (2020) 'The midwife case and conscientious objection: new ways of framing abortion in Sweden', *International Feminist Journal of Politics*, 22(3): 312–34. DOI: 10.1080/14616742.2019.1608841

Shevtsova, M. (2023) 'Resisting "liberal values": the intersection of gender, religion, and sexuality in Ukrainian heteroactivism', *Acme*, 22(3): 1025–46.

Sime, D., Tyrrell, N., Käkelä, E. and Moskal, M. (2022) 'Performing Whiteness: Central and Eastern European young people's experiences of xenophobia and racialisation in the UK post-Brexit', *Journal of Ethnic and Migration Studies*, 48(19): 4527–46. DOI: 10.1080/1369183X.2022.2085678

Sólveigar- og Guðmundsdóttir, L. (2023) 'North-to-North queer migrations: privileged subjectivities and belonging in Iceland', *Gender, Place and Culture*, 0(0): 1–21. DOI: 10.1080/0966369X.2023.2249250

Spade, D. (2013) 'Under the cover of gay rights', *N.Y.U. Review of Law & Social Change*, 37(79): 79–100. DOI: 10.1525/sp.2007.54.1.23

Spade, D. and Belkin, A. (2021) 'Queer militarism?! The politics of military inclusion advocacy in authoritarian times', *GLQ: A Journal of Lesbian and Gay Studies*, 27(2): 281–307. DOI: 10.1215/10642684-8871705

Spivak, G.C. (1988) 'Can the subaltern speak?', in C. Nelson and L. Grossberg (eds) *Marxism and the Interpretation of Culture*, Basingstoke: Macmillan Education, pp 271–313. DOI: 10.4135/9781446212233.n7

Spivak, G.C. (2004) 'Righting wrongs', *South Atlantic Quarterly*, 103(2): 523–81. DOI: 10.1215/00382876-103-2-3-523

Srivastava, S. (2006) 'Tears, fears and careers: anti-racism and emotion in social movement organizations', *The Canadian Journal of Sociology*, 31(1): 55–90. DOI: 10.1353/cjs.2006.0028

Stengel, F.A. and Shim, D. (2022) 'Militarizing antimilitarism? Exploring the gendered representation of military service in German recruitment videos on social media', *International Feminist Journal of Politics*, 24(4): 608–31. DOI: 10.1080/14616742.2021.1935289

Stern, M. (2006) '"We" the subject: the power and failure of (in)security', *Security Dialogue*, 37(2): 187–205. DOI: 10.1177/0967010606066171

Stern, M. and Strand, S. (2021) 'Periods, pregnancy, and peeing: leaky feminine bodies in Swedish military marketing', *International Political Sociology*, 16(1): 1–21. DOI: 10.1093/ips/olab025

Strand, S. and Berndtsson, J. (2015) 'Recruiting the "enterprising soldier": military recruitment discourses in Sweden and the United Kingdom', *Critical Military Studies*, 1(3): 233–48. DOI: 10.1080/23337486.2015.1090676

Strand, S. (2019) '(Re)inventing the armed forces: a governmentality analysis of Swedish military marketing and outreach in the era of voluntarism', PhD thesis, University of Gothenburg.

Strand, S. (2022) 'The birth of the enterprising soldier: governing military recruitment and retention in post-Cold War Sweden', *Scandinavian Journal of History*, 47(2): 225–47. DOI: 10.1080/03468755.2021.1997797

Strand, S. and Kehl, K. (2019) '"A country to fall in love with/in": gender and sexuality in Swedish Armed Forces' marketing campaigns', *International Feminist Journal of Politics*, 21(2): 295–314. DOI: 10.1080/14616742.2018.1487772

Sundevall, F. (2014) 'Porr i vapenskåpet och bögkompani på Gotland', in A.M. Forsberg and K. Kronberg (eds) *Lumpen: från mönstring till muck*, Stockholm: Atlantis, pp 150–71.

Sundevall, F. and Persson, A. (2016) 'LGBT in the military: policy development in Sweden 1944–2014', *Sexuality Research and Social Policy*, 13(2): 119–29. DOI: 10.1007/s13178-015-0217-6

Svensson, T. (2015) 'Alla rasifieras!', *Mana*, pp 1–5, Available from: http://tidskriftenmana.se/alla-rasifieras

Thorén, M. (2022) 'SD stoppar sagostund med dragqueens i Trelleborg', QX, Available from: https://www.qx.se/samhalle/240752/sd-stoppar-sagostund-med-dragqueens-i-trelleborg-de-var-mycket-tydliga/ [Accessed 8 February 2023].

Thunell, T., Södergren, C., Sundin, C., Andersson, C., Helander, J. and Sandkvist, E. (2014a) 'SD-HBT: kinkysex och fisting förstärker fördomarna om HBT', Nyheter24, 23 August, Available from: https://nyheter24.se/debatt/775614-sd-hbt-kinkysex-och-fisting-forstarker-fordomarna-om-hbt [Accessed 20 November 2016].

Thunell, T., Södergren, C., Sundin, C., Andersson, C., Helander, J. and Sandkvist, E. (2014b) 'SD-HBT om Pride: HBT-personer ska inte visas upp som ett djur på cirkus', Nyheter24, 2 August, Available from: https://nyheter24.se/debatt/774220-sd-hbt-om-pride-hbt-personer-ska-inte-visas-upp-som-ett-djur-pa-cirkus [Accessed 20 November 2016].

Tlostanova, M., Thapar-Björkert, S. and Knobblock, I. (2019) 'Do we need decolonial feminism in Sweden?', *NORA: Nordic Journal of Feminist and Gender Research*, 27(4): 290–5. DOI: 10.1080/08038740.2019.1641552

Tonini, M. (2016) 'The ambiguities of recognition: young queer sexualities in contemporary India', PhD thesis, Lund University, Department of Gender Studies.

Towns, A., Karlsson, E. and Eyre, J. (2014) 'The equality conundrum: gender and nation in the ideology of the Sweden Democrats', *Party Politics*, 20(2): 237–47. DOI: 10.1177/1354068813520272

Tschalaer, M. (2020) 'Between queer liberalisms and Muslim masculinities: LGBTQI+ Muslim asylum assessment in Germany', *Ethnic and Racial Studies*, 43(7): 1265–83. DOI: 10.1080/01419870.2019.1640378

Tschalaer, M. (2021) 'Victimhood and femininities in Black lesbian asylum cases in Germany', *Journal of Ethnic and Migration Studies*, 47(15): 3531–48. DOI: 10.1080/1369183X.2020.1772735

Tsymbalyuk, D. (2022) 'Academia must recentre embodied and uncomfortable knowledge', *Nature Human Behaviour*, 6(6): 758–9. DOI: 10.1038/s41562-022-01369-9

Tudor, A. (2017) 'Queering migration discourse: differentiating racism and migratism in postcolonial Europe', *Lambda Nordica*, 22(2–3): 21–40.

Tudor, A. (2018) 'Cross-fadings of racialisation and migratisation: the postcolonial turn in Western European gender and migration studies', *Gender, Place and Culture*, 25(7): 1057–72. DOI: 10.1080/0966369X.2018.1441141

Tudor, A. and Ticktin, M. (2021) 'Sexuality and borders in right wing times: a conversation', *Ethnic and Racial Studies*, 44(9): 1648–67. DOI: 10.1080/01419870.2021.1909743

Tynes, B.M., Schuschke, J. and Noble, S.U. (2016) 'Digital intersectionality theory and the #Blacklivesmatter movement', in S.U. Noble and B.M. Tynes (eds) *The Intersectional Internet: Race, Sex, Class and Culture Online*, New York: Peter Lang, pp 21–40.

Van Houtum, H. (2005) 'The geopolitics of borders and boundaries', *Geopolitics*, 10(4): 672–9. DOI: 10.1080/14650040500318522

REFERENCES

Voss, J. (2023) 'Regnbågsflagga i pansar skyddar mänskliga rättigheter under pride', QX, Available from: https://www.qx.se/samhalle/pride/250038/regnbagsflagga-i-pansar-skyddar-manskliga-rattigheter-under-pride/ [Accessed 11 January 2024].

Warner, M. (1999) *The Trouble with Normal: Sex, Politics, and the Ethics of Queer Life*, Cambridge, MA: Harvard University Press.

Wasshede, C. (2021) 'Rainbow flag and belongings/disbelongings: Öckerö Pride and Reclaim Pride in Gothenburg, Sweden 2019', in E. Alm, L. Berg, M.L. Hero, A. Johansson, P. Laskar, L. Martinsson et al (eds) *Pluralistic Struggles in Gender, Sexuality and Coloniality*, Cham: Springer International, pp 147–75. DOI: 10.1007/978-3-030-47432-4

Weber, C. (2008) 'Popular visual language as global communication: the remediation of United Airlines Flight 93', *Review of International Studies*, 34(suppl 1): 137–53. DOI: 10.1017/S0260210508007833

Weber, C. (2016a) 'Queer intellectual curiosity as international relations method: developing queer international relations theoretical and methodological frameworks', *International Studies Quarterly*, 60(1): 11–23. DOI: 10.1111/isqu.12212

Weber, C. (2016b) *Queer International Relations*, New York: Oxford University Press. DOI: 10.1093/acprof:oso/9780199795857.001.0001

Weheliye, A.G. (2014) *Habeas Viscus*, Durham: Duke University Press.

Welland, J. (2013) 'Militarised violences, basic training, and the myths of asexuality and discipline', *Review of International Studies*, 39(4): 881–902. DOI: 10.1017/S0260210512000605

Westerlund, U. (2015) Heteronormativitet och homonationalism: En kritisk diskursanalys av Sverigedemokraternas hbtq-politik. Department of Ethnology, History of Religions and Gender Studies, Stockholm University.

Wilcox, L. (2017) 'Practising gender, queering theory', *Review of International Studies*, 43(5): 789–808. DOI: 10.1017/S0260210517000183

Wilkinson, C. (2014) 'Putting "traditional values" into practice: the rise and contestation of anti-homopropaganda laws in Russia', *Journal of Human Rights*, 13(3): 363–79. DOI: 10.1080/14754835.2014.919218

Wilkinson, C. (2017) 'Are we winning? A strategic analysis of queer wars', *Australian Journal of International Affairs*, 71(3): 236–40. DOI: 10.1080/10357718.2017.1290049

Wilson Gilmore, R. (2007) *Golden Gulag: Prisons, Surplus, Crisis, and Opposition in Globalizing California*, Oakland: University of California Press.

Wimark, T. (2021) 'Housing policy with violent outcomes: the domestication of queer asylum seekers in a heteronormative society', *Journal of Ethnic and Migration Studies*, 47(3): 703–22. DOI: 10.1080/1369183X.2020.1756760

Wodak, R. and Forchtner, B. (2017) 'Critical discourse studies', in R. Wodak and B. Forchtner (eds) *The Routledge Handbook of Language and Politics*, London: Routledge, pp 135–49. DOI: 10.4324/9781315183718

Wynter, S. (2001) 'Towards the sociogenic principle: Fanon, identity, the puzzle of conscious experience, and what it is like to be "Black"', in M.E. Durán-Cogan and A. Gómez-Moriana (eds) *National Identities and Sociopolitical Changes in Latin America*, New York: Routledge, pp 30–66.

Yuval-Davis, N. and Stoetzler, M. (2002) 'Imagined boundaries and borders: a gendered gaze', *The European Journal of Women's Studies*, 9(3): 329–44.

Yuval-Davis, N. (2006) 'Belonging and the politics of belonging', *Patterns of Prejudice*, 40(3): 197–214. DOI: 10.1080/00313220600769331

Yuval-Davis, N. (2011) *The Politics of Belonging: Intersectional Contestations*, London: Sage.

Yuval-Davis, N., Wemyss, G. and Cassidy, K. (2018) 'Everyday bordering, belonging and the reorientation of British immigration legislation', *Sociology*, 52(2): 228–44. DOI: 10.1177/0038038517702599

Zivi, K. (2011) *Making Rights Claims*, Oxford: Oxford University Press.

Zotzmann, K. and O'Regan, J.P. (2016) 'Critical discourse analysis and identity', in S. Preece (ed) *The Routledge Handbook of Language and Identity*, London: Routledge, pp 113–28. DOI: 10.4324/9781315669816

Żuk, P. and Żuk, P. (2020) '"Murderers of the unborn" and "sexual degenerates": analysis of the "anti-gender" discourse of the Catholic Church and the nationalist right in Poland', *Critical Discourse Studies*, 17(5): 566–88. DOI: 10.1080/17405904.2019.1676808

Index

A

academic knowledge 60
activist groups 21
Adams St. Pierre, E. 60, 71
Africa 85–6, 87
Ahlstedt, S. 71
Ahmed, S. 20, 52, 66, 68
Åkesson, Jimmie 80
Amsterdam Pride 2009 83
Anderson, B. 32
annotations 71
anonymizing research material 111
Anthias, F. 34
anti-discrimination legislation 96
anti-gender and LGBTQ attitudes and policies 2, 5, 15, 26, 41–2, 74
anti-gender movements 137
armed forces 93–4
  see also Swedish Armed Forces (SAF)
ascription of race/Otherness 58–9
Asian women 119–20
asylum-seekers 15, 34–5
Athanasiou, A. 40
Avpixlat (website) 63, 76, 82

B

Bacchetta, P. 50–1, 53
bad Others 78, 107–8
'bad patriarchies' 18–19
Baker, C. 15, 94, 105
barricades 82–3, 87
Barthes, R. 35
Bazeley, P. 61
belonging 4, 31–9
binaries 52, 90, 135
Black bodies' hyper-sexuality 119–20
Black colonial Other 5
Black Queers Sweden 21
Black studies 55
blatte 14, 109–10, 120
Bleiker, R. 64, 67
b/ordering 31, 57
bordering 33–4
boundaries 5, 34, 36, 65–6, 84–6

boundary making 30–45
  collective and individual sense of self 37
  contested nature 57
  creating Self–Other distinctions 36
  existence of constitutive Others 58
  and grids of intelligibility 8, 38, 58
  instability of LGBTQ positionalities 134
  intersectionally 35–6
  making LGBTQ people intelligible 129–30
  national identities 34
  normative and deviant sexualities 11
  normative grids of intelligibility 133
  performative 35
  politics of belonging 3–4
  race–sex–gender 6–7, 48
  racialization 132
  racist hierarchies 47
  as/through bordering 34–5
  through the spectacle of the Other 32–4
  unstable 36
boundary-making moves 8, 55–6, 128, 129–30, 132–35
boundary-making processes
  ascription of race/Otherness 58–9
  being made intelligible 69
  grids of intelligibility 44, 58, 64, 126
  inclusions/exclusions 135–6
  military institutions 93–4
  nationalism and nationalist imaginaries 30–1
  racialization 47
  'Selves' and 'Others' 7–8
  sexuality and gender 3, 58
  Swedishness 128
Bracke, S. 112
Braidotti, R. 47
Breitbart (website) 63, 83
Brown, W. 86
Bulmer, S. 94
Butler, J. 3, 15, 17, 24, 38–43, 53, 55, 66, 90, 108

C

career-building social institutions 93
chains of equivalence 65, 67–8, 69
citizenship 14

civilizational discourses 54
Clinton, Hillary 22
collective identities 7, 58, 116
collective narratives 37
collective Self 57
'colonial gaze' 33
colonialism 9, 54
colonialist-orientalist discourses 87, 90
colonial past/postcolonial present 26–7
colonial racism 48
colour-blindness 21, 48–51
Colyar, J. 71
'Come as you are' campaign (SAF) 97
coming out 113–116, 123
   see also sexuality and gender identity
concepts and signification 65
Conchita Wurst (Thomas Neuwirth) 15, 27
criminalizing homosexuality 26
critical race theory 21
critique and modes of living 42
cultural racism 18–22, 47, 48–51

D

Dagerlind, Mats 82–3, 87
Dahl, U. 18
De los Reyes, P. 19
depersonalized markers 128
desexualization 119, 124
destabilizing normative intelligibility 42
Dhawan, N. 14, 23–4, 26–7, 41, 42, 74
discourses 8, 64, 67
discursive analyses 8–9, 64–70
'drag queen story hours' 81–2
Duggan, L. 2, 12, 13, 23, 27
'Dutch values' 83
Dyer, R. 51

E

Eastern Europe 6, 13–14, 15, 51–2
Edenborg, E. 15, 35
election campaign 2010 80
El-Tayeb, F. 17, 48–50, 116
empirical material 71
Enlightenment 14, 53
equivalence and differentiation 65
eternal migrants 14
ethical and political values 32
ethics and positionality 72–5
Europe 13–22, 78, 89
Europeanness 80
EuroPride Festival 2018 98
Eurovision Song Contest 15, 27
'exotic other' (Laskar) 123–4
exotification 118–19, 121–3, 131
expository writing 71
externalization 105, 127, 132–3
externalized Other 33, 57, 90, 123, 128, 130

F

Facebook 96, 103
'false beginnings' (Colyar) 71
Fanon, F. 50, 52
feminist foreign policies 5, 18, 102
feminist movements 20
feminist research approaches 60, 65
fetishized exotic objects of desire 124
'field of the recognisable' (Butler) 108
En flagga värd att försvara campaign (SAF) 92–3
'the flesh' (Weheliye) 55
folkhemmet 20
Försvarsmakten 103
Foucault, M. 64

G

gay-friendly countries 13, 116
gay-rights-as-human-rights 12, 22–6, 28, 54, 135
Gays in Angered 21
gender as performative (Butler) 38–9
gender equality 18–19, 21, 80, 109
gender identity see sexuality and gender identity
Gender Trouble (Butler) 24, 38–9
Germany 14, 85
Global South 22–3
Goldberg, D.T. 49
'good [racialized] other' (Sabsay) 107
'good Sweden'/'good whiteness' (Hübinette and Lundström) 20
grids of intelligibility 3, 44–5, 66
  and boundary making 8, 38, 58
  boundary-making moves 134–5
  boundary-making processes 44, 58, 64, 126
  defining 30
  Instagram 69–70, 131
  LGBTQ non-White and/or Muslim 120, 124
  LGBTQ rights 34
  masculinity and femininity 118
  normative violence 42
  race, gender and sexuality 74
  repetitions 44–5
  sex, gender and desire 38, 109
  social norms of recognition 39–40
  subjectivity/identity 40, 44
  violence 44, 54
  Whiteness 52
  working in practice 39
  see also intelligibility; normative grids of intelligibility

H

Habeas Viscus (Weheliye) 54–5
Halberstam, J. 43, 64
Hansen, L. 67
Haraway, D.J. 75

Haritaworn, J. 13, 17, 79, 80, 112
hate crimes 115
'hateful Others' (Haritaworn) 17, 112, 113, 117–18, 131
hateful racialized Other 16
haunting 33, 43, 57, 58
hegemonic gazes 67
hegemonic Whiteness 19–20, 22
'here–there'/'us–them' 35
herising, F. 60
HoF (Homo-, bi- och transpersoner i försvaret) 96
homo-colonialism 106
homogenous gender-conscious identities 19
homonationalism 2, 7, 79–82
  academic disciplines 11
  binary narratives 135
  Europe 13–22, 78, 89
  geopolitical and historical location 27
  Global North 26
  and homonormativity 12–13
  as a politics 73
homonationalist boundary making 8, 15, 63, 137
homonationalist language 79
homonationalist narratives 23, 72–3, 77
homonormativity 2, 7, 12–13, 27, 100
homophobia 79–80, 87–9, 90
homophobic hate crimes 16, 41, 77
'the homophobic Other within' 136–7
homophobic racialized Other 70, 90, 130
homophobic spaces 87–8
homophobic threats 128
homosexual, bisexual and transsexual (HBT) 81
Horton, B.A. 116
Hübinette, T. 20, 21
humanity 55
human rights 23, 24, 40
human subjectivity 59
Hungary 14, 15
hyper-sexuality 119–20

I

identity narratives 37
'imagined communities' (Anderson) 32, 33
inclusive othering 79
India 26
'inside'/'outside' 36
Instagram account for racialized LGBTQ 74–5, 107
  grids of intelligibility 69–70, 131
  intelligible as 'externalized other' 123
  intelligible as LGBTQ-phobic 127
  pictures captions 63
  privacy settings 110–11
intelligibility 37, 41, 108, 129
  see also grids of intelligibility
internal and external Others 57

International Gay and Lesbian Human Rights Commission 24
intersectionality 21, 109
intolerant Other 85–7, 132
Islam 2, 86–9, 128
  see also Muslims
Islamic Sharia law 85
Islamophobia 20, 22, 75, 107

J

Jivraj, S. 116
Jong, A. de 116
Jungar, K. 19

K

Kapur, R. 17
Kehl, K. 94, 102
key signifiers 65, 69
'kiss-ins' 85
Kuntsman, A. 13

L

Lagerman, J. 102
Langlois, A.J. 24, 25
language 8
Laskar, P. 119, 123
LGBTQ activism 1, 21, 23
'LGBTQ, but not left-wing' 81
LGBTQ emancipation discourses 75
'LGBTQ-free zones' 33
LGBTQ-friendliness 62, 129
LGBTQ identities 86, 102
LGBTQ-inclusiveness 19
LGBTQ love 105
LGBTQ organizations 76–7, 89–90, 112
LGBTQ people
  affectionate in public 81
  boundary markers 33
  double positioning 69
  excluding from national communities 2–3
  inclusive othering 79
  SAF campaigns 127
  sexual deviants 80, 81
  Swedishness 57, 126
  victims and/or protectors 130
LGBTQ people racialized as non-White and/or Muslim 59, 69–70, 107, 108, 110, 117, 129, 131
LGBTQ-phobia 41–2, 120, 127–30
LGBTQ politics 23, 73, 136
LGBTQ refugees 16
LGBTQ rights
  becoming recognizable 40
  boundary drawing 13–14
  defending 99, 102
  delimiting who belongs 2
  Global South 22–3
  homonormative and homonationalist narratives 23

human rights discourses 40
LGBTQ positionalities 129
nationalist boundary makers 73
nationalist mobilizations 1
New Cold War sentiments 15
political actors protecting 78
racialization 6
rainbow flag 69
and SD 76–7, 80
Swedish nationhood 18–19
Swedishness 49, 57, 126–8, 132
tolerance, modernity and backwardness 22
Western values 13–14, 107, 116
LGBTQ rights holders 69, 106
LGBTQ soldiers 69, 93–4, 99, 104
London Pride 2008 93–4
Lundström, C. 20, 21

M

Marcouch, Ahmed 83
marginalized identities 110
'marked racialization' (Svensson) 51
marriage laws 100
Mårtensson, Emelie 82
Martinsson, L. 19
McQueen, P. 43
Middle East 85–6, 87
migrants 7, 87–8
military service 24, 93–4
    see also Swedish Armed Forces (SAF)
Mills, C. 41
Moffette, D. 54
Molina, I. 19, 46–7
'More important now than ever' campaign (SAF) 92–3, 103
Mulinari, D. 19, 49
multidimensional critiques 26
Muslims 1, 17–18, 19, 47
    see also Islam
'myths' (Barthes) 35

N

national identity 34
nationalist boundary making 7, 30–1, 35, 73
nationhood and belonging 133, 136
NATO 6, 18, 103
Neergaard, A. 49
Netherlands 14
Neuwirth, Thomas (Conchita Wurst) 15, 27
New Cold War 15
non-belonging 4, 53
non-European Russian Other 128
non-intelligibility 41–4
'nonintroductions' (Colyar) 71
non-performativity (Ahmed) 68
non-public LGBTQ identities 116
'non-redistributive recognition politics' (Rao) 12
non-Western Others 14

non-White and/or Muslims
bad Others 107–8
'constitutive outsides' 2
cultural differences 15–16
externalized through racialization 50
LGBTQ activists 21
LGBTQ in White Swedish contexts 63
LGBTQ-phobic backwardness 107
non-Western Others 14
non-Whites 51–4
#NoOrlando 76
Nordic countries 9
normative grids of intelligibility 7, 43–4, 53, 126, 133–4, 136
    see also grids of intelligibility
normative intelligibility 3, 41, 43, 44–5, 58
normative sexuality and gender 58, 74, 93, 137
normative violence 41, 42
'norms of recognition' (Butler) 108
NVivo (software) 64, 70

O

'old White Sweden'/'good feminist Sweden' 20
Omar, Mateen 76
'open' White LGBTQ people 115
oppressive narratives 17, 22
'the Other' 53–4, 119
    see also 'the Self' and 'the Other'
Othering 14, 16, 19, 61, 69–70, 86
Otherness 38, 46, 49, 128

P

Parker, N. 34
Pekgul, Nalin 88
Peltonen, S. 19
performativity (Butler) 39, 42–3, 55, 66, 90
'phenomenology of whiteness' (Ahmed) 52
pictures' captions 63
placement of flags 125, 126
'planned flexibility' (Bazeley) 61
pluralist approaches (Bleiker) 64
plural logic of and/or 28, 35, 55–6, 69, 134
Poland 14, 15, 33
policing racialized and queer subjects 54
'political racelessness' (Goldberg) 49
politics of belonging 3–4, 31–2, 34, 57
populist right 40–1, 61–2, 90
positionality 10, 72–5, 123
Posocco, S. 13
postcolonial critiques 19
postcolonial societies 26–7
post-racial Swedish society 20
post-structural analyses 64–5
Price, A. 103
Pride Järva 76–91
    'appropriation' of LGBTQ issues 61
    boundary making 34

exclusionary Swedishness 89
integrating into LGBTQ/pride
  structures 84
international audiences 72
LGBTQ rights 91
Othering 62–3, 107
right-wing homonationalist projects 84
SD rhetoric 80
Sweden and hateful Others 67–8
Swedish gender exceptionalism 127
teaching hateful other a lesson 113
Pride Järva 2015 82–3
Pride Järva 2016 1, 76–77, 83–4
progressive Western Europe 15, 22, 127
psychological violence 41
Puar, J.K. 2, 12–13, 17, 23, 27, 28, 73, 79
Pulse nightclub, Orlando 76
pussa (chaste kisses) 85

Q

qualitative research 60–1, 70
queer and feminist methodologies 60–75
'queer art of failure' (Halberstam) 43
queer critiques 23–5
Queer International Relations (Weber) 26
queer intimacy 17
queer logics of analysis 25–8
queer-of-colour organizations 16, 79
queer research approaches 60
Queers against Fascism and Racism 83
queer theory 11, 24, 25, 28, 54
queer vulnerability 25

R

race 3, 5, 47, 48–9, 54
race–sex–gender boundary making 6–7, 48
racial grammar 54
racial hierarchies 21, 50, 57
racialization 30, 46–59
  ascription of race and Otherness 47, 58–9
  boundary making 47, 132
  defining 21
  and exotification 118–19
  'fleshly surplus' (Weheliye) 55
  grammatical form 46–7
  grids of intelligibility 53, 109
  human and non-human 56
  LGBTQ-phobic Other 128
  and migration 9, 52
  and racial hierarchies 50, 57
  and religion 2
  social construction 53
  social hierarchization 58–9
  social process 128
  social relevance 48
  and society 47
  Western Europe 109
racialization processes 48, 52, 109
racialized as White 121

racialized LGBTQ people 62, 110–11
racialized masculinity/femininity 118
racialized Othering 89–90, 136
racialized people as non-White and/or
  Muslim 15–18, 49–50, 108, 112, 113,
  116–17, 121–3, 133
racialized positionalities 21
racialized queers 21–2
racialized Swedish LGBTQ activists 1
racism, sexism, homo-, bi- and
  transphobia 73–4
racist and Islamophobic othering 107
racist hierarchies 47
radical Islamist ideologies 88
rainbow flag
  cultural symbol 1, 94–5
  forged from tank armour 6
  key signifiers 69
  nationalist narratives 2
  SAF's pride campaigns 68–9, 92, 101–2,
    104–6
  SAF's public image 96
  soldiers' uniforms 125
Rainbow Refugees Sweden 21
Rao, R. 12, 22–8, 74
rasifierat 109
recognition 40–1
'relay accounts' (*stafettkonto*) 110
religion 2, 48–9, 128
representation 120–3
(re)presentation and (in)visibility 67
reproductive heterosexuality 5
rescue narratives 16, 77, 79, 112, 113
resignification 43, 53, 66
Richardson, L. 60, 62, 71
'right' and 'wrong' kinds of Others 78–9
'right kind of queers'
  boundary markers 17
  grids of intelligibility 109
  and homonormativity 12
  LGBTQ rights 49
  normative grids of intelligibility 9, 133
  racialization 137
  as White 121, 124
  and 'wrong' kinds of queers 3, 32, 65, 126
'the right to be who you are' 102, 106
right-wing news websites 63
Rinkeby, Stockholm 76, 84–6, 88
Russia 14, 15
Russian invasion of Ukraine 6, 18, 24,
  103, 128

S

Sabsay, L. 13, 107
Sámi population 10, 50
Scandinavia 18
'SD-HBT' 81
'the Self' and 'the Other' 7–8, 31, 53–4,
  57, 65

Self/Other distinctions 36, 69, 90
self-reflexivity 72–3
sexual and gender rights 22
sexuality and gender 3, 4, 19, 20, 70, 78, 93–5
sexuality and gender identity
  asylum seekers 15
  boundary making 5, 11
  coming out 123
  discrimination 102
  grids of intelligibility 120
  pride-related campaigns 104
  as private issues 81
  race and racialization 7
  Scandinavian identities 18
  'the Self' and 'the Other' 53–4
  social construct 9
  Swedish gender exceptionalism 4, 73
sexualized exotification 33
sexual liberation 14
sexual orientation 15, 81, 102
signification and subjectification 58
Sjunnesson, Jan 1
  analysing speeches 67–8
  backwardness of the 'East' 90
  binary Self/Other distinctions 90, 130
  defending LGBTQ rights 99
  homophobia 87, 127
  intolerant Other 84–6
  Islam 87
  Pride Järva 62–3, 76–8, 82, 83–7
  protecting LGBTQ people 40
  rhetoric 14, 89–90
  and the SDs 80
  Swedish gender exceptionalism 127
  "transsexual called Jack" 88
Slotervaart, Amsterdam 83
social locations 31–2, 36
social media 1, 61, 63, 82, 96, 102–3, 110–11
social norms 2, 9, 39–40, 99
South Asia 85–6
Spiller, Hortense 55
Spivak, G.C. 16
state-adjacent civil society actors 23–4
'state feminism' (Dahl) 18
state-related power and protection 24
stereotypical visualization of minorities 67
Stern, M. 106
Stockholm Pride 1, 61, 82–3, 89, 95, 96, 98
Strand, S. 94, 102, 106
strange Other 33
subjectivities 36, 38–41, 44, 58
suburbs (*förorten/orten*) 87–9, 113
subversion and meaning-making 42
Svenska Dagbladet 99
Svensson, T 51
Sweden 14, 18, 132, 137

Sweden Democrats (SD) 1, 5–6, 18, 20, 40, 63, 80–1, 89–90
Swedish Armed Forces (SAF) 1, 61–2, 92–106
  campaign images and posters 63, 68–9
  classical military iconography 104
  defence of LGBTQ rights 102, 105
  equal opportunities employer 96–7
  exchanging flags 125
  externalizing anti-LGBTQ sentiments 128
  gender and sexuality 92
  LGBTQ personnel 95–7
  making LGBTQ people intelligible 127
  mobilizing LGBTQ 94, 130
  pride campaign 2018 98–9
  pride campaign 2019 99–100
  pride campaign 2020 100–1
  pride campaign 2021–2022 101–4
  pride campaign 2023 6
  rainbow flag 57, 68–9, 92–3, 96, 101–2, 105–6, 125
  and Swedish progressiveness 94, 127
  territorial defence 34, 102
  visual materials 67
Swedish Classification of Diseases 96
Swedish exceptionalism 6, 19, 21, 80
Swedish Federation for Lesbian, Gay, Bisexual, Transgender, Queer and Intersex Rights (RFSL) 82–3, 89, 96
Swedish gender exceptionalism 4, 6, 18–19, 77, 85, 90, 127, 132, 136
Swedish LGBTQ exceptionalism 136
Swedishness
  boundary making 34, 34–5, 128
  contemporary constructions 132
  distant LGBTQ-phobic Others 130
  grids of intelligibility 34
  homonationalist boundary making 63
  on the international stage 136
  LGBTQ-friendly 62, 127–8, 131–2
  LGBTQ rights 34, 57, 126–8, 127
  national traits 19, 109
  progress, secularism and rationality 80
  racialization and boundary making 132–3
  at Rinkeby and Tensta 88
  Whiteness 20–1, 99, 105, 123, 132–3
Swedish (post) coloniality 9–10, 50
Swedish progressiveness 61, 94, 106, 126–7
Swedish Queer Initiative Syd 21
'Swedish White We' 19
symbols and identities 94

T

Tatchell, Peter 84
territorial defence 34, 102
text-based meaning-making processes 64
theoretical approaches 57
'Thou New, Thou Free' campaign (SAF) 1, 97
threat and protection narratives 17, 38, 78, 79, 89, 90, 116, 127, 132

tokenism 117–18, 120, 123–4, 131
tolerance 1, 86–7
traditional Eastern Europe 15, 51–2
traditional Swedish identity 20
traditional values 2–3, 14, 15, 24
transgender people 5
transphobia 41, 80

U

Uganda 26
UK Armed Forces 93–4, 105
UN Human Rights Council of an Independent Expert on Sexual Orientation and Gender Identity 22
unintelligibility 41–2, 43
United States 12, 13
universalism 23–5, 27
unmarked racialization 51
'us–them' rhetoric 33, 35, 79

V

Vadasaria, S. 54
Vaughan-Williams, N. 34
victimhood 130
'victim subject' (Kapur) 17
violence 41–2, 113
Voss, J. 6

W

Weber, C. 26, 27, 69
wedding cakes 105

Weheliye, A.G. 46, 48, 51, 52–6
'We let Sweden be at peace' campaign (SAF) 97
Western European societies 13–18, 107, 116
Westernization of LGBTQ identities 23
West Pride, Gothenburg 125
White melancholy 20, 21
Whiteness 51
  contextual 51, 52
  feminist movements 20
  neutrality/'non-race' 109
  and racial hierarchies 21
  Swedishness 20, 99, 105, 123, 132–3
White people 20, 58, 99
White purity 20
White solidarity 20
White Swedish LGBTQ 1, 79–80, 90, 114–15, 123
Wilcox, Lauren 39
Wilkinson, C. 15, 25
Wilson Gilmore, R. 47–8
writing as analytical work 60, 70–2
'wrong kinds of queers' 3, 9, 32, 65, 126, 137
Wynter, S. 52, 55

Y

Yiannopoulos, Milo 83
Yuval-Davis, N. 31–2, 34, 37, 48, 57